C000076498

YOUN9Y

THE AUTOBIOGRAPHY OF
ALAN YOUNG

I would like to dedicate this book to my four wonderful children: Wesley Alan Young; Jordan Lewis Blake Young; Kyle Alexander Kilby Young; and last, but by no means least, my beautiful daughter, Sophie Isabella Young. XXXX

First published 2013

The History Press
The Mill, Brimscombe Port
Stroud, Gloucestershire, GL5 2QG
www.thehistorypress.co.uk

British Library Cataloguing in Publication Data.
A catalogue record for this book is available from the British Library.

ISBN 978 0 7524 9716 7

Typesetting and origination by The History Press
Printed in Great Britain

CONTENTS

ACKNOWLEDGEMENTS

I would like to thank the following people and organisations: the lads from Bentley's Roof; The staff of the Six Hills Hotel, Leicester LE14 3PD for endless coffee during the many recording sessions; Declan Flynn at The History Press; East Midlands Today (T.V.); Sir Geoff Peters; Simon Kimber; *The Fox* fanzine; Mr Gary Lineker; Mr Gary Newbon; Jon Armstrong Holmes (Gary Lineker's agent); Colin Slater, BBC Radio Nottingham; Harry Griggs of The Brighton Argus; The *Leicester Mercury*; Dean Eldredge (Oporto Sports Managements Ltd. and Soar Media L.T.D.); Steve Lambden (Football Correspondent); Tasha!; John 'Jock' Martin Bokus Wallace (6 September 1935 – 24 July 1996); Gary Silke; Neville Chadwick Photography; Ian Davidson at Leicestershire County Cricket Club; David Smith for career statistics; John Hutchinson, Leicester City Official Historian Clive Burgess for providing the inspiring book, The Team From a Town of Chimneys by Stewart W. Beckett; Kyle Young for the original idea behind the front cover design; Andy Lochhead; and Fiona Foster

Photograph credits:
Neville Chadwick Photography
www.fox-photos.co.uk

The author and publisher have made every effort to contact copyright holders for permission and apologise for any omissions or errors in this regard.

FOREWORD
BY GARY LINEKER

The slightly crooked smile, the extremely bandy legs and the now oh so common Scottish accent were the immediate observances of one Alexander Forbes Young. We're going back over three decades ago, to the era at Filbert Street of Jock Wallace and 'McLeicester City'. Jock came south with, what seemed to us young English lads, half of the Scottish League. He also brought with him his infamous training regime, which included the never to be forgotten sandhills. I lost count (and sleep) of the number of players that clambered over Hadrian's Wall to join Jock's tartan army, but the one who stood out, the one who made the biggest impression, the one who was the loudest (alright Martin Henderson may have edged him in that department) was Alan Young. He was cocky, vibrant and talented. He was also Jock's boy, and for good reason.

I was still only coming to the end of my teens when he arrived but Alan made an early impression on me. He was the star centre forward but was always generous with his support and advice, and it wasn't too long before we became strike partners, although my initiation into the City first team was on the right wing. Once the absurd notion that I would ever make it as a wide man was cast aside, I vied with a certain Jim Melrose (who I'm sure will feature in this book for a variety of reasons) for the privilege of pairing Youngy up front.

He was an old fashioned aggressive centre forward. He possessed, though, a delicate touch and finesse that belied his big target man status – the perfect partner for a nippy little goalhanger trying to make a name for himself.

There were many highlights in his hundred-plus games for the Foxes, but if I had to select one match that epitomised his indomitable spirit it would have to be the 1992 F.A. Cup quarter-final against, of all teams, Shrewsbury Town. It was a ridiculous game which we eventually won 5–2, and will be remembered for the unusual statistic that in a game of 7 goals, two keepers kept clean sheets – one of whom was a certain Alan Young, acting as an emergency keeper for the injured Mark Wallington. He then got injured himself, Steve Lynex replacing him between the posts. If my memory serves me correctly Youngy bravely returned to the field of play after treatment. I'm sure this heroic encounter will feature in the book so I will leave the rest to Alan.

After a very successful career, largely around the East Midlands, Mr Young has had his ups and extreme downs, all of which, undoubtedly, will make for a fascinating and emotional read.

Gary Lineker, 2013

1

EARLY DAYS

My Mum's name is really Isabella and my Dad's is William, but they were known as Ella and Ron and they met in 1950 in the Labour Club on Hunter Street in Kirkcaldy, Fife. That's where my parents got together and that was the start of it. Now my Mum doesn't know that I know this but I worked it out and she must have been pregnant with my older brother when she got married. My brother turned out to be a horrible bastard – I won't even mention his name in this book.

I was born and raised in Kirkcaldy in Fife; the first house that we stayed in, No. 133 Dunairn Drive, was the middle tenement of a block of flats. I lived there with my elder brother and parents and then along came the twins, Lynn and Ronnie. My Mum was absolutely taken aback because she didn't know she was having twins. My Dad at the time had just come out of Bowhill pit where he had worked as a coal miner since he was fourteen. His brothers had all gone to war but my grandmother said to him, 'You're the youngest boy, you're not going to war.' However, despite missing the conflict he did nearly lose his life in a roof fall underground. He has the biggest scar you can imagine on his back; it goes from top to bottom and there are branches of the scar coming off – he calls it his tree.

Mum and Dad used to like to go up to the Temple Hall Tavern for a pint or two and that was in the days when the women couldn't get in the bar, so Mum would have to go in the snug. They would leave the twins with me and my brother and the two of us would just end up fighting and I remember during one fight he put my head through the veranda window. Incredibly I didn't get a single cut from that but when Mum and Dad came back the curtains were blowing everywhere so we couldn't really hide it. We both got a good hiding for that, no messing about.

Another time we set fire to the airing cupboard because we were messing around with matches but this was par for the course for us and each time we got a good hiding; we expected it and got it. I can remember when I was about five years old, I pulled a hot pot of tea all over my chest and I still have the scars. They put a huge piece of lint smothered in Germolene on it. That hurt but not as bad as when I broke my leg when I was six years old. We used to have a little slope on the path outside the house and it was gritted because there had been snow. However, we could still slide on it because we were tough! Anyway, the scullery window overlooked the pavement and I remember sliding and falling over and landing on the path and I felt a crack and I thought 'Oh shit!' I looked up to the window and shouted, 'Mum! I've cracked my leg!' She appeared.

'You what?'

'I've cracked my leg,' I repeated.

'Well, if you've scratched your leg, get up and I'll have a look at it.'

'No! I've cracked my leg!'

Sure enough, I had broken it, so I went off to the general hospital down near Ravenscraig Castle to have it set in plaster. I can always remember how itchy it was and when they took the cast off, three knitting needles and a fork and some other stuff fell out that I had stuffed into the cast trying to scratch the leg. I nearly shit myself when they came to take the cast off because I thought that gun device with the circular saw on the end was for cutting right through the plaster but it wasn't, it only vibrated. I had to be held down while they took it off, because I was screaming and thrashing around until it was removed.

I do know that as a child I was very happy, even though we had nowhere really to go and play. There were flats all around us that were ready for demolition so we used to play football in the close which was 10 yards long and 6 yards wide. We would play keepy-uppies, headies or football-squash against the door. I used to shit myself when the downstairs neighbour, Shug Nicholson, would come out when we were playing football. He kept ferrets and when he came out and got a load of stick from us, he would say 'Right, I'm going to fetch Snowy!' We would scatter in all directions because Snowy was this mean, white ferret and we were terrified of it! Then there was Mrs Martin who lived on the other side. If the ball ever went in her garden she would just put a knife in it. Horrible person she was.

Christmases were great! You always looked forward to Christmas but you never expected anything; it was just the way you were conditioned, Mum and Dad were skint, they never had any money. Very poor, my Dad had just come out of the pit and was working for Rent-a-Set which became Radio Rentals and eventually Thorn Electricals. He wasn't on a great wage, while Mum was at home looking after the kids and that's how it was. But you always hung a sock up and you always got an orange and an apple and some nuts (still with the shells on usually). One year my Dad made me a fort out of hardboard. He made the turrets and the towers with a hacksaw and then he painted it; he must have spent ages on it. And they got me some toy soldiers to go in it as well. I adored that fort.

The next Christmas I was about seven years old and I got a bike. I thought, 'How the hell have they managed to afford this lovely red bike?' and I assumed it was for my brother until they opened a bedroom door and there was a slightly bigger bike which *was* for him – so the red one was mine. The elation that I had was amazing but not anything near the joy I had when I got my first football boots. Oh Christ almighty! Timpson Shooting Stars they were called and they were black with four blue stripes and even if they were too big or small I wouldn't have cared, they were not going back. I was straight outside, deep snow (proper snow!) to play in them. They were *my* football boots.

We eventually moved to Valley Gardens because up until then my two brothers and I had slept in the same bedroom – the same bed! – and with no central heating – it was freezing cold. My sister Lyn was sleeping in Mum and Dad's bed. Valley Gardens was a whole new world to me and I was enrolled for Valley Primary School which was half a mile up the road – that was when the football really started. I got another pair of boots from my Dad and these were proper Adidas boots with screw in studs, the absolute business. I remember sitting in the bath with them to soften them up in hot water, and afterwards stuffing them with newspaper.

When I was about nine, I got into the primary school's team which was unusual because you usually didn't make it into the team until your last year at school, but I was good enough at nine. The man in charge of the football team was Mr Reeckie and he didn't have a clue – not a Scooby! He was tall like John Cleese and knew nothing about nothing, but he picked the team so you stayed on the right side of him. He picked my brother to play in the same team as me and he really was useless. I played on the right wing-back then and my brother played centre half because he was tall and that's all he was, tall! He couldn't trap a medicine ball in cement. The strip comprised green and blue hooped shirts and any colour shorts and socks that you wanted. We played Wednesday afternoons when everybody else was in classes unless there was the slightest spot of rain in which case it was called off – that breaks your heart when you're a kid. You have had the build-up and you've been waiting all morning and then at lunchtime you got changed! There was fierce rivalry between the local primary schools and the Valley headmaster, Mr Wood, was superb. He was like another Dad and he would always come and watch on the touchline. Great times my primary school days.

Where we lived in Valley Gardens was better for playing football than my previous residence. There was a lot more 'green' and on the other side of the road from us was a cul-de-sac which had a big sign at the top that read 'No Ball games'. Well, we used that for a goalpost! The coppers would come along and we were frightened of them back then, we thought we could go to jail for playing ball games there so if we saw a copper we would scarper and then creep back when we thought it was safe. We would play after it got dark and my Dad would come and look for me and shout 'Alan!'

I would dive out of the way and one of the boys would say, 'He's not here Mr Young,' and my Dad would say 'Well if you see him tell him to come home.'

'Aye I will Mr Young.'

As soon as he was gone the ball would be out again and we would carry on playing although, the next time Dad came and he caught you, you would really be in trouble.

When it was brighter we would go along to Hayfield Park and play matches up to twenty-a-side. It would start with maybe five or six of you, throw the jumpers down and off you go, and by the end of the day there would be fifteen or twenty on each side – we used to love it. They were very happy days, especially when my grandparents came to visit; Granny Forbes and GrandDad Forbes (who I'm actually named after). He was nicknamed 'Wingy' because he only had one arm (he lost it in a press at work) but he pushed a bike until he was sixty-five collecting insurance in all weather. My grandDad was a small, thin man (a bit like the old 'Steptoe' character) with very short, cropped hair. He would have a tot of whisky every day and say, 'That's to kick start my day'. He liked a fag as I recall and he always smoked Park Drive – my outstanding memory is that when you walked into their house it always smelled of fags or damp wool. Or both! He would be in the window of the front room studying his 'Bible' (his horse handicap form book). He would have a drag on his fag and then put it behind his ear while he wrote something down, and he had a big nicotine stain all up that side of his head. It was a sad day when my granny got knocked over in a road accident by a hit-and-run driver. She eventually died of her injuries after which my grandDad lasted about three weeks before he was taken into hospital. He had a bottle of whisky brought in for him and of course he wanted to be near a window so he could have a crafty fag. I remember the nurse seeing these and taking them away and she actually said, 'I'm going to take these away from you Mr Fforbes because all they will do is kill you.' He died the next day.

My parents' discipline was physical. The expression, 'Wait 'til your father gets home' was never more true or feared than in our house. If we misbehaved then you would be sent to your room to wait for Dad to come home and you would be quaking. You could hear him come in, hear the argument at the bottom of the stairs and then he would be coming up the stairs taking off his belt and he would come in the bedroom. He wouldn't even ask you anything, he would just wallop you a few times. But we were always out the house playing football and when I joined the YMCA, then the serious football started. That was at the same time as I got into Kirkcaldy High School when I passed the eleven-plus because I was clever enough, as was my sister. My brother, however, was another matter. He used to copy off of me and in one test when I wrote an answer of 'I don't know', he wrote 'I don't know either'!

I was playing football for the YMCA, the Boys' Brigade and several representative teams so every weekend I would play Saturday morning, Saturday afternoon, Sunday morning and sometimes on Sunday afternoon as well. That was four games some weekends! I remember that a few of us from the Boys' Brigade thought that it would be good fun to hitchhike one weekend up to Inverness and go camping. I would have been about fifteen or sixteen at this point. Well, we got about 6 miles without getting a lift so we got the train instead. When we got to the campsite in Inverness we were amazed to find out that the Kirkcaldy battalion of the Boys' Brigade were also there on an organised trip. So I found Mr Methren, the Kirkcaldy Boys' Brigade leader, and asked him how on earth I didn't know about this. He smiled and said, 'You were told Alan but you told us you were playing football.' I couldn't remember it for the life of me! Anyhow, there was match arranged between the Kirkcaldy Brigade and the Inverness Brigade and Mr Methren asked me to play but I didn't have any boots. They managed to borrow a pair for me and they were actually baseball boots that belonged to Rankin Grimshaw, chairman of Raith Rovers at the time. I played the match and ripped the guts out of those baseball boots but he didn't seem to mind because afterwards he invited me for a trial at Raith Rovers down at Stark's Park. So I went along and I managed to score a goal but I was so disappointed because there were no nets in the goals so my shot went between the posts and just trickled on to the running track – I wanted to see the net bulge!

Raith didn't take me on, though. I wasn't mature enough or strong enough or fit enough at that time – I was only a kid. I used to go and watch Raith, though, they were my local team and we would sneak in over the railway line for free. We couldn't afford to watch football and to be honest we preferred playing. We would walk miles just to play a game of football, the sport was everything to us back then. When I did watch Rovers my hero was a guy called Ian Porterfield who I eventually played for at Sheffield United. When he first started at Raith he was known as the new Jim Baxter.

Sadly most of the coaches at YMCA lacked any real football knowledge and most of the training sessions consisted of running and fitness work. But we still enjoyed it because we didn't know any different and I used to love playing. There was fierce rivalry with teams like Leven Royals and Dunfermline but we feared no one because we had good players like Martin Henderson – who was eventually my best man. But it was more than just the football; I used to live at the YMCA and they would have discos on a Saturday night and me and my mates would turn up drunk having been to the off-licence on the way!

I remember there was a tournament in France that the YMCA was invited to and they asked me to go with the seniors which was a big deal for me. The problem was the cost, Mum and Dad never had a pot to piss in so when I asked them I didn't expect them to say yes – but they did. They somehow found the money and I went to Grasse for this tournament for a week. I went back to the guy who was running the trip, Jim Cooper, and gave him the good news straightaway because I was elated, really chuffed.

We played a team from Saint-Remèze and a side from Grasse, the local French town. I didn't play in the first two games but I was picked for the third and, basically, if we won that then we would win the tournament. There were about ten minutes to go when their centre half played a dodgy backpass to the keeper and I was in on it like a flash and slid it past the goalie into the net. However, just as I played the ball the centre-half came in late on me and slashed all down my calf. I was in agony on the ground and a big fight was broke out all around me; Tom Stirling came hurtling up the pitch from our penalty area and kept on running and then stuck the heed on their centre-half. Bang! And then all hell broke loose.

I was taken to the local hospital because they thought I might have ruptured a blood vessel. I hadn't as it turned out but they gave me some cream to help with the bruising. We had a few drinks after and then went back to the accommodation. Now I'm not sure if he was pretending to be drunk or actually drunk but Jim Cooper was acting very strange on the way back. We all went to bed in the dormitories and I was just dropping off when Jim came into my room and said he wanted to put some of the cream on my calf injury. Now bear in mind I was only fifteen at the time, was half asleep and I had no real understanding of what it was to be gay (in those days we would have said 'poof') and although I hadn't heard any rumours about Jim, I was still a bit uncomfortable with this. I lay on my side and he put some cream on my calf and the next thing I know he's got his hand on my dick. That snapped me awake and I jumped up and told him to fuck off. Now keep in mind that I was only fifteen and the first thing I thought of was that I would get in trouble for telling Jim Cooper to fuck off, even though I knew that what he did was wrong.

I needed to tell someone about this so I told a pal of mine, Angelo Grieg. He was a goalkeeper and only had one eye, as it happens. Angelo said, 'Right, don't you worry, I'll look after you,' and he was the only person I ever told because I didn't want any mockery or trouble, it was a different world then. But many years later a number of people came forward to say that they had been sexually assaulted by Jim Cooper and came to a big court case in Kirkcaldy. I chose not to come forward with more evidence because the logistics of getting to and from Kirkcaldy would have been difficult and, to be honest, I didn't want to get involved in it given where my career was at the time.

Jim Cooper was found 'not proven' (which in Scotland means unable to prove guilt or innocence) and stripped of his MBE (which he had for youth work) but the case was hampered by a number of witnesses withdrawing their statements and he kind of got off with it. He was a very lucky man, but I knew. At that age I trusted adults and nobody ever admitted to being gay because if you did then you would be persecuted.

✳ ✱ ✳

Kirkcaldy High School was a bit daunting to be honest. We had to wear uniform for the first time (collar and tie) and the teachers all wore gowns and mortar boards. A proper school! My first couple of years there we didn't have a football team – it was all rugby, volleyball and basketball. I didn't play schools football until I was eighteen. What 'got me' was playing football in the playground with a tennis ball and I would be taking all the lads on and beating them and then coming back for more and people thought, 'This kid's a bit good, I want to be his pal.' So I was accepted fairly early and I actually enjoyed my time at secondary school. My uncle (my Dad's brother) was an RAF man all his life and he helped me choose my O-Level subjects, so there I was doing Physics, Chemistry, Maths, English, PE and German, believe it or not. I actually got an O-Level in German! The standard of football stepped up once I had done my O-Levels and I used to play with Robbie Graham (who was on Rangers' books) Martin Henderson (my best friend, he was at Glasgow Rangers), Ken McNaught (Aston Villa) and Andy Blair (who went to Coventry). We would all be playing against each other. We had a maths teacher called Mr Ritchie and in the Monday morning lesson there would be no work done because he always wanted to talk about the game at the weekend and wanted to know how we had got on.

Miss Trotter, my English teacher, was absolutely gorgeous. I was in love with her! In the seven years at that school, hers was the only class where I sat at the front. Every other class I would be at the back, but not hers. I wonder where she is now. Now Mr Gilchrist, who I had for Chemistry, I was not so fond of. I never understood a word he said and he would give you the belt for the slightest thing. He drove a bubble car so one morning we got to school a wee bit early and carried this car into the assembly hall between a dozen of us. As everyone arrived from all over the school for assembly and the laughter subsided, the headmaster (The Bod) stood up and asked, 'Does anyone have any information as to why this vehicle is in the position it is in?' And we cracked up then, and all got pulled out by the teachers, and then taken to wait outside The Bod's office. There were letters to the parents, threat of expulsion and all sorts.

All in all I managed to get nine O-levels and two A-Levels and needless to say I failed Chemistry twice!

The reason I stayed on after O-levels was that, up until then, we hadn't played football but they were going to introduce it at last – and we had a team and a half! I was captain of the volleyball team and the basketball team and I was doing alright to be honest. I loved my PE teacher Terry Trewartha, he was fantastic and the only teacher we could call by their first name; we would call him 'Terry' or 'T' and he called me 'Youngy'. He coached us for everything and he introduced football and made me captain, meaning I was responsible for picking the team. We went on to win all sorts of trophies and I got capped for Scotland Schoolboys. They used to have trials for what they called 'Secondary Juvenile' tournament and then there were further trials for the international team. I failed the Secondary Juvenile tournament disastrously. It was played at Dens Park, Dundee, and it saw East of Scotland play West of Scotland. I remember the pitch had an awful lot of grass on it and I had a shite afternoon! We then had separate trials for the international team. I remember my Dad took me along to those and in the first game they played me wide on the right again and I played quite well before they took me off.

'How did I do?' I asked my Dad.

'You're doing alright,' he said.

Then in the next game I scored 2 goals early on before they took me off again, and again I said 'Dad! What's going on?'

'You're alright, relax,' he said, and then in the third game I didn't play. By the fourth game I was concerned but looking around I could see players like Errol Dowe and John Paterson (who went on to play for Rangers) and they had already been successful at the Secondary Juvenile tournament previously, so I started to think that maybe I was doing alright after all.

FIELD OF PLAY

Duration: 40 minutes each half

Any team changes will be announced by loudspeaker

ENGLAND
(WHITE SHIRTS)

1. Trevor Henderson
2. Timothy Rutter
3. David Tatam
4. Alan Potts
5. Stephen McDonald
6. Graham McKenzie
7. John Worrall
8. Anthony Galvin
9. David Chandler
10. Tadeusz Nowakowski
11. Shane O'Neill

SCOTLAND
(BLUE SHIRTS)

1. Ian Cassells
2. John Brogan
3. Henry Murtagh
4. Sam Lynch
5. Steven Patterson
6. Tom McGuire
7. Alan Young
8. Lindsay Muir
9. Chris. Robertson
10. Norman Anderson
11. Atholl Henderson

Substitutes

Nigel Fenner
Adriane Goode
Richard Wilson
Ian Scott
Graham Heys

Hamish Morrison
Leonard Fair
Ian Gibson
Errol Dow
Brian Ross

Referee: P. BIRCHALL (Bolton)

Linesmen :

D. M. HOLLOWELL
(Nottingham)

D. A. HARPER TARR
(Carlisle)

TO ALL OUR YOUTHFUL SPECTATORS

May we appeal to you to respect the property of this fine stadium and to refrain from causing damage or encroaching on the playing pitch.

Programme produced by R. Travers, Esq.
Printed by A. Cook & Sons Printers Ltd. 278 Manchester Road, Audenshaw

I played well again and played the whole game. At the end of the tournament my Dad came across and said that there was this guy wanted to talk to me and it turned out he was a scout from Southampton, and he invited me down for a two-week trial.

The trial at Southampton took place the same time that Lawrie McMenemy was in charge there. They put me up in this big old house which was ok but, of course, I was on my own so I went out into town to have a look around and I ended up going to the cinema and watched *The Exorcist*. I was sat in the second row and by Christ I nearly shit myself! There were people being sick and fainting but the bit that really got me was when the father has come back for the exorcism and he's sat on his own in a room with just a bare lightbulb. He's drained and exhausted and then the music starts to build (you know, 'Tubular bells') and I'm thinking, something's gonna happen here and the tension is building and guess what happens? The fuckin' phone rang in his room! I jumped 6ft in the air and then looked around saying, 'I knew that was coming, didnae scare me that.' Then I had to walk home through this big dark park and in through the big front door which creaked as it opened. None of this was helping me I can tell you so, when I turned off the light switch, I was in bed before the light went out!

Now Lawrie Mac was manager overseeing the trials but they turned me down. The next time I saw Lawrie was after I scored twice against Southampton in the F.A. Cup at Filbert Street. He stopped me in the corridor after the game and said, 'Whatever happened to you? Why didn't you sign for us?' I said 'Your loss pal!' He then made out that he knew nothing about me being rejected and that he had wanted to sign me.

I was also offered trials at Nottingham Forest in 1974 and Tony Woodcock was on trial there at the same time. We played three games in seven days; I got a hat-trick in the first, he got a hat-trick in the second and we both scored one each in the third. So what did they do? Fucked me off and kept him! To be honest it was probably the right thing to but it makes me smile to think about it. This was before Cloughie of course; Allan Brown was manager at Forest then.

But even bigger than these trials in England was the news that I had made the Scotland team! They announced it at the end of the Secondary Juvenile trials and said, 'This will be the team to play England at Old Trafford.' Not a squad – the team! When they said 'Alan Young' I thought, 'Bloody Hell! Did he just say my name?' and I looked at my Dad who turned and walked away to have a little moment to himself. I never imagined I was that good but since then whenever I have taught kids or coached them in any way, I have always told them that if you are in the right place at the right time, doing the right things and being seen by the right people, then that can be what gets you your break, because that is how I got started on my professional career. And that applies in any walk of life, just do those four things and you never know.

My Dad was very supportive of my career, especially in the early days. Sometimes when I came home from football he would ask how I got on and I might say that I'd done okay or scored a couple. But he would always ask questions about where we had played or who we had played against as if he hadn't been there. Then one day, when I was explaining what had happened in the match, he said, 'Aye, but what about that one you missed?' I looked at him.

'How did ye know about that one? Were ye there?'.

He just smiled and nodded and that was the first time he admitted that he had actually been there. It turns out for years he had been watching me from a distance or hidden. I have never really discussed it with him; why didn't he come and stand on the touchline with the other Dads? He only came to Filbert Street twice but he loved it because Jock Wallace made a big fuss of him and generally he would come to games when he could – which wasn't very often.

So we went to Old Trafford and drew 1–1 with England and I set up the equaliser. I was the only player in the Scotland side, or on the pitch for that matter, who wasn't associated with a professional club. In the stands that day was a guy called Colin McDonald, he had been a goalkeeper for Burnley and maybe Scotland. He approached me and said that he was from Oldham Athletic and asked me to sign for them. So a few weeks later he came to Valley Gardens in Kirkcaldy and sat in our dining room and there I signed my first contract – it was a one-year full professional contract.

2

COMING TO ENGLAND – OLDHAM ATHLETIC

I went to Oldham with my Dad and my grandDad to have a look round and get prepared. We then returned to Scotland and I started to get everything sorted for leaving permanently a week later. On my own for the first time in my life, away from my family and friends, I was wondering what would happen. I was full of trepidation and basically shittin' myself if I'm honest. But I decided to say my goodbyes at home because I didn't want everybody at the train station; I would have just broken up so my Dad took me and we never spoke a word. Not a word, all the way to the station. The first thing he said was, 'Go and get yer ticket,' so I did and we went on to the platform. The train arrived and he still wasn't saying anything; he put my bag onto the luggage rack in my carriage and then got back out. I got on the train and pulled the window down (because you could in those days) and I leaned out and he shook my hand and said, 'Just remember one thing son. Don't you ever lose your accent.' At the time I remember wondering why he would say that, thinking that maybe they wouldn't understand me down there or something.

I arrived in Manchester Piccadilly, was picked up by Colin McDonald and got taken to a part of Oldham called Werneth. It was Coniston Avenue to be exact, and I stayed there with Tony, Barbara and Tracey (the daughter) and she was a right pain in the bollocks. They were big people and they liked to eat; they used to make this huge tray of something called Parkin, which was like a big treacle sponge cake, and the Sunday dinners they made were fantastic.

I started my first preseason as a professional footballer which was a really new and strange environment for me. I was earning £30 a week as a professional footballer in a professional club, paying only £10 a week for digs – by Christ did I feel loaded! I settled in eventually, but I was homesick as hell for about five or six weeks. However, it ended suddenly because preseason was over and I found myself in the first team, so I had something else to think about. We were playing away at Manchester City in the Texaco Cup. Only six weeks earlier I had been playing on the fields at Valley Primary School pretending to be Denis Law in a Scotland v England game (as we used to call it) and here was Denis Law on the pitch with me! And so was Colin Bell, Mike Summerbee, Rodney Marsh and Franny Lee and I just thought 'holy shit!' I remember running over and deliberately bumping into Denis Law just so I could say 'I touched Denis Law'– he was a hero of mine.

And that was my full debut. I got taken off even though I had a good game (I've got newspaper clippings that I have read and it looks as if I did okay and did enough to deserve a run in the team) but I gave Tommy Booth a hard time so he came over and clattered me as if to say, 'fuck off! Don't you take the piss out of me!' So that was that. But I did okay and the older pros started to accept me in the dressing room. When I first got there I was in what they called the

26 COMISTON AVE,
WERNETH,
OLDHAM.

Dear Folks,
　　　Here we go again with some more newspaper cuttings off our game against Cardiff.
　　　I'm really looking forward to seeing all the cuttings together again. It should be quite good as I've forgotten all I've done.
　　　Anyway hope all is well at home and until I phone or write again Cheerio,
　　　　　　　　Love,
　　　　　　　　　　Alan xxx

Reserve Team Dressing Room with the reserves and some of the younger kids. It was difficult to talk to them because they knew that I was a pro and they gave me some stick for that, but once I made my debut I was moved into the first-team dressing room. There were some very strong characters in there and some lovely people and I made some friendships that have survived to this day, like Les Chapman, who is the kit manager at Manchester City. Despite this, I still had to go to training everyday on the No. 420 bus, which dropped me off at the top of Sheepfoot Lane – Boundary Park being at the bottom of the road. But I didn't mind that, I knew I hadn't arrived yet and I certainly wasn't famous. I remember talking to Ronnie Blair who was a miserable Irish bastard, but he did give me some useful advice early on in my time at Oldham. He told me, 'Make the most of it 'cos it doesn't half go quickly' – and not a truer word has anybody said to me because your career is over before you know it. One minute you're making your debut and the next minute you are retiring from the game, but at the time I didn't really think about it.

Back then I was used as a sub a lot and I remember a young pro called Ian Buckley who would take some dumbbells and weights under the Main Stand and build his strength like that, so I started to join him. We also used to do extra sprints on the track with spikes. Back then this was unusual because the club didn't really worry about building up my strength, but I knew that I needed to when I looked at the other guys in the first team.

I settled into the first team eventually and held down a regular place. They were great times even though the club was poor and we never had anything like the facilities that they have now. Take the team bus for instance; we didn't have toilets on board, we had to pee into a plastic container and put a lid on. Then Andy Lochhead would empty it out of the window – you didn't sit behind the window or you would get covered in urine if it was windy. And we didn't have post-match drinks or nutritional meals, if you were lucky you got fish and chips on the way home.

Training was mostly about running. I don't think I ever got coached properly until I was at Brighton and Sammy Nelson was coach there. He came from Arsenal with lots of good ideas. Jock Wallace and Ian Macfarlane at Leicester were never coaches; they were more motivators and man managers. I suppose the exception at Oldham was Andy Lochhead, he was the first person who ever took a real interest in my career. We used to go to Clayton Park training ground which was close to Boundary Park but wasn't actually a proper training ground, people walking their dogs could join in if they wanted to. I remember Bernard Manning came by one day in his Rolls-Royce and wound the window down and started taking the piss. He was performing at Ian Woods' testimonial years later as the star attraction and at one point when he was doing his routine he pointed at me and said, 'See that c*nt Alan Young? If he had taken six shots at John Lennon then the bastard would still be alive!' I just shouted 'Fuck You!'

But Andy Lochhead would take me out to the park with a bag of footballs and an empty goal (we would even put the goal net up ourselves) and it was awful conditions because the pitches were shite – unbelievable! But me and him would be out there in all weathers and he would throw them to me and say, 'Hit the net!' and it didn't matter if it bobbled in or flew in, I just had to hit the target. He would say that for every one I missed I would have to give him ten press-ups at the end of the session. And that was how we did it and it was good for me, he would be calling out, 'Right foot, left foot, take a touch, first time, turn.' Big Andy must have seen something in me, having played in that position himself. I must have played two or three times alongside Andy for Oldham and he was a huge influence on me because I was in awe of him; I was a little bit scared of him in fact. I don't think today's young footballers have the same respect for senior professionals; they have a certain swagger because they have the nice cars and the nice watches and everything. Take Patrick van Aanholt who was on loan at Leicester City in 2011; he thought he was Ashley Cole and he wasn't even close, especially when it came to defending. I think it is a process where you learn your trade and develop that confidence and self-belief as you get better, but now the young players don't have that. Too many of them are giving it the big 'I am' and we just wouldn't have behaved like that then. You worked your bollocks off and if you didn't then you didn't make the team. Simple.

Big Andy Lochhead looked after me on the pitch as well. He was a great talker. I learned how to give useful instructions to my teammates from Andy, you know the sort of thing – 'Man on, turn inside, get it wide, etc.' I made my league debut at Portsmouth when I came on as sub, and soon after we got a corner. Now I don't know why I was standing where I was, just inside the box, but the ball came across and it was half-cleared and I just hit it and it flew into the back of the net. Well, catch me! Come on, if you can. There must have been about three Oldham supporters in the corner so I ran to them and I felt fucking great! I felt fantastic and all the lads came over and said 'Well done' and so on but I felt unbelievable that day. I'm thinking I love this game! And it's a feeling you never get tired of, every time you score it feels like that. You celebrate in different ways but on that day, the first, coming on as sub, evening kick-off, staying in the Holiday Inn, bring it on! I loved it because it was all new – it's better than an orgasm! But in the midst of all this Andy Lochhead came across, calm as you like, and said, 'There's twenty fucking minutes to go. Screw the nut and focus.' Andy was making me do his running at the time and I was challenging everything and running around like crazy and then suddenly I'm lying on the ground, poleaxed. Somebody had smashed me in the face but I only found out that it was Eoin Hand when, a few minutes later, he was out himself as Andy had absolutely mullered him.

Andy virtually knocked him out and Eoin Hand was a big lad, but there he was on the ground with blood all over his face and Andy standing over him saying, 'Leave the fucking kid alone.' Hand went on to manage the Irish national team when he retired from playing.

That sort of retribution doesn't happen as often these days because there are cameras everywhere. I would always wait for corner kicks and then get one in when the referee wasn't looking and if you didn't then someone else would do it for you. That's how it was then.

After that game I was flying. I sat at the bar in the Holiday Inn having a pint of shandy and this gorgeous girl came over and started talking to me. We were chatting away and I thought, 'I've made my debut, scored, and this gorgeous girl is talking to me!' And then in came Woody, Gus, Les, Maurice Whittle, all big time Charlies and what did they do? Straight into her and that's me bombed. Not that I would have known what to do back then but as it turns out they did me a favour – she was a hooker! I know for certain that one or more of that group had to visit the doctor when they got back to Oldham.

I made my full league debut away at Cardiff and I scored again but I had another run-in, this time with a real animal called Richie Morgan. I didn't go looking for trouble and that was never part of my game when I was a youth player, but I suppose I was thinking that I was playing against real men and I needed to take care of myself. So I was elbowing him and knocking him whenever I got the chance and what happened? I got knocked out again. But then I got booked by that twat, Keith Hackett! Because I was annoying the centre half! But he had punched me! Anyway, we drew 1–1 and after I scored I ran past Morgan and said, 'Fuck you!' Maybe the centre-halves union were on the phone to each other or something because they seemed to be after me. But that never bothered me – I loved all of that.

Boundary Park didn't have great facilities, we used to do a lot of running up the hills around the area and we certainly didn't have dieticians telling us what to eat. In fact, if we played away from home you would have a pre-match meal. Usually it would be a light lunch; some would have fish or scrambled eggs or toast and then Andy Lochhead would come into the dining room and wander among the lads asking what they were eating.

'What are you having there Chappy [Les Chapman]?'

'Scrambled eggs and beans, Andy.'

'Aye that sounds nice, might have that myself,' and then he would walk over and put his hand on my shoulder and say, 'You can have some chips today son.' That meant you weren't playing! If you got the hand on the shoulder then you knew you could have chips, the unhealthy option, because you weren't picked. It didn't just happen to me but it was happening more often because it was my first season and I was still trying to establish myself in the side so whenever he would walk around the dining room I'd be thinking, 'Fuck off you big bald bastard!' But if it was somebody else then we could all enjoy it and the lads would be saying, 'Can we get some salt and vinegar for my pal?'

But the day when I realised that I had changed was when I first went back to Scotland after about three months in Oldham. I kept intouch with a lot of my mates – like Graham Dickie, Tom Fleming and 'Gogs' McGarry – and we had arranged to go out for a drink down the road. What I noticed was that they all seemed like giggly little girls to me and doing daft things. When we got out the pub they were throwing bottles up the street and I thought, these guys are still kids. They haven't changed and I've moved on. I had responsibilities now and they were still with their Mums and Dads. And after that night I didn't bother keeping in touch and I didn't go home much. I had to get on with my life and what I had to do and stay focused. If I had kept my association with them then I might have got myself into a wee bit of trouble. I realised that night that I had matured and a lot had happened to me in my life but nothing had changed in theirs. So it was back to Oldham and back to work and the environment that I was comfortable in, I loved it.

❊ ✳ ❊

I remember a refereeing decision involving the legendary Jack Taylor. Now Alan Groves, 'Gus', was very well endowed and a bit of a legend, but we always left him up on the halfway line because he was safer there, he couldn't mark time! I forget where we were playing but this corner came across and I managed to trap it and clear it away over the halfway line and Gus was after it, the linesman flagging for offside. I went to Jack Taylor and said 'Jack, he couldna been offside, he was in his own fuckin' half'. Jack replied, 'Al, if he didn't have such a big fuckin' donger he would have been on side.'

Referees at that time were more humorous. Take Bernard Mcnally for instance. Bernard was a bit rotund and thinly thatched (like Andy Lochhead) and he sounded a bit effeminate and he was gay. Anyway, one evening after a night game he came into the dressing room and said, 'Excuse me, the shower in the referee's room isn't working, can I use yours?' He said in his funny voice, 'can I have a bath with the boys?' Of course all the lads were having a laugh shouting 'let's play hunt the soap!' The relationship with referees was better and refs like Pat Partridge and Clive Thomas were human and you could talk to them. I think they made just as many mistakes then as they do now but refs now are totally scrutinised and so it seems like they are worse, but they're not.

✳ ✱ ✳

Now and then I would come home and there was Ken McNaught (who was at Villa by then), Martin Henderson and Andy Blair (who was at Coventry) and we would go for a round of golf and get bladdered together in the clubhouse until midnight, followed by a taxi home to Martin's house. We always went to Martin's because there was a bakery nearby and the smell of baking bread would wake us up in the morning and we would go and get some hot rolls for breakfast. I enjoyed going to my Mum and Dad's as well, but at that stage I didn't really think too much about my parents after I had got over the initial spell of homesickness. But the thing that did stay with me was that when I was seventeen I met a girl called Fiona Foster and it was like, wham! We were together all the time, every spare minute. Even the football took a back seat occasionally because I was totally and absolutely besotted with her. She was a beautiful girl but more than that, she seemed a lot older and wiser than me, working as a hairdresser when I was still at school. We had some fantastic times together; I remember when I broke my foot and I was in plaster but I still walked her home to her house in Grampian Gardens (and it was up a long hill so it felt like climbing the bloody Grampians) but I knew what I would get at the end of it. There was some groping took place there I can tell you, and we steamed up her porch window many times, but we had a great time together and we were great together. She always said that I just left her and broke her heart when I came down to Oldham but I don't remember it that way. I still feel a bit shit about that because, if I did break her heart then, she didn't deserve it. I often wonder 'what if?' Of course we didn't have mobile phones then, it was much harder keeping in touch and the relationship might have lasted if it happened today. I remember that Fiona was very supportive of me and whenever I had injury problems she always came to see me. Mum and Dad loved her too. She was a huge part of my life for eighteen months and I was very proud to be seen with her when we were out holding hands. One or two people, including my Dad, would say, 'What's happening with the football then?' He would be telling me to concentrate on the football and I'm thinking, 'if you were getting what I'm getting you wouldn't be saying that!'

During my return trips to Fife in 2012 I started to see Fiona again and we got pretty serious for a while but I messed things up and lost her all over again. We were doing stuff together again and visiting our old haunts and basically I fell in love and it felt great. I got a bit carried away with the euphoria of being with Fiona on a trip to Fort Augustus and I felt really good and had too much to drink and completely missed how much I had upset her. It was a tense weekend all round after that and it went downhill and brought about a cooling-off period. Basically she thinks I have been single for too long and to be honest, Fiona's lifestyle just doesn't suit me anymore.

Anyway, back to Oldham, and I started to get established in the first team and started to score goals on a regular basis. Occasionally the television cameras were there as well and I was getting good reviews. On one occasion I was interviewed by Ian St John after the game and that was all new to me. I think it went alright, it was on Granada television and I was getting noticed which was great. I was also getting bigger and stronger physically and learning the game – things were good. I think I did well for Oldham; they weren't the greatest of teams but they were a good set of lads and I enjoyed it, but I wanted to play at a higher level. I was going from £30 and a one-year contract, to £40 and a one-year contract, to £50 and a one-year contract, to £60 and a one-year contract and every year at the end of the season, I was shitting myself in case they were going to let me go. I was never confident enough to go and bang on the manager's door to demand a five-year contract, but it is just as well I didn't because if I had, I would have tied myself to the club and then I would have been trapped.

So eventually during the last year I was beginning to resent things because I knew that some of the other lads in the team were on two or three times the money I was on. That was around the time I scored a hat-trick against Leicester in the F.A. Cup and Martin Henderson spoke to me and said that Jock Wallace had asked him to talk to me and say that he liked me and wanted to talk. That was a strange night all round because my best pal, Martin Henderson, was playing for Leicester and I also nearly got knocked out by flying concrete from the Leicester end where some of their fans were throwing lumps on to the pitch. But that hat-trick was the best thing I ever did because it got me my move to Leicester.

Funnily enough we nearly didn't play Leicester in the cup that year. We played Stoke away in the third round and, because it was snowing, they rolled the snow and marked the pitch with blue lines so the referee said the game could go ahead. Anyway, we were getting nowhere and we were 2–0 down in no time. When we came in at half time, Jimmy Frizzell said, 'Right, get your kit off and get in the bath. We are not fucking going out for the second half'. We looked at each other and one of us said, 'You can't do that Jim, that's not allowed surely.'

But he was adamant – 'Get in that fuckin' bath!' – and he was away to see the referee to tell him that he wasn't letting his players come out because it was dangerous and that they were all in the bath. So the ref had to call the game off and we played the match again at the Victoria Ground a few days later and we beat them 2–0 on a really boggy pitch. You would never get away with that these days either – managers had power then. Players never had power, the referees never had power, and the F.A. never had power. The power then was with managers and they dictated how football was run. Managers are coaches now, they don't run the football clubs like they used to.

I got on fine with Jimmy Frizzell but he always had a problem with me calling him 'Boss' – he didn't like it. It didn't matter whether we were at the club or away from the ground and mixing socially, I would always call him 'Boss' and he would say, 'Call me Jim.' But I couldn't because he *was* my boss – the gaffer.

I remember playing for Oldham at Leicester on New Year's Day in 1979. It was the day Gary Lineker made his debut and the pitch was hard but playable because Leicester had this protective tent. It's funny, even if the conditions are horrible and freezing like that, you still want the game to go ahead. But the conditions never bothered me although, these days there are some pros that will take a look and think, 'I'm not going out on that today.' It's unusual to have frozen pitches anyway these days because of undersoil heating and so forth. But when I was a kid I would play in any conditions and I would be gutted if the match was called off. I had good balance and a decent touch so I could get by on that type of hard pitch. And anyway, if you've trained and prepared all week you *want* to play, there was nothing worse (as a player) to be told that the game was off.

My contract at Oldham was almost up, so with freedom of contract I was free to leave. Oldham had offered me a new one-year contract but I had said no because I knew that Jock was interested in me. I went down to Leicester to meet him. Gerry Gow was the first to move under freedom of contract, when he went from Bristol City to Manchester City, and I was the second. I remember Jock saying to me, 'There's a bandwagon on the move, a rollercoaster, and if you want tae get on board then sign yer name on that fuckin' contract.' So they signed me and they said they would sort it all out and off we went on a tour of Sweden. I went back to Oldham and told my wife, Julie. We had had Wesley by then of course; he was born right opposite the football ground in Boundary Park Hospital just hours after Louise Brown (the first test tube baby) in the next cubicle. Anyway, when Oldham heard what I had done they went mental! I was accused of all sorts of things and the *Manchester Evening News* called me a traitor in a big article. It was only afterwards that I learned Manchester City had been promised first dibs on me if I decided to leave. Jimmy Frizzell was very good friends with Tony Book and I wouldn't have been surprised if some sort of unofficial deal was done although I can't know that for certain.

Oldham wanted £400,000 for me and Leicester offered £100,000 so it went to the tribunal and they fixed the fee at £250,000. I like to say a quarter of a million because it sounds more and it certainly did in 1979. I am also told that Richard Dinnis at Sunderland, Sammy Chung at Wolves and Mr Stein at Leeds wanted me but I didn't know anything about this interest, not a dickie bird, until afterwards. I didn't have an agent but there was more trust in the game then. Had I known about these other clubs would I have made the same decision? Abso-fuckin'-lutely! Because of Jock Wallace. And then I was a Leicester City player.

3

A FOX
IN THE BOX

I didn't drive in 1979 so I went down on the train and was met at the station by the (then) Leicester City secretary, Alan Bennett. He drove me to the Four Seasons hotel and I started to think, 'this is more like it! This is what I have waited for!' We took a detour via Filbert Street and had a wee look in there and already I was starting to feel very good about the move. Compared to what we had at Boundary Park, this was the business. So we ended up at the Four Seasons and the contract was already written up (that would never happen these days) and there was Alan Bennett, the gaffer and me in this hotel bedroom and Jock said again, 'This is one giant fuckin' rollercoaster, get yourself on it, sign this contract, don't miss out.' The contract was a four-year deal at £200 a week and that was more than double what I was on at Oldham and with win bonuses and a signing-on fee (which was £10,000 but it was taxable so I would have got about £7,000) I was feeling very happy about life. So Jock gave me the pen and said, 'Sign it.' And I did. I never questioned anything, I wasn't tempted to say anything like 'I want another £100 a week', or 'I want another five grand signing-on fee'. If I had I might have got it but I was convinced by Jock and I bought into it totally. There was an affinity for Jock Wallace from the first moment that I shook his hand; there was a thrill about working for Jock that I never lost. I was genuinely excited; I was thinking, 'When is the first game?' I couldn't wait to start. Once I signed it he shook my hand and said, 'Congratulations! You've just made a fucking great decision.' At the back of the room was Alan Bennett who squeaked up 'Welcome to the club' and all that. And that was it, I was a Leicester City player. I had to get back to Oldham, get all my stuff together and get myself off to Sweden for the preseason tour.

But before I did that I had a visit at the Four Seasons that night from Beverley Blackshaw who worked in hospitality at the football club, and I think at the time she was also Miss ATV. Now Bev was quite a looker and by all accounts Martin Henderson had been in touch with her to let her know that I was in town, on my own. So she showed up and said, 'Hi, my name's Bev, do you fancy a night out?' So we had a great night, ending up at Granny's nightclub and then back to the hotel. And then the next time I walked into the changing rooms everybody knew! That bastard Henderson had set me up and I knew he had when he said, 'That's it then, Bev only needs a wide left midfield player and then she's had the entire team.' I have no idea whether it was true or not but Bev was lovely and great fun, really good company.

Then things started to go much faster; Monday became Tuesday became Friday and suddenly I was off to Sweden with the team. I'd been back to Oldham to sort things out. I'd bought my first house up there by that time, a three-storey, three-bedroom terraced house near Oldham in a place called Hayside. I bought it for £5,950. I'd actually forgotten the solicitor's fees so when I walked out of the solicitor's office after signing the contract I had five pence to my name. But I had my house! I had my first son at that point, of course, and I was very happy. And now I had to put it on the market and get a new place in Leicester.

I went to Sweden while Julie had to start the business of selling the house. I'll tell you what really opened my eyes up, I had never seen a preseason tour like this. I had been to Anglesey with Oldham Athletic and it was all running, no drinking in the evenings (well not me anyway, I was drinking orange juice then) but the Sweden tour was something else. We stayed at a place called Hindusgarten with a guy called Nester Lauren. He organised the whole tour for us – 'nest o' tables' we would call him! He was a great guy and anything you wanted he would sort out for you. It was a great training camp with great facilities and a lovely surface to play on and above the pitch was a ski jump. In the winter the skiers would land on the pitch from this ski jump. There was a massive pine tree hanging over the pitch as well. Everything about that tour was top drawer, even the diet with fresh fruit and cereals and all the good stuff an athlete should be eating.

In that clear air you could hear things much more sharply. I woke up one morning and could hear this growling sound from outside and I remember thinking that it sounded like the gaffer. So I opened my curtains and sure enough there was Jock halfway up this ski slope on the steps. Jock had just had an operation on his knee to have it straightened and the plaster had been taken off just before we went to Sweden – he was shouting to himself to encourage himself to get up all those steps. When he eventually got to the top he stood up straight and, spread his arms out and went, 'Yeeeesssss! Come on!' And I looked at this and I thought, what a man! My admiration for him just grew and grew every time I was in his company. I would seek his company even though he was the Gaffer and I was just a player, I loved listening to him and being around him – but he would control the relationship so you were only pals when he said so. I really grew to respect him and we became great friends and we respected one another and we loved each other as I found out later in life.

We had nine games scheduled in the three weeks that we were there and I managed to get 19 goals in those games. Now good old 'Hans Christian' Bill Anderson was with us from the *Leicester Mercury*. The lads called him Uwe Seeler because he resembled the thinly thatched German midfielder but he made the mistake of letting it be known to us that he didn't like being called 'Uwe', which meant that we did it even more. Anyway Bill was doing his reporting and obviously this was getting back to Leicester and I was getting good reviews and loving it; I couldn't wait to wake up in the morning. The Gaffer would have us going to bed at nine in the evening but we did it without question and if you played fair by him then there would be rewards. You might get a night out some time or training would be broken up with a bit of fun stuff like a head tennis tournament. If players nowadays went to Hindusgarten for three weeks they would go stir crazy. They want Marbella, Dubai, the Far East or California but give me Hindusgarten any time; it was all about the football there. The highlight for me was a story involving little Dennis Rofe – or 'Sid' as we called him because he resembled Sid James with his strange haircut and his Cockney accent. He was a fantastic captain but on this occasion we had been let off the leash for the night. Jock said to us, 'Get yerselves off, enjoy yerselves but look after each other. If I hear that any of ye have left one o' yer pals anywhere, ye'll be for it boy! I want everybody at the fuckin' breakfast table at 9 o'clock. Ah dinna care if ye don't get back in until eight thirty, ye will be at the breakfast table at nine!' The rule was that if one person let the team down then everybody got fined £100 (half a week's wages).

Jeans, t-shirt, white belt (seriously) and white trainers, a load of aftershave on and off into Gothenburg we went. We found a bar where beer was £1 a pint! Even back thenSweden was expensive. Mind you if you fancied a snack then a reindeer sandwich would set you back a fiver! Anyway, we were in this pub and we are getting more and more merry, standing on the tables and dancing and stuff. Then this lovely Swedish girl hooks up with us and we went with her to a party. She was gorgeous but then they all are over there aren't they? We went off to this party, four of us: Me, Eddie Kelly, Martin Henderson and Bobby Smith. There was an umbilical cord joined the four of us together, wherever one went we all went. So I walked into this party and I was having a good time with this Swedish girl and I lost track of time because when I came out the rest of the lads, Bobby, Eddie and Martin were all waiting for me. They wouldn't leave me behind. It turns out that they couldn't get in but they didn't want to abandon me. I remember being in the party wondering where they had got to and I was a little bit worried because I didn't know where I was and how I was going to get back to the training camp. But when I got outside the first thing they said was, 'Did ye fuck her?' and I told them to mind their own business. After that it was just four pals walking back to the Hindusgarten and having a laugh. We got back alright but one person didn't – Sid! Some of us had only had like an hour's kip and some of the lads, the boring bastards like John O'Neill, Tommy Williams, Larry May, had been in bed early and had a full night's kip.

When I say 'boring bastards' I mean it with affection because they were great lads and I loved my teammates. Everybody was there at breakfast except Sid Rofe. It was now gone quarter to nine and there was no sign of him. Mark Wallington and Sid used to room together so we were asking him where he was and 'Duke' was saying 'I don't know, we got split up last night.' We were getting really pissed off now because there was a £100 fine waiting for us and the lads were starting to mutter among themselves about giving him a good hiding for this, you know, shut the door, turn off the light and wham! Then there was a couple of minutes to go and Jock started to count down the time. Then he said, 'In fifteen seconds you will all be fined a hundred quid,' and who should jump out from behind this tree outside but Dennis fuckin' Rofe!

'Awright boys, cor what's the time? Bloimy, look at that. It's 9 o'clock exactly, I'm jast in time.'

We couldn't do anything but laugh when he walked in with the swagger and the whistling. Bastard! But it had all been a set-up. Jock told me later that he had pulled Sid to one side when he got back and asked him if any of the lads had seen him get back. When Sid said that they hadn't, Jock told him to stay in his room until the very last minute. Jock didn't tell me that until a year later.

But things like that built team spirit. The way the room just lifted when he turned up was brilliant and the relief at not losing half your week's wages was immense. Jock was a master of player psychology and team building. A lot of this stemmed from his army days of course. If we went running in the woods everybody would be at the same pace with everybody putting the left leg down at the same time. The problem when we were out running was always Gary Lineker. Now he was only a baby then but he was incredibly fit and quick, so he would be away at the front of the pack on a run and Jock would be shouting, 'Come on Gary, step it up son,' and we were like, 'Slow down son, this is fast enough.' Then Jock shouted again 'Come on Lineker, get tae the fuckin' front!' and we said, 'Gary, do you want to take him on or do you want to take the rest of us on? Stay where you are.' Poor Gary didn't know what to do.

But Jock was always looking for an opportunity to bring everyone together. In most teams you will find cliques of three or four players but Jock simply wouldn't allow that. He might tell us that we were going to the local pub that night so we would meet in reception at 7 o'clock (and God help you if you were late, Jock wouldn't tolerate lateness) and we would all walk down to the pub together. Jock would get the drinks in and he would ask around the lads 'Anyone fancy a beer? Who wants a pint? Any of you ladies want a glass of wine love?' (meaning Tommy and Larry). And then all the daft stuff would start on the way home, trying to chuck each other in the lake and larking around, but we were all friends. Only one player didn't fit into that category but he wasn't there in that first season – Jim Melrose. If he had been there at that time then it would have been totally different. There was a closeness and friendship between all of the players and it remains to this day. If I see any of those lads now it is always a big hug and, 'How are you doing Big Man?' In all my time in football I have never known a team spirit like it before or since.

The only time that came close was when I was at Brighton and that wasn't down to the manager, that was down to the players. The manager then was Chris Cattlin and he had got Jimmy Melia sacked – he was a complete twat! He should have stuck to selling rock on the seafront.

After training there would always be about a dozen or so of us headed into town to Woody's Wine Bar and we would be there all afternoon. Two o'clock became 5 o'clock which became 8 o'clock and so on, into the night. We were good pals on and off the pitch but at Leicester we were a tighter bunch of players and it was more like a family. We would look after each other and that could make it difficult for players coming in, like Geoff Scott who arrived from Stoke in the second half of that first season. He never really fitted in; he was a bit of the big 'I am' and a bit reckless to be honest. Don't get me wrong, he did alright for Leicester. But that side was very consistent with not many changes and a few players were present in every match. But the team spirit started in Sweden and that was where Jock's experience with Glasgow Rangers kicked in. He had done it all with Rangers, all over Europe and he brought a lot of that with him to Leicester. He knew when to give you a kicking and when to give you a pat on the back. Some nights he would say, 'Right! Me and Ian [Macfarlane] are going out tonight, you lot all stay here. Don't you dare walk through that door.' Now that was fine by us because we could enjoy a bit of high jinks but you wouldn't dare disobey him.

The next time we went to Sweden he asked me to come to his room. He wanted a chat with me. He said, 'Listen! You're going to be fuckin' great manager one day. Yer intelligent, ye listen and people respect ye fer that. And ye dinnae suffer fools and yer good with people. You've earned the respect of others and ye have everything ye need tae be a good manager one day.' I never did, though. I remember him calling me when he was at Colchester and he told me that the Leicester City job was up for grabs again and he wanted me to partner him. The way he put it was that, 'Aye big man, I'm trying tae get back in at Leicester but I need some legs.' Roger Page was trying to get Jock back to Filbert Street and he called me first to let me know that Jock was going to phone. I told Jock I would be there for him and I would have loved that. Imagine, back at Filbert Street as Jock's lieutenant. But I never heard any more about it, which was such a shame.

My relationship with Jock was crucial for me. I wasn't scared of him even though he was a big imposing man – I knew he was a softie. Nobody saw that compassionate and caring side of him, or that smile that would greet you in the morning when you came into training; he would put his arm around my shoulders and say 'Aye, mornin' Big Man!' He made you feel great when you saw him at the club and it was a fantastic feeling to be in the same place as a man like Jock. He was a real family man and I remember when my first marriage wasn't going so well, he could sense it. He was very perceptive and his expression was that he could 'smell' something wasn't right and he knew about me and Julie, he just knew. I hate saying ,'he used to' because it reminds me that he isn't around anymore. I wish so much that he was still here. I still talk to him, though, maybe have a wee chat before I go to bed, maybe ask him 'What would you do?' if I have a dilemma.

He drove you hard and expected 100 per cent from everyone, no exceptions. He demanded application and dedication but he also believed in education. He liked to educate his players, not so much in football but in life. He would make sure the young lads knew about bank accounts for instance and he wanted to know if you were getting enough sleep and if you were eating right – even back then he had that sort of attention to detail. I remember young Stuart Hamill making his debut against Manchester City at Filbert Street in November 1980. Jock had been to watch the kids play at Belvoir Drive in the morning and 'Wee Hammy' was flying that morning. Jock said to Eddie May, 'Right, get him aff'. When Hammy came off Jock said, 'Right you, get a collar and tie on and be at Filbert

Street at 2 o'clock, you're playing against Manchester City.' He stuck him in and he slaughtered Bobby McDonald in the first half and set up my goal; he beat McDonald, drew the 'keeper and rolled it across for me to side-foot in. Perfect!

And then two minutes into the second half McDonald got him, in fact he absolutely murdered him. Hammy had stud marks down his front, McDonald was all over him. Bastard! And that was the end of young Hammy, he had to go off after that. You could tell that McDonald had had enough of this young upstart turning him over. But I got him back – he got a sore one and then he had to go off; we looked after each other. But Jock would approve of that because he likened the camaraderie and togetherness of his mates in the army when they were in the Burmese jungle, to the togetherness that he was trying to build at Leicester City. This was all part of it.

People have questioned Jock's tactical ability and maybe they are right. Before a game he would put the team up on the board in the physio's room and this is typical of his coaching; Wallington, Williams, Rofe, May, O'Neill, Smith, Lynex, Kelly, Peake, Young, Henderson – Lineker couldn't get a game at that time! And then it was, 'Wally, you know what ye're doin' eh? Back-four, you know yer jobs. Midfield, Ted [Eddie Kelly], sort it out. Big man? OK? Right, get through, get changed.' And that would be his team talk. I've learned since that if you try and give players too much information then it doesn't always work. I've been guilty of this too when I was coaching and at half time in a game you are going through five, six maybe seven points. It doesn't work, they can't take it in. Keep it to one point – 'Every time you get the ball, take him on', or 'Win your headers', or 'Hold the ball up' and 'Get your crosses in'. All individual things, not general points but Jock wouldn't even do that, he was very much concerned with general team orders. The last thing he would say was instructing us to have a wee swig of team spirit which was a bottle of whisky that would be sat on the table in the middle of the dressing room. And we all would, even the English lads like Tommy Williams and Larry May and watching their faces as they took a swig was always amusing. Tommy would usually spit it out and Jock would say, 'Dinnae waste ma fuckin' whisky you!' Then the last thing he would say before we went out would be, 'Right! Siddown! Have a wee think. Look at me, let me see yer fuckin' eyes. Do ye ken yer job? Cos if ye don't there's a fuckin' substitute sat there and he will dae it fer ye. Right get oot there!' We would be tearing the door off its hinges to get out on to the pitch after that. And it wasn't just Jock. He had been there a season before I joined and he had been starting to change things, giving the youth players a chance for instance. He wanted a young side, he believed in lads who were not yet twenty-five and he thought they would be at their most hungry for success. And the Leicester public was already buying into what Jock was doing and he had a good rapport with the fans. It wasn't easy, but I had the most fantastic start although having said that I was very nervous. I remember on my debut, just outside the dressing room door, I turned to Martin Henderson (my best pal in football and my best man) and I said, 'Martin, look after me.' That is not like me at all but it shows how nervous I was. With Jock it was probably nervous excitement rather than nervous tension. I remember the roar of the crowd at Filbert Street for that first game and I had never known a welcome like it. I had come from Oldham with crowds of 3–4,000, terrible pitch, awful conditions and then there was this stadium and what seemed like a vast arena to me. The Kop and the double-decker behind the goal and the big Main Stand; I thought – this is what I want, this'll do me. And then everything fell into place against Watford on the opening day. I got goal of the season for one of the goals I scored that day. The first goal, the ball fell kindly to me after it rebounded off of Eddie Kelly and I just wacked it from about 12 yards and it flew in. The second goal was less straightforward – Ian Wilson took a throw-in parallel to the 18-yard line, straight to my feet and I was going to give it straight back to 'Willie', but one of their players read it and came in front of me. I thought, 'I can't go there,' so I put my foot on top of the ball and dragged it back, outside of my right foot and turned and found myself on the edge of the penalty area. What do I do now? Now I'd never been known as a dribbler but I dropped my right shoulder and the defender in front of me took it, moved to my left, next defender came across so I dropped my left shoulder and made some space for myself. I thought about hitting it then, made like I was going to hit it and dragged it across with my right foot on to my left foot and then just smashed it with my left foot. And it went in! It went in! What's going on here? I had 2 goals to my name and I felt fantastic, the greatest feeling in the world. My only disappointment in that game was not getting a hat-trick. I don't recall getting a hat-trick opportunity either because the second half was a bit of a disappointment in comparison to the first. Watford started to take a few more chances to try and get back in the game and don't forget, Watford were a decent side back then; they had Jenkins, Blissett and Barnes. But despite not getting a hat-trick I was delighted with the ovation I received from the Leicester fans.

It didn't take long before I had my own song – 'He's here, he's there, he's every fucking where, Alan Young, Alan Young.' It came a few games later and it started because whenever we lost the ball I would try very hard to win the ball back and I got really annoyed with anyone who didn't do the same. I would chase back to the full-back if necessary but Jock didn't like that, he would get annoyed and tell me to get up front and do my job. And if Tommy Williams bombed forward from full-back then I would go back and cover him because I was incredibly fit back then and it just came naturally to me but it would really annoy Jock. Anyhow, that's where the song came from and as a professional footballer you like to hear the fans 'give' you your own song. You know they like you then. I loved that song; I thought it was really funny. Every home game when we went out and warmed up I was getting a great reception and that made me feel like a million dollars.

The Watford result was a great start to the season and although I don't recall specific games very clearly, we seemed to be doing the right things and picking up points fairly consistently, so we were always there or thereabouts at the top of the table and looking good. We knew what we had to do in the run-in and it was in our hands which was how you want it. We knew that if we beat Charlton at home then we were as good as promoted and I scored one of my favourite goals in that game – and it was on television as well. I have a great photograph of me celebrating that goal, jumping up in the air with my arms out and my tongue sticking out. Beautiful!

I remember going back to Oldham in October of that season and what a reception I got, my God! I never knew that my wife (Julie) was so promiscuous! It seemed that half the Chaddy End had shagged her according to them and the lovely song they were singing. But I scored at that end and I ran behind the goal with one finger up because they had been giving me pelters and I had given them five seasons for a pittance and I remember thinking fuck you! That turned me against them because I didn't deserve that from them; I extended Vic Halom's career by two seasons by doing all his running for him and Andy Lochhead will tell you that I gave him another season by doing his running for him as well. I did all this on lousy wages for Oldham Athletic because I loved football and I was prepared to do whatever it took and whatever I was asked to do. So I scored and ran behind the goal just to let them know and then I ran back to my own half past the home dugout and did something stupid – I spat. I didn't spit at anyone but I spat on the ground as I looked at Jimmy Frizell. I would love to have punched him but you couldn't have got away with that. David Holt equalised second half so we came away with a 1–1. Even after the game there was still some animosity lingering because when I scored I muscled Ian Wood off of the ball and he (typically) fell over like a screaming baby. After the game he was still arguing with me and I said, 'Ach, ye need to get in the gym son, get some muscle on ye and then ye won't get muscled off the ball so easy.' He just told me to fuck off which was disappointing because we used to get on really well when I was at Oldham. Some of the other lads came over and chatted and asked how it was at Leicester and I told one or two of them to get out of Oldham because it was a graveyard for footballers you know. Anyhow, it was nice to score, I played well, and the more they gave me stick the better I played and the more I smiled about the idea that they had all shagged my wife … maybe they had, I don't know. Julie had been around a bit before I met her so who knows! Only kidding!

❋ ❋ ❋

There was a spell in the middle of the season from December through to mid-February when I didn't score but I was playing my best football. How many strikers would keep their place these days if they weren't scoring? The important thing was that we were winning and I was contributing but it was on my mind and I would have liked a goal, not because I was out of form because I wasn't. What I was missing was that buzz that you get from scoring a goal. But Jock was great, and he said to me, 'Have you got many videos of matches when you've scored?' I said, 'Aye, I have,' and he replied, 'Go home and watch them and see what you did right when you scored those goals. See how you took the goal, how you made space, was it left foot or right foot?' Funnily enough when I did this I realised that I had scored most of my goals with my left foot even though I'm right footed – I have a redundant right. But that was Jock's therapy for me to get me back in the scoring habit again. So I did that and it never made any fucking difference! But you did as you were told and if the Gaffer told you to look at the videos then you did it. The goalless spell ended when I scored at West Ham after I got on to the end of a corner. For some reason they had Trevor Brooking marking me at the corner. I mean for fuck's sake, Trevor didn't like to get his hair messed up so he wasn't going to like it too much when I was fighting for the ball and he was up against me. No contest!

Despite that goalless run I still feel that my time at Leicester was when I played the best football of my career; I was in the 'zone' if you like. Those three seasons I was flying. I still had some stinkers, don't get me wrong and I always knew if I was going to have a poor game, even during the warm-up before the game. I would take a ball out to juggle with during the warm-up; I juggled it all the way to the edge of the penalty area and then volleyed it into the net. If the ball flew in and if I didn't drop it, then I knew I was going to have a good game, but if I dropped it or the ball didn't go into the net when I volleyed it then I would think, 'Oh bollocks!' I was very superstitious and I would be sure that I was on for a poor game. I'm being a bit flippant here because of course it wasn't just about my juggling trick in the warm-up. Once the game started, if you won your first header or you got a shot in at goal early on and you felt good, then maybe you could be sure you were going to have a good game. Some games you would feel invincible, what some players refer to as 'being in the zone'. You feel as though you could climb Everest. You just want the ball at your feet, you run around demanding it. Maybe that was why I got booked so often, because I could be so pumped up some days and I would contest every decision. If the ball went out over the goal line I would be demanding a corner. Every throw in, every free kick, I wanted it to go to us. And I usually believed it was ours as well. Just occasionally I would shout regardless because I had this determination to win and you just hope to get it from the ref. This made me unpopular with refs sometimes and I talked myself into a lot of bookings and Jock hated that. He would give me hell when it happened.

'Shut up fer fuck's sake, leave the ref alone.'

My defence didn't seem to cut any ice with him when I would say, 'Ah canna help it Gaffer, I just have to win, I hate to lose and I contest everything.' But Jock would just shake his head at me. I had such a competitive streak in me and I loved to hear the final whistle after we had won, I loved to see the ball burst the back of the net and I couldn't get enough of that feeling – it spilled over into being too competitive some days and the refs didn't like it, and neither did Jock!

A lot of my good form at this time was down to confidence. I felt invincible, like I was the greatest player in the world. Obviously I wasn't but I believed I was a good player. I wasn't the quickest but I had a nice touch, I was good in the air and I could see things that other players couldn't and, of course, Jock gave me massive self-belief. I played a game for the Leicester Legends a few years ago (a veterans team) and Jon Sammels played as well. After the game he said, 'You know what? I have had more balls back from you today than I had in three years with Frank Worthington.' Frank would hold on to it but I would take one or two touches and give them a ball that gave them time to make their next pass and it was always a good ball, an easy ball – a ball that they could play first time. I was brave as well, too brave sometimes which I am paying for now but that was me. Always chasing the impossible odds or a lost cause. Now I can put my hand on my heart and say that I never gave anything less than 100 per cent in every match that I played and the supporters would back me up on that. I never gave up, I was an absolute trier. I might not have been everyone's favourite but I was well-liked. Even today I get an affectionate attitude back from Leicester fans who now know me as Alan Young, the guy on the radio. But back then I wanted to do the best for my manager, the best for my teammates, supporters and even old Clarice who made the tea. She would get the buzz from the team when we were winning and she would stop her ironing or whatever and come across and say, 'Isn't it lovely when we win?' Jock loved her too and treated her the same as his players. There were no superstars at the club, he would come down on any player like a ton of bricks if they started to give it the big 'I am' and get ideas above their station. I tell you what he really hated (and you see it a lot more in the modern game sadly) – when a player gets wide and into the box, instead of crossing he takes the shot and misses. If the guy in the middle throws his arms out and starts complaining because he was in a good position then that would really annoy Jock. He would take you off if he caught you doing that. He thought it was very disrespectful to a teammate and he would launch into anyone who did it, 'Don't you dare do that! By all means think it or have a quiet word later but don't you *ever* make a big display of your anger at a teammate. If you want to play that game then you can come off and sit beside me for a while.'

And he was right of course.

❋ ❋ ❋

We went to Orient on the last game of the season and knew we needed to win to secure promotion and the title. Sunderland were at home to Cardiff and their kick-off was delayed fifteen minutes because there were so many fans trying to get into the ground. Anyway, it was a nervous game and I missed a sitter that day. Eddie Kelly got to the byline and cut the ball back and all I had to do was side-foot it in, but I missed from about 3 or 4 yards out. Maybe I was so shocked at Eddie Kelly being so far up the pitch, I never saw him in front of me so maybe I was waiting for his nosebleed to start instead of concentrating on the game! Fortunately Larry May scored the only goal and we won and it was a big, big day for the club. The Leicester fans seemed to have taken over the whole ground and there must have been 10,000 from Leicester there that day, oh the noise was fantastic! When the final whistle went we just had to get off the pitch somehow, it was every man for himself and poor Martin Henderson ended up walking into the dressing room with just his pants on! Then we were waiting in the dressing room, all the fans were on the pitch going mental but I didn't realise that some of the lads had gone up into the Directors' Box to see the fans. I didn't go because I was waiting for the results elsewhere and at the final whistle we hadn't won anything yet. I remember Jock was in the dressing room as well, pacing up and down waiting for the results. He didn't just want promotion; he wanted us to go up as champions. I sat there and we both knew what the other is thinking. When the results came through we all went mad in the dressing room – it was a great feeling.

But it wasn't just about that game, we knew we were good enough to go up right from the start. We won 4–1 at QPR quite early in the season and from then on we expected to win every game,; it wasn't a question of 'if' but of 'how many'. That's how confident we were even when we had a slight dip in form after Christmas. Towards the end of the season we started to smell the title and I would look at the league table on Sunday morning in the papers and think to myself, 'We don't look bad here do we?' But Jock never mentioned it and we didn't talk about it in the dressing room either. He made an exception the following season when we were in Division One and he said on television, 'We want to win this,' which of course we were never going to do. He should have kept Eddie Kelly but that's another story.

We never really felt any pressure during the run-in to be honest and once we put Charlton to bed to all but guarantee promotion, then the pressure was really off, However, that didn't mean we relaxed or sat back, Jock wouldn't allow that. Never! It didn't matter if you were playing Real Madrid or Accrington Stanley (with no disrespect to Accrington Stanley) he would prepare the same. He wanted consistency and approached every game with the same mindset. And I think the team line-ups reflected that during that season. Mark Wallington played every game, so did I, while at the back you had Tommy Williams, Larry May, John O'Neill and Denis Rofe (replaced by Geoff Scott mid-season). In the midfield you had Eddie Kelly, Andy Peake, Bobby Smith, Ian Wilson and Pat Byrne. A lot of players played a lot of games and that tells you the benefits of stability and consistency and makes a mockery of squad rotation and all that nonsense.

The only blip in this wonderful season was the F.A. Cup exit at Harlow Town. I believe that Ian Wilson has a lot to answer for on this matter. We were 1–0 up with about seventeen minutes remaining at Filbert Street when we won a free kick in their half. I was over the ball when Will spotted something and said, 'Gi' us it, gi' us the ball man.' I was looking around for something else but he kept on – 'Gi' us it Big Man' – and so I did. I went for the return pass but it never came, he tried to turn away and got caught in possession. They went up the pitch and a few passes later they had scored. Eddie Kelly went mad.

'What the fuck were you thinking? It's a few minutes to go, don't go doing stuff like that fer fucks sake!' I was trying to defend myself and tell 'Ted' that I wanted it back but on reflection Ted was right. Maybe I shouldn't have played that ball to Willy in the first place and Willy certainly shouldn't have tried what he did. So that was that and it finished 1–1 and we had a replay at Harlow Town. Well, what a shit heap that place was. But we really went for it and threw everything at them and we must have had about twenty shots that night. We battered them to death and couldn't score and they got the poxiest of goals and that was that, we were out. Jock's approach was interesting; he was disappointed of course but almost immediately he was saying, 'Let it be, we have bigger fish tae fry!' On the way home we stopped in at a pub and it was pints all round and we took a load of beer on to the bus for the rest of the journey. As far as Jock was concerned that was it; Harlow Town was done and dusted, it never happened. A lot of time after away games he would walk down the bus and he would go over something that happened in the game with one or more players. Then he might walk back down and, finding one of the younger lads who had done well that day, would ruffle their hair and say, 'Well done son.' It was little things like that that made the difference and made Jock the brilliant man-manager that he was. He wasn't one for watching videos of games that was for sure. He would have teams watched of course but he rarely practiced set pieces; he would leave you to play what you saw at the time. Make your decision and do what you think is right at that moment and in a football match you are making hundreds of decisions without even thinking about it: do I go inside? Do I go up for this one? Should I follow him? Should I take him on or pass it? And you can't coach that, you need intelligent players that make more right decisions than wrong ones, and the successful sides are the ones that have more players that make more right decisions. I used to get a bit annoyed at corners, though, because Jock used to want us to hit Larry May but I knew I was just as good as him in the air, so I would go near post instead. Another thing that irritated me then was that Jock made Bobby Smith the penalty taker that season; if he had let me take the penalties then I would have had about 30 goals!

But the games were coming thick and fast and the preparation was always the same. Tuesday was 'work day' and I loved it. One of the pitches at the Belvoir Drive training ground was on a higher level and it had a slope. Now we would start at the top of the slope and Jock had four lanes marked out for us to run round. We would all be fighting to get away first and we were really competitive and Jock loved this. The problems started if you ended up in a 'four' with Gary Lineker. We would be whispering to him, 'You stay with us, don't you go blasting your way out to the front.' We would let him break away for the last 50m but at the start we would be holding his shirt to stop him getting away. Jock used to clock this and halfway round he would be bellowing 'Lineker! Stop fucking around!' and we would have to let him go then. But Jock knew what we were up to and he knew that Lineker was only young and he wanted to know about his character; in other words, are you going to do what these buggers are telling you or are you going to tell them to fuck off? And Jock would come across and talk to me about Gary Lineker. He would say, 'Have we got one here or what?' and I would say, 'Aye, he's certainly quick Gaffer.' Gary learned a lot at that time and we loved him. But it wasn't just about speed because he spent the early part of his career on his arse, he needed to be stronger and that came eventually. Training was good at Leicester and every day was different. Jock would have us using hurdles, but not in the conventional way that you see at athletics meetings, he would have us bouncing over hurdles in two-footed jumps and they were spaced apart such that you would have to have control over your whole body in order to clear the hurdle and then the next and the next without stopping. He would have us competing in threes like this and it was really hard. Most of the players really wanted to win these contests, there weren't many who were cruising it. In the sports hall it could be fierce for six- or seven-a-sides. You didn't pull out of anything and I remember once young David Buchanan and I were going after a loose ball and I knew that the first thing to do was get across the ball and block the opponent, cut off his route to the ball effectively. Now 'Buck' was a bit inexperienced and he was going at full tilt thinking he was going to get it but I just got my body across the ball and he bounced about 5 yards and landed on his arse. Jock was laughing out loud and said, 'Let that be a lesson to ye Buchanan, get yerself in that fucking gym!'

I only fell out with Jock on one occasion, and that was when he left in the summer of 1982. I never found out why and I still don't know the full ins and outs of his departure back to Scotland, but it made a big impact on my decision to leave Leicester City. We were never told officially, we read it in the papers. I was very sad I have to be honest. I lost a manager, a guy that I admired and I lost my best friend. But you have to move on and I wasn't named in the squad for the preseason tour of Ireland because I was unsettled and wasn't really getting on with Gordon Milne who was in post by then. So I stayed behind and played in the County Cup final. I played centre half and I have to say, I loved it there. Billy Gibson was made captain, though; I wasn't pleased about that. In fact, I never captained Leicester City and I would like to have done. When the rest of the squad came back the writing was on the wall for me. By then I had been contacted by Ian Porterfield who was manager of Sheffield United and I rang Jock to ask his advice and he told me to go for it and that Porterfield was a good lad. It meant dropping a division which I didn't really want to do and my fee was about £180,000 so my value had dropped about £70,000 already. But it was a move I should never have made and at the time I blamed everyone but myself; I blamed Gordon Milne, I blamed circumstances, I blamed certain situations I was faced with and it is only recently that I have admitted to myself that actually I was to blame. During that phone call with Jock (who was installed as the Motherwell manager by then) he said that he wanted to bring me and Lineker to Scotland but that he couldn't afford us with Motherwell's transfer budget. He said Motherwell would walk the league if he had us (he actually said, 'We would scoosh it!' – one of his favourite words). I never questioned why he left Leicester even when I had the chance and he never said anything. I think he went back to Scotland because he wanted the Scotland job and he had more chance of that by being successful in Scotland. The Scotland job was one of the few things left for him to go for to be honest.

The next time I saw Jock was after he had managed in Spain. I mean, Spain! Can you imagine him taking a training session with a load of Spaniards that can't understand a word he says? I wonder if he had them running up sandhills.

4

TOUGH AT
THE TOP

My only season in the top flight of English football came the following season at Leicester. This was 1980/81 and we knew it would be tough, but when Jock went on television on the eve of the season and told the world that we could win it, we all believed him! Now it might look like a daft thing to say with hindsight but that was Jock all over, he wasn't afraid of anything and he didn't want his players to be either. I won't criticise Jock for saying that, but I will say here and now that he made a mistake letting Eddie Kelly go when he did. Eddie told Jock that he wasn't sure if he could hack it in the top flight and while I don't ever believe that was the case, I also think that maybe Eddie felt that he was coming towards the end of his career and he was looking for another pay day and a transfer out was the way to get it. But whatever the reasons, it was a big mistake to let him go and we missed his influence badly; his steadiness, his encouragement, his instructions on the pitch and all the good stuff that he brought with his knowledge of the game. There is no doubt in my mind that Eddie's absence contributed to us being relegated. I remember the opening game of the season at home to Ipswich; we lost to an 89th-minute goal and I remember thinking that we would get away with a point until they scored so late because the difference was very apparent right from the first minute. And this was against a team that we expected to beat at home even though they were a decent side with good players like Beattie, Wark, Mariner, Gates, and Muhren and Thijssen – the two Dutch lads. But they outplayed us and made us realise how tough it was going to be that season.

That said, there were some highlights. We beat Manchester United 1–0 at home and I remember young Paul Friar and Joe Jordan had a set to at the Filbert Street end. Joe had the ball and wee 'Tuck' slid in and dumped Joe on his arse. Jordan immediately jumped up (with no teeth in of course) and so did Tuck – he was only 5ft nothing and 8 stone soaking wet and there he was going eyeball-to-eyeball with big Joe. Jordan said something like, 'Ya wee fuckin' bastard,' but Tuck wasn't giving any ground at all, stayed where he was, looked up at him and said, 'Fuck off!' Joe just walked away with a big grin on his face. I was in earshot of the whole thing and it was funny to hear, but wee Tuck wouldn't take any prisoners. He was a brave wee fella with a decent left foot and he was quick, but he was never going to be a great player so I guess he must have enjoyed his time at Leicester.

Then there was the home game against Liverpool early in the season. We won 2–0, it was our first win of the season and I remember it mostly because I missed a sitter on my left foot. I remember Phil Thompson moaning continuously throughout that match– I was beating him to everything and giving a right going over, getting in the odd elbow or kick when I could and he hated it. I just said, 'Shut fuckin' up ya big nosed bastard!'

I would say the biggest difference between the Second and First Division was speed and strength – quickness of thought and reactions. It was really noticeable and even though I was in my prime physically at this time, I was feeling it. And there was a better calibre of player; there wasn't a huge difference man for man but there were more players facing you each week who might get into any team in the land, while if you looked at Leicester you might pick just two or three. That was the difference and maybe Jock should have brought in a few more quality players to strengthen the squad, but maybe he wanted to keep faith with the lads who had got us there and perhaps that was a mistake. But who am I to question Jock's judgment because, even though we got relegated, we had a great time. Even though it was a relegation season we still kept believing that we would win whenever we went out to play a game.

We got a couple of spankings that season; I remember losing 5–0 at Nottingham Forest and Manchester United in successive weeks and we got beaten 1–0 at Arsenal soon after and the scoreline doesn't tell the full story; Arsenal battered us. But the reason I remember the Arsenal game so clearly is that it was that night that I met Karen. I went to the Turnstile pub with Peter Welsh when we got back to Leicester because I had called Julie (as I always did after a game) and asked her if she fancied going out for dinner and, as usual, it was a 'no'. So me and 'Welshy' went for a few in the Turnstile and then on to a place in Leicester called the 'Bali Hi'.

✳ ✱ ✳

The biggest result of the season for Leicester City (or any club for that matter) was Liverpool away when we won 2–1. They had an incredible record of 85 games unbeaten at home spanning two-and-a-half seasons, but we still felt that we had a chance despite Liverpool being invincible at Anfield. Maybe we were still getting a buzz from playing at bigger grounds like Anfield but I can still remember the wood-panelled walls in the dressing rooms which made it feel like someone's front room, totally different from Filbert Street. I can remember touching the sign above the tunnel (Welcome to Anfield) because everyone else does! I'm pleased to say that I can blame Ian Wilson for what happened next; we were defending the Kop in the first half and Willy's job that day was to pick up Terry McDermott when we didn't have the ball, only Willy got injured in a tackle and Liverpool got possession. Willy was still lying in the centre circle and McDermott set off on a run, so I thought I had better go with him. I was running back towards my own penalty area with McDermott who had run to my left side just as Alan Kennedy had hit a lovely cross to the backpost where David Johnson headed it back across goal. By now I was in line with the penalty spot and I could see the ball just ahead of me – I know that Terry McDermott was on my blind side so unless I got a piece of this, then he had a free header at goal. So I did get a piece of it – but it was too big a piece of it and it flew into the top corner. The Kop went mad and I just stood there. I didn't feel bad because we had been playing well enough and I turned around to the lads and said, 'Come on, don't worry about that. Let's go again!' I helped to get the equaliser in the second half. It was a similar ball across and Ray Clemence came for it and I thought, 'I'm going to clatter him.' I did but I also got a head on the ball and it ran for Pat Byrne who had an easy side-foot into the net. Clemence went berserk!

'That's a foul ref, surely that's a foul!'

'Shut up you fucking twat!' I said.

Then Melrose got our second and we managed to hang on and defend it, incredibly winning 2–1. After the game our supporters were fantastic but so were the Liverpool fans and they stayed behind to applaud what had been a good, honest performance from us – they understood and appreciated that. They like triers in Liverpool and that's what we had been that day. I had a nice surprise later on when it turned out that there were man of the match awards for the home team and the away team – when it was announced that I had won the prize I had to go to the sponsors' lounge to collect it. I was surprised because even though I thought I had played reasonably well, I didn't think it was nearly enough to win man of the match. Anyway, Graeme Souness was already there and he was the Liverpool man of the match. He handed over a big hamper to me full of goodies: food and booze (I still have a picture of it with me and Wesley stood beside it). As we are getting on the coach I was giving it the 'big one' saying to the lads, 'Hey, gi' us a hand wi' this big hamper lads, it's really heavy!' I only found out the truth some years later when I was at Notts County. Kenny Dalglish had come to watch Mark Draper and he asked me what I thought, so I told him that Mark was a decent lad, took care of himself, and had a good future ahead of him if he carried on doing the right things. But when I said that Mark didn't drink, Kenny turned around and said 'Well he's no fuckin' good tae us then!' But after that we got talking again about the Leicester game at Anfield that day and I reminded him how big the hamper had been and how I had been winding the lads up asking them to help me carry it. He stopped me and said, 'You didn't think you got that for being man of the match did you?'

'Aye, of course.'

'We gave you that because you scored for us!'

And I had gone all those years thinking I had earned the hamper for my performance!

Incredibly, the fallout from that match at Anfield is still going on. About two years ago my daughter, Sophie, was on holiday in Ayia Nappa and by the end of the second week she was skint, checked out of the hotel, killing time until the flight home which wasn't until 7.30 that night. She was walking around with her Liverpool shirt on (she is daft about Liverpool, so are her brothers but they also have a fondness for Leicester City, naturally) and she went into a little bar because she spotted a guy behind the counter also wearing a Liverpool top. She explained her circumstances and ordered a glass of water because she was broke. So she got chatting to the guy about Liverpool and they talked about their favourite players and how long they had supported the Reds, etc., and it turns out this guy had followed them for about forty years. Then Sophie said, 'My Dad scored for Liverpool.'

'Really?', said the guy, 'who's that then?'

'Well actually he didn't play for Liverpool but he scored an own goal when he was a Leicester City player,' said Sophie.

'That's Alan Young! Your Dad is Alan Young isn't he?' he said straightaway. And suddenly it was like this guy was a lifelong friend and he allowed Sophie and her friends to put their bags at the back of the bar in a safe place, he fed them and wouldn't take a penny for it and all because of the Liverpool connection.

It was bizarre in that season in the First Division just how much the results swung one way and then the other. We did the double over Liverpool and yet we got beaten two weeks on the bounce at Forest and Man United. The great thing about Jock was that he would handle the wins and defeats in the same manner. In fact, he might take the blame for those 5–0 defeats and say that he picked the wrong team or played the wrong tactics, but he would never blame the players. When we won at Liverpool he would say that it was only what we deserved but he had the press on his side too. He was stronger than the press and he would tell them what to write half the time because they were scared to write something too derogatory about his team. He would also use a lot of reverse psychology after a disappointing performance; we played Bristol Rovers at home on New Year's Day and we were 2–0 up at half time but it could have been 5–5; we were atrocious. He came in at the break and said, 'Sit fucking doon!' and he ripped straight into me. I had missed a few chances but I wasn't the worst offender by any means but it was me he came to. He was only inches from my face

'Ye big fuckin' prima donna you! Ye think yer a big superstar don't ye?' he said in his tirade. 'That second one ye missed, ma Granny could have put that in wi' her left tit!' Spit was flying everywhere and then suddenly he left. He just walked out of the dressing room and the place was deathly quiet for a moment. Then Tommy Williams came over and said, 'Are you alright big man?'

'Fuck off Tom, leave it!' I said. And then Andy Peake, who was only a baby, he came across and started trying to console me and I told him to fuck off too and eventually I turned round to them all and said, 'I'll sort ma game out, ye lot sort yer own game out. I will show that specky bastard what for!' And I did. But he had got to the rest of the players through me. He could have ripped into all of us that day because we all deserved it but he wasn't one for doing that or throwing tea cups around, he relied on the power of the word. We won the game comfortably after that and improved no end in the second half. He wouldn't publicly criticise the players, ever.

There were some tough runs of results in the First Division and after one game that we were genuinely unlucky to lose, he walked into the dressing room and we were expecting some sort of reaction from him. Instead he just said, 'Right, see you Tuesday!' and walked out. We were all looking at each other thinking, 'Monday off? That was unheard of.' So when we all came back on Tuesday we were all thinking it would be a really hard shift. We were used to Jock insisting that you had your shirt tucked into your shorts and your tie-ups tied on your socks; train as you mean to play. But it wasn't what we expected; we did the usual warming up exercises in twos up and down the pitch and a few stretches and then he came jogging up to me and said, 'Aye, the troops are looking great this morning Big Man.'

'Aye Gaffer, we're all ready for good session this morning,' I said. Then he stopped and looked at us all and said, 'Right, fuck off home! Yer as fit as fiddles.' We were asking for a bit longer, maybe a five-a-side or something, but he was adamant.

'Take the missus shopping or something, yer all fit as fuckin' fiddles, now fuck off home!'

And that was it. We all left the training ground feeling 10ft tall – invincible. Jock used that sort of psychology to very good effect.

The other thing Jock was very good at was understanding and respecting the supporters. He always reminded us that the supporters paid good money and we had a duty to do our best for them. It wasn't the case that we had to go out and get results because the supporters demanded it; he knew that they paid good money and in return they needed to see that the players were giving everything, even if the results weren't going right. And the fans kept turning up because of this belief; they went everywhere that season in their thousands. Even on the last day of the season at Norwich when we were already relegated, there were thousands of them turned up and made a great atmosphere and we won 3–2 with Melrose bagging a hat-trick.

Now Jim Melrose was a player that I didn't get on with. He was 'Billy Big Time' and a very selfish player. It wasn't that he didn't fit in with Jock's team spirit belief, but he was different in many ways. He wasn't wholly accepted by the senior players but that didn't come onto the pitch. When we played together I was there to help him and he was there to help me – the team came first so you left your personal feelings behind once the match started. Off the pitch it was different. I remember one morning he came into training and it was around the time that I met Karen. Melrose said something derogatory about her that I won't repeat, but I took him through to the drying room and I was going to knock the shit out of him and give him a good hiding but I stopped myself because that would have meant big trouble for me no matter what the reason; Jock wouldn't have tolerated it. I had to be better than that, so instead, I lifted him up on the pegs and hung him up even though I knew it would get back to Jock; I knew he might not approve because it was over a personal issue and that was the wrong reason to do it. Jock liked all of his players to be married and settled with kids, he wanted stability in your life. Maybe at that time I didn't have stability and I was very close to giving Melrose a good hiding. But he wasn't popular and he was often ridiculed as well. One of the routines we had was for the players to be in a circle and keep possession of the ball with one man in the middle and on this particular occasion Melrose was in the middle. He was getting frustrated and he took it out on Gary Lineker; the ball went to Lineker and Melrose went right through him, studs showing, and ripped his sock open and everything.

Well, we gave Melrose the biggest beating. We all piled on and had a go, everybody was there and then Jock stepped in and said, 'That's enough. Right Mr Melrose, let that be a lesson for ye.'

But it wasn't, he didn't change. We thought he was divulging information to Bill Anderson at the *Leicester Mercury*, his best mate, confidential stuff from the dressing room. We would call him 'Buzz' or 'Jaffa' because he only drank orange juice. The 'Buzz' nickname came about because in dressing room discussions he would always have his hand in the air first with an answer to the gaffer's questions so we would be going 'Bzzzz! Melrose, University of Leicester'. He was a good player though.

The odd thing about that season was how much we enjoyed it even though it was hard to win points and sometimes hard to even get a goal. We only contemplated relegation once it was mathematically impossible for us to stay up. We loved going to some of the grounds and playing the best sides in the country like Arsenal and Everton; Mike Lyons and Roger Kenyon at the centre of defence for Everton were very hard players and made Goodison a tough place to go. It was a right shithole too! And Arsenal had a really small pitch I remember, making it hard to play when you weren't used to it. Southampton was a tight ground; the fans were on top of you there and they had a good team then as well. Jock played me in midfield there – what a mistake that was! We were 4–0 down at half time and I can categorically say that I am the worst midfield player in the world. Steve Williams ran rings around me and I didn't have a clue.

I didn't know it at the time but I would eventually play for Brighton. When we played them over Easter in 1981 I got sent off for the only time in a Leicester shirt, so I wasn't that fond of the place then. Before the game the Gaffer had said that the 'keeper, Graham Moseley, had got a pea heart and told me to get into him and hammer him if I got the chance. The idea was that he wouldn't come for crosses if he knew that I would have him, but it didn't work out like that. There were only a few minutes gone when a cross came in and Moseley went up for it. Well, the match was played in April but I hit him in May! I really got into him and I got booked for it and that was fair, I deserved it. But the second booking that led to me being sent off was not fair at all. It came during the second half; the ball fell in midfield and bounced up as me and Steve Foster both went for it. Well we both missed it but he went down holding his knee but I hadn't touched him, nowhere near the ball or his knee. The referee came over and told me I was going off and I looked across at Fozzie who was still on the ground – he was pissing himself laughing by now because he had done me. That was made worse because we had to win that game to give ourselves a chance of staying up. I maintain to this day that I shouldn't have been sent off and we even appealed the decision at the time, but the Football Association added another game ban and a £250 fine. Tossers! They didn't know their arse from their elbow.

I sat in the dressing room after the sending off and felt totally desolate. I had let myself down, let the supporters down, let Jock down, and the team – in fact, it has to be one of the low points of my time at Leicester to be honest. While I was sitting there mulling this over, I heard the clatter of studs coming down the tunnel and in walked Kevin McDonald –

he'd been sent off as well! That was a long journey home that night, truly awful. Even now I think if I hadn't been stupid with my challenge on Graham Moseley then I might not have been booked, then I wouldn't have been sent off and we might not have lost which would have given us a better chance of staying up. I've had bigger disappointments in my life after football but at the time I was very upset. Funnily enough, when I signed for Brighton after I left Sheffield United I went for my medical in the treatment room and who should be lying on the next bed but Steve Foster. He saw me and started holding his knee saying, 'Oh my knee, send him off ref!' I have to admit I thought that was funny and me and him became great friends.

5

CUP GLORY AND THE PUB QUIZ QUESTION

'Oh fuck! That hurts. Oh Christ, is ma career over, how long will this take tae get over, when will I play again?'

I'm lying on the plastic pitch at Loftus Road. It's September 1981 and my career has just changed forever, but the story starts a few days earlier …

The build up to QPR game wasn't really any different to a normal game. We drew 1–1 with Chelsea on the previous Friday night at Filbert Street and came in on the Monday as usual and did the stretches. Tuesday was a work day – as it always was with Jock Wallace. You did your hard running on the Tuesday and normally got Wednesday off. But he brought us in this particular Wednesday because we were doing something a little bit different – playing at Queens Park Rangers and on their plastic pitch that Saturday. So we trained indoors at Belvoir Drive – the Leicester City training ground – on the carpet, which sort of replicated the plastic pitch at QPR. Still it wasn't ideal because we wore flat shoes on the indoor training surface at Belvoir Drive and the plastic pitch at QPR was AstroTurf, which behaved totally differently.

I know that Jock Wallace wanted to protest about the QPR pitch – in fact he had wanted to make a protest at the start of the season and I'm sure he did. But as we got nearer to the day of the match Jock didn't want to put it into the players' minds that QPR had an advantage, even though they did, and so he waited until after the game before he made his thoughts known. Much to the annoyance of a certain Mr Venables, who said that Jock should have made his protest before the game.

On Thursday we came in as usual and worked (as usual) on the set-pieces and free-kicks and the formation. Now sometimes, when we were playing in London, we would travel down on a Friday and other times it would be on the Saturday morning. On this occasion Jock took us down on the Friday and said, 'Come on, we'll go doon early and ha' a look at this shite pitch and have a walk on it.' So we got down and got sorted at the hotel. Then went to Loftus Road, but they wouldn't let us out on the pitch. It was frustrating but we turned that to our advantage. We adopted the attitiude, 'Well sod them! If they're not going to let us look at the pitch then we'll come back tomorrow and stuff them'; you know, siege mentality. So we came back the next day, so we did and, in the meantime, unbeknownst to the players, the Gaffer had ordered a load of AstroTurf boots. We got into the dressing room and there was a box in the middle of the floor, full of AstroTurf boots – or 'pimples' as we called them. They were just the job! They were the proper chaps to be using on this surface. I got a size nine, which I didn't really like because I usually took a size eight, but we went out to warm-up and I found it alright. I think that was because I had a decent touch; you can hammer the ball at me but I'll deal with it. The surface was a lot quicker and the ball bounced an awful lot higher; you had to be a lot more sympathetic with your passes and the way you passed had to be just right, otherwise it came on too fast or it went out of play or bobbled up.

I remember later on in my career when I met John Burridge, the 'loony' goalkeeper. Now John knew that I had done my cartilage on the plastic pitch and he had played for QPR for a while and he was actually suing them because he reckoned that his career was shortened because he had to play and train on the plastic pitch. We lost touch and I don't know if he actually went through with it. Anyway, the plastic pitch didn't last much longer at QPR after that.

As for my own experience that day; there was about twelve minutes gone, there was an attack down the left and I got a nice pass from Andy Peake, I took it on my left foot just inside the penalty area and I thought I would take on the full back (Ian Gillard). Turning on the pitch was a bit dodgy because if you were square on then it was difficult to turn round. Well, I got it past him and I was about 2 yards from the goal line, I planted my right foot and set to square it across the goal. What would normally happen is that your right foot, as it twisted, would take a divot out. But on this surface my right foot stayed exactly where it was and my whole body twisted around it. The pain in my knee felt as if I had been shot and I ended up behind the goal line where my momentum took me into a policewoman who was walking behind the goal at the time; we both ended up in a heap. I recall at the time that the *Leicester Mercury* didn't get it quite right; they reported that I tore my cartilage when I hit the policewoman. Wrong! I tore my cartilage because of the plastic pitch. I can state that quite categorically. I knew straight away that something was seriously wrong. I didn't know it was cartilage then but I knew without doubt that there was something extremely wrong with my knee because of the pain and I heard and felt the tear and I just knew. I've since had a knee replacement and I thought that was painful but I remember back then how serious the pain was. John McVey, the physio says 'Lie still' and all I can think about is the pain and then that turns into 'Oh Christ, is ma career over, how long will this take tae get over, when will I play again?' and John is just trying to placate you because any kind of movement might make it worse. John was very good at his job and a marvellous physio. I remember him holding my hand and calming me down as we went around the pitch and down the tunnel. And we lost the game 2–0, so it was a bad day all round.

✳ ✱ ✳

After I was carried off they put ice packs around the knee and that's how it was managed back then. You didn't go straight for scans or anything like that. Eventually we went back home to Leicester. I spent the next day in bed and on Monday morning I went into the London Road private hospital to have my cartilage removed by Mr Chan, the orthopaedic surgeon. I didn't really get told anything about it, I wasn't told that I had done my cartilage or that it was coming out, no details about the prognosis or rehabilitation. Nothing. Not a sausage! By now my knee was huge and I had on it what they call a Gibson's bandage and all I knew was that I wanted the pain to go away, I wanted the job done quickly.

John McVey told me afterwards that when I was under anaesthetic waiting for the operation, Mr Chan came into theatre, looked at me and said: 'Why is this man's knee not shaved?' and the theatre orderlies all looked at each other. In the meantime Mr Chan got his scalpel and ran it down my knee to remove the hair and them wiped it on his gown before he opened up my knee with the same scalpel! Back then, of course, if there was a problem with the cartilage they took the whole thing out. These days they can trim it, sew it, put little balloons into cushion it, they can do all sorts of stuff to make it right. But that was me back then – out it came and so I played the rest of my career without a cartilage in my right knee.

I remember on the Tuesday night after my op, Leicester were at home to Preston in a League Cup tie and Jock came into see me at the hospital on his way to Filbert Street and he was telling all the nurse how to do their jobs. He says to me, 'Are ye alreet?'

'No. I'm not fuckin' alreet. If I was alreet I'd be playing! So anyway Gaffer, how are the lads?' I said.

'Aye they're fine, they're fit and they're up fer it tonight,' he said; and so we just talked football for a while for about twenty minutes. Then a nurse came and took my blood pressure and it was through the roof, she told me I had to relax or they would have to give me something to get my blood pressure down. 'I don't have high blood pressure, I have never, ever suffered from high blood pressure,' I said.

Jock turned round to the nurse and said, 'Dinnae be so stupid. It's not high blood pressure, it's battle fever!' The two of us talking about the game got the adrenaline going.

So that was the start of my recovery and then I was released from hospital. Within four or five days I was in the gym working on my upper body and my core and middle, working the left leg and leaving the right leg alone. There were lots of hot and cold baths as well and that's how it was until the big bandages came off in about the second or third week, when I started to walk unaided. I had lost a lot of condition in my right thigh, my right quads, and it was still damn sore so I was throwing painkillers down my throat in order to try and build it up. I didn't have any specific targets but for some reason

I can remember that six weeks was in the back of my mind. I think I had read somewhere that that was how long it took for a cartilage. And come the fourth or fifth week we started to run in straight lines, no turning, straight long run after straight long run, boring as hell, but Jock would be stood at one end of the line and Ian MacFarlane would be stood at the other end balling at you to keep your knees up and keep your arm action going – push it harder. Then they would shout 'last two!' and then last two would become 'last five' and then 'one last one' and after you would fall into the bath. When you got home you would fall into bed, no time for the kids or the missus. You just wanted to sleep. Dead. Leave me alone. No food, shut the door, shut the curtains and leave me alone.

Come the fifth week it got harder; the double-decker stand at Filbert Street behind the goal was my apparatus. I went up every single step of the double-decker with a bag of cement on my shoulders. That was how we got fit back then. None of the psychology and bicycles and all that nonsense. I had a bag of cement on my back, I went up one flight then there was a landing, second flight, another landing, third flight. Then you dropped the bag, ran to the end of the concourse, came back, picked the bag up and ran down the stairs again. Health and Safety would go crazy if they knew what was going on then. Jock would be waiting at the bottom shouting at me. I was physically sick, spewing up all over the place but I had to go and do it again and I did it every day because the Gaffer wanted me fit for the cup tie against Southampton in January. And I made it! My comeback game was at Oldham the week before in a 1–1 draw. This was to prepare me for the cup tie the following week. Typically, when you are injured, Jock would come walking into the physio's room and say, 'How's he? How is he training?' He wanted to know everything. If you're not training then why not. If you've been off too long then he would say, 'Ach, he's soft as shite'. And John would go and see Jock afterwards and talk about the players concerned. But Jock would also talk you fit. He had a psychology about fitness. He'd build the players up. And that was the effect he had on me and it helped me to get back to fitness. All through my recovery and was constantly telling me how great I was, how important to the team I was, how the guys were all missing me. He once did a piece of psychology on a guy called Tom Forsyth at Glasgow Rangers who had been out for a while with an ankle injury. The Gaffer told me that Tom was really hard and before this game he told him to bring a ball outside into the tunnel. He said, 'Right, take the ball and gi' it a block tackle against the wall with yer sore ankle' and Tom did this but with his good ankle and told Jock that it was feeling fine. So Jock then told him, 'Right, now do the same with yer good ankle'. Tom did the same again and still used his good ankle, of course. So Jock says, 'Aye, yer good enough son, get changed.' Now that kind of thing stayed in my mind, the sort of things that Jock brought to the club and worked wonders for me. I didn't kick a ball until the last week before I played, they wouldn't let me near a ball and when I did I was nervous because you have to strike it 'just so'. I remember in the cup tie against Southampton, Ian Wilson took a throw in and found me on the left wing just outside their penalty area and as it came to me a defender came past and I thought I would take the ball and go, but as I put my foot on the ball to go with it, my right knee clicked and I thought, 'Oh no, not again, please no!' Then logic kicked in and I realised that my bones had clicked against each other for the first time and I really felt it. I didn't go off and I managed to get through the pain as it subsided but I was a bit delicate. My son Kyle loves to point out that the first goal

I scored in that game, you can see that I am having to keep my leg straight and not twist in any way. It looks silly, daft you know, but I had to make sure I had a good shape and put the ball in.

I wore a bandage on my knee for a while after that to support it. Being injured is one of the most awful things in football. There is very little you can do about it, you are in everybody else's hands. If I had got that injury now I think I would have recovered more fully and played for a lot longer than thirty-one years of age. Nowadays the diagnosis is made much quicker thanks to the incredible scanning equipment they have now. They don't automatically remove the cartilage either, they can repair it and leave it in and the rehabilitation is miles better than it was back then. There is a really comprehensive programme for this type of injury and none of it involves bags of cement. And there is sports psychology included as well now. But that was then and it was definitely the beginning of the end of my career. My knee was never the same, I would occasionally hurt it again and it took a bit longer to recover each time and then, of course, there were the problems with my back as I tried to compensate and protect my knee from further damage.

✳ ✱ ✳

After relegation back to Division Two we made a decent start with what was basically the same group of players. We expected to get back up at the first time of asking to be honest. My own season hit a wall when I got injured at Queens Park Rangers on that awful plastic pitch and my comeback in December coincided with the start of a cup run that is still talked about today in Leicester. It's funny because whenever I bump into Leicester supporters they nearly always want to talk about that cup tie against Shrewsbury. The cup run in question started with the third-round tie at home to Southampton when I got a couple of goals. The centre half for Southampton that day was Chris Nicholl; I used to like playing against Chris. I got on well against him for some reason. The first goal of the game was a side-foot but my technique looked a bit ungainly because I was wary of my knee giving way, but it went in and that's all that matters. The second goal came from a right wing cross by Andy Peake. I could tell by the way he hit it and the position he was in that it wasn't going to travel far and it wouldn't get beyond the near post, so I took a chance and got in front of Chris Nicholl and met it perfectly and it flew into the top corner. I knew that I was back and fit again and I had 2 goals behind me and that did me the power of good. In the second half, with about fifteen minutes left, a through ball went towards Malcolm Waldron, he was favourite to get it but I slid in and hooked the ball back. So I when I got up I was one-on-one with the 'keeper, Katalinic, but at that stage of the game and on a heavy pitch it felt like I was running through quicksand, but I got to the edge of the area and hit it and watched it come back off the post. If that had gone in I might have stayed on but I was spent and lay on the floor, my lungs were on fire and I was spent. That was Jock's cue to take me off; he did me a favour because it might have done more harm than good to let me finish the match. So off I came and Lineker got the third goal after Keegan had got one back for Southampton. That was one of the chances I had for a hat-trick at Leicester City, something I never achieved. But we won 3–1 and then we had a tricky tie to face at Hereford in the fourth round. Larry scored the winner and we won 1–0 but it was a shite game with two teams playing shite. We were just pleased to get through and be in the draw for the next round.

I don't recall much about the fifth-round tie which we got through 2–0 at home to Watford but I know John O'Neill got one of the goals and Steve Terry put through his own net for the other – we won comfortably to be honest. This set us up for a quarter-final tie at home to Shrewsbury and what a day that was. We heard about the draw listening in the Axe & Square in Countesthorpe; we were second to last out of the hat and the home tie with Shrewsbury. That was the best draw we could have hoped for and I remember thinking straight away, we are in the semi-final. It was full house at Filbert Street, packed to the rafters. Graham Turner was their manager at the time and I knew Ian Atkins as well, having done some coaching courses with him. We took the lead early on when big Larry scored and then a bizarre set of events took place. A ball was played through that Andy Peake should have dealt with but he didn't and it was a race between 'Wally' (Mark Wallington) and Chic Bates of Shrewsbury to get it. Had Bates done what he did in the street he would have been arrested; it was one of the most horrendous challenges I have ever seen, completely idiotic. It was something he should still be ashamed of because he was a coward to go in the way he did and his stud punctured Wally's thigh; there was a big hole in his leg. I was so angry but I stayed away because I was boiling mad and I knew I could have got into trouble. The referee didn't even book him, but it changed the game completely. Wally got strapped up which was a mistake in hindsight but, of course, you don't want your 'keeper to leave the pitch, we didn't have sub 'keepers back then. He was dragging his leg all over the place. They equalised with a Mickey Mouse goal that Wally would have thrown his hat on normally, then another followed soon after and that was just as soft. So we are 2–1 down and it was at that stage that I remember Eddie (Kelly) shouting, 'Get him fuckin' off!' so that was it, I got the signal to get in goal. I think I was chosen because we had a striker on the bench coupled the fact that I was tall and a good athlete with good hand-eye coordination. I was also brave and (mostly) sensible, so Jock could trust me to keep the back-four intact. So I'm putting on the green jersey and the gloves in front of The Kop and starting to think, fuckin' hell! I kept talking to myself to stay calm and to help me to concentrate. Fairly soon after that they started trying to test me as you would expect. They put a high, high ball into the box and I jumped like a striker with my legs crossed (which you should never do as a keeper) but I caught it and as I come down Chic Bates came in and shoulder charged me and knocked me over, but I held on to the ball, that was all I was bothered about. Under any other circumstances I would have gone mental at Bates but I was in goal and I had the ball, so if I had done something stupid it would have been a penalty. My mindset was now that of a 'keeper, thank goodness, but as I looked around into the back of the net there was Tommy Williams and John O'Neill and they had got a hold of Chic Bates and I was thinking, I should be in there. Bates got booked for that, but not for the challenge on Wally which I found odd. Then just before half time there was a most bizarre own goal from Steve Cross and we went in at half time at 2–2. Jock didn't need a half-time team talk that day because we were all still angry about what happened to Wally. Jock just said, 'Be angry but control it.' We went out for the second half and John O'Neill headed one back to me but it wasn't quite strong enough, and little Bernard MacNally closed in on it, which he was entitled to do. He may have even tried to pull out of the challenge but he went underneath me as I grabbed the ball; I was holding on tight to the ball so I couldn't break my fall and as I rolled over the top of him, I landed on my head. It is only through looking at video footage since then that I know what happened at that moment. I vaguely remember Jock moving my head but I couldn't see properly and I felt sick. I was telling John McVey (the physio) that I couldn't see so he took me down the tunnel into the dressing room and slowly things started to come into focus again. Big Ian MacFarlane came in at that point wanting to know what was going on and John told him that I would be ok. So I went back on, but up front this time. However, I know I went back in goal later because I've seen it on the video but I can't remember any of that. I went back in goals and Steve Lynex came out on to the pitch again and helped us to win the game. Melrose got a couple and Eddie Kelly played a couple of lovely passes to set up 2 goals; but he was involved in them all. We were cruising in the end and at 5–2 up I am feeling very confident and hoping that someone would have a shot. The back-four protected me brilliantly and the only thing I had to do was collect a corner and I shouted 'KEEEEEPPPEEERRRRSSSSS!!' and took it cleanly. I could see Melrose free, wide right, so I released the ball to him but he let it run out of play, the twat, otherwise it would have been a great piece of goalkeeping.

I remember after the game the crowd went mental and when we got back into the dressing rooms I felt a bit out of it. The rest of the lads were really bouncing but I felt lethargic and I remember going straight home and not joining in the celebrations. I wasn't allowed to drive so somebody had to drive me and I didn't sleep well that night; I kept waking up with a blinding headache and I still had it the next morning when I got up. I don't remember much about that match but I know I have never played in a match like it before or since. I know I saw Stevie Lynex going in goals on the television; he was given the gloves but he didn't put them on, he threw them into the back of the net. And that was when I remembered what happened when I went back in goals – I was panicking because I didn't think I would have enough time to get the spare jersey on and the gloves that I had found in the back of the net. They were wet of course and that made it even harder to get them on and I was thinking, please just give me enough time to get these fuckers on before you blow your whistle.

If we had got the right draw in the quarter-final then we had the worst draw for the semi-final, even though we had beaten Tottenham twice the previous season. As it turned out they won comfortably in the end and it turned into one of the most disappointing days of my life. Afterwards Jock said, 'I don't want to see you until Thursday.' Which was good because it gave you time to get it out of your system, because we really felt like we had let Jock down. But on reflection, that semi-final defeat was probably the worst day of my life (in football), even worse than getting relegated because I had fully expected us to beat Tottenham. I thought we were good enough on the day and if today's rules had been in place then Chris Hughton would have been sent off. He twice brought down Gary Lineker when he had broken away from Hughton and would have been clean through. We were on top of them for parts of the game, even though we weren't playing great ourselves but then neither were Tottenham. But after Tony Galvin broke Tommy Williams' leg he should also have been sent off. Earlier in the game Galvin had flattened me at the near post at a corner as well; he wasn't like a lot of wide players, he was solid and hard too.

But I didn't have my best game that day. I had been out injured for a while with a groin problem but I had to play. There was no option, so I was throwing pills down my throat and I had a painkilling injection just before kick-off. The whole experience left me devastated to be honest; I didn't go home for three days. I went to a hotel with all of my friends because there were two bus-loads down from Scotland. All of the lads came down and so did my Mum and Dad and even some other family members. I managed to get them all tickets as I fully expected that we would beat Tottenham. I was up against Grahame Roberts at centre half – no problem, bring it on! I really didn't worry about facing him. The rest of their team were pretty useful (Hoddle, Ardiles, Galvin, Archibald, Hughton, Crooks, Hazzard, Perryman) but as the match progressed we competed with them and got to half time at 0–0. The groin was still sore but I was coping. I took some more painkillers and went back out for the second half, still confident that we could win. Then I remember going for a ball in the centre circle with Paul Price and I felt another tug on my groin as I jumped; I knew before I landed what had happened. I wasn't bothered about the pain but I couldn't run properly when I picked myself up. I couldn't run so I knew I had to come off. Jock saw it from the dugout straight away and that was that. The walk off the pitch was heartbreaking, knowing that my game was over. I looked up at the Holte End, half-filled with our fans, making a tremendous noise, and I felt as if I had let them down. In hindsight that sounds daft because I did my best and gave everything. I ran my socks off up front and came back and did my defensive duties when I was needed to, I challenged for every header and didn't let them settle. So Jim Melrose came on as substitute for me and it wasn't long after that Tottenham took the lead. The thing is, in a match every player has attacking duties and defensive duties. My job was always to mark the near post when we were defending a corner so when Melrose came on he should have taken that role but he didn't. When Spurs won their next corner he was standing on the halfway line but he should have been back defending. Spurs took the corner short and Ossie Ardiles took the ball along the byline towards our goal into the penalty area; if Melrose had been where he should have been then he could have stopped that because he should have been out to meet Ardiles. Our routine at Leicester was always that, if there was a short corner taken then the near-post man went out to meet the players at the corner and the back-post man came across to take the near post. But Melrose wasn't there so Ardiles had time to pull the ball back for Crooks to stick it in and we are 1–0 down and chasing the game. So where was Melrose? On the halfway line picking his nose! I wanted to kill him after the game; I had a quiet word and said 'Did you forget your duties? Are you too good to come back and defend?' He just told me to fuck off. He very nearly got a right hook.

Ian Wilson then had appalling luck to score the own goal that put the game beyond our reach. When the ball arrived at his feet he could have done anything with it other than what he did, which was lift it over Mark Wallington's head and into the net. I have an ongoing thing with Ian Wilson that he is to blame for EVERYTHING! Everything is Willie's fault. Thank Christ the little shite is up in Aberdeen and out of harm's way! I met him at Bobby Smith's funeral two years ago and reminded him of the problems he had caused me at Leicester City and we had a laugh about it. But Ian was a tough little nut and he went on to have a good career after Leicester, especially at Everton. He was what we called a 'choochter'. That was somebody from the north of Scotland, a yokel if you like. When they see a bus they go, 'Oh look, a hoose on wheels!'

Anyway, after the game Jock was quiet so we knew that he was hurting as well and he just said, 'I dinnae want tae see ye 'til Thursday. Go away and get it oot yer system.' So that was that.

Afterwards I just got together with all my mates down from Fife on the coaches. Now some of them were a bit mad to be honest so it was always going to get messy. As it was we all descended on the Wigston Stage Hotel, just outside of Leicester, where they were all booked in. And that is where I stayed until they all went back on the Tuesday, remembering of course that Jock had already told us he didn't want to see us until Thursday. In the evenings some of the lads went mental; they were climbing along the roof space between rooms and dropping into other guests' rooms! There was a guy called Jimmy Cooper who covered himself in shaving foam and was stark bollock naked underneath, he went knocking on guests' doors just for the hell of it. It was a mad, mad few days but it helped me. It took my mind off everything but I was terrified that they might overstep the mark so I was trying to keep a lid on things wherever possible – I couldn't relax completely.

So when we got back into training on Thursday Jock called us together and said, 'I don't want anybody mentioning the semi-final again. It's gone, it's over and there is nothing we can do about it. Now let's win the league!' But we never kicked a ball after that and we went on a poor run that saw us well out of the running for the title by the end of the season. I know we were fifth in the table after the semi-final and we had games in hand so we were well placed, but it just didn't happen. The strange thing is that I remember very little about the run in. Up until the semi-final I can remember every detail of the games we played, but after that I am blank. I know the final match of the season was a 3–0 defeat in a meaningless game at Orient in front of about 2,000 fans. I mean what a contrast to the glorious day at Orient just two year earlier when we won the league and what a terrible anti-climax to a season that was going so well. I sometimes wonder if that influenced Jock's decision to go back to Scotland. If we had been promoted in '82 then he would have stayed put and so would I.

6

YOU'RE NOT MY GAFFER – LEAVING LEICESTER

Preseason came around for the 1982/83 season and that was when I found out that Jock was gone. We all turned up for the first day of training in early July and Alan Bennet came to the training ground and informed us of what had happened. We also discovered that Gordon Milne was already lined up to replace him, even though he wasn't actually there for that first day back. This was a massive blow for me. A huge, huge blow because I loved that man. I loved everything about him. I loved his passion and his anger and even when he got his words mixed up and got foreign names wrong; he called Johan Cruyff, Johan Croof and Pele was Peelie! But you didn't dare let him catch you laughing because he would come over and give you a slap. But he was always prepared to laugh at himself and he could be a very humble man. A lot of what he did was genuine, very real, but there were two sides to Jock. Everybody saw the passionate, serious man but he was also very compassionate. I don't mean turning up at charity functions and drawing raffles, I mean his caring, human side; he knew if you were unhappy and he wanted to know why because he cared. He turned up at my house and knocked on the door at half seven one morning shouting, 'Get the bloody kettle on! Where's them bairns? Get them up too!'

And I'm thinking, 'Whoa, what's going on here?' I had never known anything like this before but he thought this was normal. The reason he did it was because he thought something was wrong at home with me and Julie. And he was right, of course! He said that he could 'smell' when something wasn't right. This applied to all sorts of things and he said he could smell fear as well in our opponents, a bit like Bill Shankley. He would often come in the dressing room before a game and say, 'I've just seen them in the corridor, they are shitting themselves. I can smell the fear!' He also knew when something was wrong and he would have to go and find out for himself, or 'smell' it as he would say, and that's what he was doing that morning. He would always expressions like that, 'Ah can smell success', or, 'Ah can smell a couple of goals for ye today big man', or, 'Ah can smell a clean sheet for you today Wallington and it's aboot fuckin' time!'

But when he went, that was when the doubts set in straightaway. The training was different immediately and I noticed that a couple of the lads had their shirts outside their shorts and their socks round their ankles and I knew that it wasn't going to be the same. It had only taken two days but it was already happening and discipline was slipping. If Jock caught us with our shirts outside our shorts he would say, 'Ye look like a fuckin' Celtic player!' and that was the biggest insult he could give you. It was in one of those early sessions that I jogged over to Gordon Milne and introduced myself properly and said, 'Morning Mr Milne, welcome to the club. You've got a good bunch of fit, honest lads here and I think we will have a very good season.'

To which he replied, 'Well thank you very much but from now on it's "Boss".' I think after the socks and shirts and discipline issue I just thought, 'Ach, fuck this'. Despite the fact that I believed we would have a good season and I loved the club and the supporters, I didn't think my heart would be in it. I went to see Gordon Milne and I started by saying, 'I think we have a problem.' He asked what it was.

I said, 'Jock was my boss'.

'So why is that a problem for you?' he said.

'That is my problem. Jock was my boss'. Then he offered to circulate my name and basically let me leave. I stayed behind when the lads went to Ireland for preseason and I played in the Leicestershire Senior Cup Final at centre half alongside Billy Gibson and Stu Hammil. I enjoyed the game but there was a sadness that I couldn't shake off; even if Milne didn't like me as a person then surely he would have considered me as a player. I would have worked hard for him and given everything and he would have only have had to ask around to know that. Even though we didn't see eye-to-eye, and he wasn't Jock Wallace, it was still Leicester City and that still meant so much to me. But he didn't really pull up any trees to try and make me stay and that was a clear indication that I was better off leaving and going somewhere else. Shortly after that I was pulled in and Milne told me that Sheffield United wanted to talk to me and that a fee had been agreed. I asked how much the fee was and was told it was £160,000. I knew that Ian Porterfield was the manager but they were in the Third Division and I wasn't too keen on that even though I knew that Sheffield United were a huge club with great support and a good stadium. So I phoned Jock at Motherwell and he was dead straight with me as always and told me: 'I want to get you and Lineker up here but I cannot fuckin' afford ye!' I asked him about Sheffield United and he told me to go and get myself up there, told me that they were a big club and described Ian Porterfield as a 'decent boy'. And he was, maybe too nice to be honest. Certainly too nice to be a football manager, he didn't have a harsh word to say about anybody. If you add in the fact that I used to go and watch Porterfield when I was a kid and he was playing for Raith Rovers then you can start to understand why the move felt right. Of course, I was also offered a decent contract with decent money and a decent signing-on fee which helped.

When I moved from Sheffield United to Brighton a year later I agreed terms with Jimmy Melia; Sheffield United were happy with the transfer fee and so were Brighton but I went back to Reg Brealey and said that I needed another five grand because the standard of living was so much higher on the South Coast compared to South Yorkshire. Now Reg said, 'You can have it if you will trust me and we will meet up when it's convenient at a later date and I'll give it to you then.' So I remember driving up from Brighton to Sheffield for a midweek evening game (I can't remember which one exactly) and I went into the manager's office and Reg Brealey came in and handed me a plain brown envelope and it contained three and half grand in readies and a cheque for one a half grand. Five thousand pounds in total ... so I didn't stay for the game, I was away back down the road.

But Reg was as good as his word, which is more than I can say for Tommy Cannon (from Cannon and Ball) because he still owes me five thousand pounds. This goes back to when I signed for Rochdale; I met the manager, Vic Halom, on a Motorway junction on the M62. No café or service station, just on the motorway roundabout. Vic asked if I fancied joining him at Rochdale and helping him out. I wasn't sure he would be able to match my salary but he assured me that he could, but that I wouldn't be getting a big signing-on fee. What he did say, however, was that they would arrange for £5,000 relocation expenses in readies. When I got up there, there was nothing of the sort; Halom denied all knowledge of it. That really pissed me off because I had given him two more years as a player at Oldham because I had done all of his running for him. He wasn't liked at Oldham; the players used to call him 'The Hamburglar' because he ate too much fast food. All he knew was running up and down hills, no football knowledge at all.

I liked it at Sheffield United when I got there; they had some good players like Tony Kenworthy, John MacPhail, Keith Edwards (the best striker I have ever played with), Colin Morris, and Terry Curran. The thing that really struck me when I got there was a serious lack of discipline; what a contrast to Leicester. They had a lot of flamboyant characters there and this was epitomised by Terry Curran who became a good friend and, incidentally, still owes me two months' rent! He came to stay the night and ended up stopping for two months. He was one of many good players at Sheffiled United but the same couldn't always be said of the back-room staff. Cec Coldwell was a Sheffield United legend. Whispering Cec we called him, he was old brigade but he was fine and always got his point across and I liked him. And there was a guy we called, 'Jim the Jog' because all he wanted you to do was run. He was hopeless and didn't know the game at all, which was why his sessions always consisted of running. There was also John McSeveny, the Assistant Manager and he was a snake; I remember being in the manager's office trying to sort out my personal details when I was negotiating the transfer package and I opened the door and John nearly fell in because he had been listening at the door. I suspect he was more the odd job man than anything else, didn't really have much input into training.

They call Sheffield 'Little Rome' because it is built on five hills and our training ground was built on top of one of them. If it was 30 degrees centigrade at sea level it could be snowing on top of our hill! They weren't the greatest training facilities but it wasn't a problem for me; I guess I had been spoilt at Leicester. As I said, it was a decent side with Little Colin Morris on one side, Terry Curran on the other wing, with me and Keith Edwards up front. There was Monty at the back with Mick Henderson (from Sunderland) and Tony Kenworthy and Kevin Arnott. We had two good 'keepers: Keith Waugh and a young lad called Conroy. So, I had every reason to believe this was going to be enjoyable but when preseason came I was amazed to find that all we did was run. Run, run, run, run and run!! They took us to a public park one day that was on the side of a huge hill with a path that swept down in an 'S' pattern and when we got there who should be running on it but Seb Coe! His Dad would wait at the bottom of this hill and time his run up and down this hill. He did about twenty reps and each rep was about 300m. When Jim the Jog saw this he was hooked: 'What's good enough for Seb is good enough for us' and that was that. Jim could run mind you, he was a big tall Geordie and he loved running.

Even when we trained at Bramall Lane it was still running, running, running! Not on the pitch, on the gravel track around the pitch. He introduced me to Fartlek running (it comes from a Swedish word meaning 'speed play' apparently) which is basically interval training but if you listened to Jim the Jog then you would think he had invented the bloody thing. Now I was fit, but it was even too much for me because I could always feel this niggle in my groin which didn't go away through my whole time at Sheffield United. This was the injury I aggravated against Spurs in the semi-final, so I was never fully fit, but I just ran through it. Ironically the knee was fine at this point but the groin may have been aggravated because I was protecting the knee in the way I ran. So anyway, I started off ok at Sheffield

United, scoring on my debut. In fact, I scored on my debut for all of my clubs except Notts County, and I even scored on my debut for Shepshed Charterhouse when I played non-league football. Not being fully fit I knew myself that I wasn't playing to the best of my abilities; I was tiring before the end of matches and that was unusual for me. I put that down to the injury not letting me run as freely as possible and the training, which was taking too much out of me. So I mentioned this to Jim and told him that I wasn't peaking on Saturday afternoon, I was leaving half of it on the training ground and what I needed was a different training programme; don't get me wrong, I was prepared to run but he had to decide if he wanted me to be running for ninety minutes on Saturday or seventy-five minutes. Unfortunately he wouldn't accept this and said, 'If you are fit, you're fit. It's about total fitness.'

'But I feel fatigued with ten minutes to go in the game and that's not like me in fact when I was at Leicester City I was at my BEST with ten minutes to go so I know the difference,' I said. But he wasn't having any of it. It was a different approach, and so was the psychology of fitness at Sheffield United. I've mentioned about Jock Wallace talking you fit ('You are as fit as fuckin' fiddles') and he could have you walking away feeling 10ft tall and invincible. Nobody bothered with that at Sheffield United and they were more concerned with your times when you were doing your sprints and reps. If you came in half a second slower than they wanted it was frowned upon and it seemed at times as if that was all they were bothered about. And that's how it was, but off the pitch things were going well; I moved into a lovely cottage in a village called Dore and Karen moved in with me so that was the end of my marriage to Julie effectively. I left Julie the house on Van Dyke road in Oadby, it cost £23,000 and that was with a deposit of £6,000, so there was a mortgage £17,000; it had a lovely back garden. I gave that to Julie in the divorce settlement so that the boys had a decent home. The courts also decided that I had to reduce the mortgage by £5,000 so that my maintenance payments would cover the cost of the mortgage for Julie. So I got screwed and there was a lot of money to be paying every week, £99.00 to be exact. If she had sold the house then I would have got my £5,000 back. And she did sell it a few years later for £75,000, so she did very well out of me. But fair play; the boys are terrific (Wesley and Jordan) and I have a great relationship with them and I always have had. I'm very proud of them. She eventually met another guy and they started a business up in Rochdale where she still is. I admit that the reason the marriage failed was entirely my fault but you can't legislate for falling out of love with someone. You can't turn love on and off like a tap. The thing is, Julie never wanted to come to games or go out after the games, so that was when we started to grow apart, plus the fact that professional footballers who have a high profile (as I did at the time) get a lot of attention from girls when they are out which doesn't help. That goes with the territory I suppose, but I never played away from home.

So it was off to Sheffield where we had a lovely little cottage in Twentywell Lane in a super little village and I became great friends with Emlyn Hughes in the local pub which was called the Rising Sun. We would be at the end of the bar and we had a right laugh together. He was manager of Rotherham at the time and he was always saying, 'Come to Rotherham big man, I'll sell that Ronnie Moore. I can easily get rid of that twat!' I didn't want to leave Sheffield United, I had played at Rotherham and it was a dump. I said, 'You will not get me there Emlyn and anyway you can't afford me', but he kept trying and even though I kept saying no we remained good friends.

In fact, we were friends with Emlyn and his wife Barbara and his kids Emlyn and Emma (he had a bit of an ego did Emlyn naming his kids Emma and Emlyn). When I moved to Brighton, Karen moved in with Emlyn and his family for a while. We had to vacate the cottage because it was only rented, so Emlyn stored all of our furniture in his garage. Unfortunately that didn't work out quite as we had planned because it took so long to find somewhere to live in Brighton (I was living in rented accommodation and a hotel) that by the time I bought a house I signed for Notts County just a few weeks later!

Karen and I had a fantastic life, it was absolutely fabulous. Her parents, Dot and Colin, knew that we were seeing each other before I went to Sheffield because they asked me if we were when I was in Grannies nightclub. Of course I denied it because it was too early to admit something like that to them. We used to get on famously with Karen's parents and we went on holiday together, they would come and watch Leicester City, and when I moved to Sheffield United they came up there for the games as well. Me and Colin regularly used to go out and we would quite often go to his Conservative club for a game of snooker and a pint. Colin also loved hanging around with me and Emlyn in the Rising Sun pub. Even when I went to Brighton they would still come down and watch the games and spend time with us. They loved being with us and I loved having them around, they were very, very happy times for me because I was very much in love with Karen at the time. It felt like that first love feeling that you get when you are seventeen years old and I haven't felt like that since Fiona back home.

I forged a really good friendship with Tony Kenworthy and we went everywhere together and we looked out for each other, if there was any trouble then Tony would be on my side and vice versa. We would fight the world Tony and I! My other pal up there was Keith Edwards, but he was the worst trainer in the world, all he wanted to do was get the ball and smash it into the back of the net. Keith was a great finisher, really quick across the ground and he had a great touch and he knew it. He knew he was the best and he had a look about him that said 'I am the best'. But I always used to tell him you were born offside. Time and time again the linesman's flag went up and it was Keith who was offside and I remember telling him once, 'For fuck's sake Keith bend your run, you are quick enough.'

His reply was, 'Listen Youngy, one of these days that twat is going to get it wrong and keep his flag down and that is when I will go on and score the winner and get you your win bonus, so shut the fuck up'. And he was right, of course. Keith never played at a higher level even though he was a prolific goalscorer in the lower leagues. Maybe he was just content with his lot or maybe the Scouts from top-flight clubs didn't want to take a chance on him. Either way I was delighted because he was in my team and he would give us 20 to 30 goals a season. You also have to remember that it was a different game back then and there was not the stupid sums of money floating around in the higher division that would attract a player like Keith Edwards.

My best mate at the club was Tony Kenworthy and he could be a bit of a lad; he had a wife and a girlfriend and Karen and I would often socialise with him and Michelle, his girlfriend. One night we went to see Shalamar at the City Hall in Sheffield and halfway through the show Tony leaned across and whispered to me, 'Big man! My fucking wife has just walked in.' So I had to grab Michelle and pretend that she was with me and have a few dances with her whilst Tony went and sorted out his wife. I have no idea what he did but he did manage to get it sorted somehow and he got away with it.

He wasn't always that lucky and I have a feeling that he spent some time in jail, despite that if I meet him now, we will have the biggest hug because I absolutely love the guy. When I was at Notts County I was driving the youth team minibus to Mansfield on the A60 one day when we had to stop at some roadworks. I looked up and there was Tony Kenworthy holding the stop-go sign at the roadworks so I leant out of the window and shouted, 'Oi, Shetland' (that was what he was nicknamed at Sheffield United, either that or 'fatty' because he had a weight problem). By the time he realised it was me driving the lights had changed to green and I had to go but when we drove back down the A60 on the way home he wasn't there. I saw him one more time after that in Ibiza, I was in the sea on the beach at San Antonio and as I came out of the water I looked across and saw the little guy up to his waist in the water with his hands on his knees, staring into the sea. I thought, it can't be, surely not and then I noticed that he was wearing a pair of football shorts with a number six on them and I knew it was him. So I went across and shouted, 'Oi fatty' and he looked up and recognised me.

He pointed into the water and said, 'Have you seen these fucking fish?' After all that time that was the first thing he said to me. After that we had an incredible night that seemed to go on forever; Carol and Michelle went off and left me and Tony to get absolutely bladdered. That was the last time I saw him, that holiday. I would love to know where he is now, I've searched everywhere for him because I would love to see him again. He was always smiling even though he had constant problems with his ankles – they were always sore because he had a very high instep. In fact, if I think about it, he wore size 5 boots because he only had small feet, but he wasn't afraid to tackle and he had a terrific left foot.

I was playing for Sheffield United when I picked up one of the worst injuries I have had in football, but it didn't feel like it at the time. We were at home (I can't remember who we were playing) and I went to the near post for a diving header and as I landed I put my hands out to break my fall and I caught a stud between my little finger and my ring finger and it needed stitches. I went off and had a couple of stitches put in and came back on and finished the game. Now that was on Easter Saturday and we were due to play at Bradford two days later. We had a day off on Sunday and had to report to travel to Bradford that Monday morning. On the Sunday night my arm became sore and started throbbing and I had to (believe it or not) wrap a curtain around the arm whilst I was sleeping to try and keep the arm above my heart. As soon as I brought my arm down it started to throb really badly and hurt like hell. Anyway, I turned up as planned and went to Bradford with the squad and changed and went out on to the pitch to warm-up but I felt dreadful; I could hardly move my legs. So my warm-up lasted about a minute and then I came back down the tunnel and said to Ian Porterfield, 'Ian, I don't feel well'.

'What's wrong?' he askd.

I showed him my arm and said, 'I don't feel well, in fact, I feel terrible.' I rolled up my sleeve and it was red and swollen and the veins were standing out and it was becoming really scary.

Ian took one look at this and said, 'You'd better see a doctor'. So the Bradford City club doctor came through and very quickly said that I needed to go to straight to hospital. So that's what happened and no sooner had I been admitted than I was in a bed, I had a big needle in my arse injecting God knows what, and I had drips coming out of each arm and one arm was held up by a sling. I was in for three days with (as I later found out) advanced septicaemia. I could have lost my arm apparently and if untreated I could have died!

We had good times in Sheffield though and I made some great friends, none more so than Emlyn Hughes, even though I nearly killed him one day playing golf. We were playing at Topley and there was one tee on a dog-leg; it was an elevated tee so Emlyn went to the end to watch my drive. Well he did more than watch it; I caught the ball with the heel of the driver and it went very flat straight into Emlyn's midriff, just below the rib cage. He went down as if he'd been shot and because it was an elevated tee I couldn't see him straight away. I went running across and he was lying on the ground moaning and rolling around. I couldn't get a word out of him for a while and I was saying to him 'Em, tell me you're okay, do you want an ambulance?' But he just carried on moaning and told me to fuck off when he eventually could speak. Well he was okay but he had a perfectly round bruise in his midriff that went all colours of the rainbow. He would show it to everybody down the pub and tell them that I tried to kill him. Overall I just played the one season at Sheffield United, 26 games and 7 goals. The fans never really took to me but I can't blame them for that. I only played about one in three games and I was never fully fit because the training was too much and Jim the Jog was running the bollocks off of me and my groin was still a problem.

Anyhow the following preseason we were over at Reg Brearley's place at Boston Spa and I remember looking around thinking to myself that we were going to have a very good season; I was feeling very happy at the prospect of another season at Sheffield United, so I was surprised when Ian Porterfield cornered me at the bar one evening after training and told me that they had received an offer from Brighton. He then told me that they were going to accept the offer and asked if I would like to speak to Jimmy Melia. So I looked Ian in the eye and asked him, 'Don't you fucking want me like?' And he made all the right noises and assured me that it wasn't his decision, that it was the chairman because they needed to get some money in and that I was the only player that they could sell right now. So I went down to see Jimmy and his wife Val and met them at a hotel in Brighton where he told me what the terms were and that my signing-on fee would be £20,000; that was when I got back to Brearley and asked him for the extra five grand which of course he honoured. Now Val was quite a spiritual individual and when Jimmy and I had finished discussing the terms of the transfer she asked me what star sign I was. When I told her I was Scorpio she clapped her hands together and said, 'Jimmy, it's perfect. We need that tough Scorpio character in the team.' At this point I am thinking, what are you on? But I was far too polite to say anything so I kept it to myself whilst Val was bouncing up and down because she had found a Scorpio.

7

I DO LIKE TO BE BESIDE THE SEASIDE

Jimmy Melia made it very easy for me to sign for Brighton; he was a real football man, football through and through and he was very popular when he played for Liverpool. He told me that he wanted me to play up front with Terry Connor, to act as foil for Terry, and that sounded good to me. We had a great squad at Brighton, back then and I was chuffed to be a part of that; we had big Joe Corrigan in goal as well as Perry Digweed and Graham Moseley as back up, Steve Gatting, Steve Foster, Chris Hutchings, Kieron O'Reagan, Jimmy Case, Danny Wilson, Gerry Ryan, Gordon Smith, Neil Smillie, Tony Grealish, and Terry Connor. That was a right good squad.

So I agreed terms and then it was into the Courtlands Hotel and where did we go for preseason? Majorca! Now I was the new boy and I had no idea that this was normal for Brighton, so this was great news to me.

I met Chris Hutchings recently when Leicester played Ipswich and he reminded me of the fantastic team spirit and friendship that we had at Brighton. Normally within a club you will get groups of three for maybe five players together,

but at Brighton there were thirteen or fourteen of us maybe
and we all stuck together. After training we would go down to
Woody's wine bar where we would all tuck into huge plates
of calamari covered with lemon and black pepper and wash
it down with a bottle of wine; then another bottle of wine
and another and then it would be off to a gentlemen's club.
There we would play pool all afternoon and nobody would
know where we were, not a soul! Jimmy Melia had no idea
about this, but we didn't abuse it because we wouldn't have
done any of this after Wednesday and certainly not the day
before a game. But Jim was great, he wanted us to play good
football, to keep the ball and pass it and get it on the ground.
Unfortunately he had an assistant called Chris Cattlin who was
one of the most horrible bastards I have ever met in football.
Cattlin played at Coventry in the seventies as a right-back but
what a complete and utter twat he was. He undermined Jim
all the time and did it in a very underhand manner, covertly
and sneakily. He, in my opinion, was instrumental in getting
Jimmy the sack because he was very good friends with the
chairman – Mike Bamber - at the time. As soon as that
happened then that was it for me; things were never going to
be the same again at Brighton. Anyway, we went to Majorca
for the preseason preparations and had games against Real
Madrid, Real Majorca and Ferencváros; just a little four-team
tournament at Majorca's ground. When we arrived where
was the first place you think we went? Magaluf. In the bar
where the ducks are, Mano's Bar (it's a famous bar). So we are
all in this bar and I remember there was a song by Malcolm
Maclaren going around at the time called Double Dutch
and there was a section of the video for the song which had
a skipping routine (Ooh ma ma, ooh ma ma etc., you know
the one) in the middle of it. The whole team were recreating

the video for Double Dutch and the whole place was going mental. Everyone joined in and it was wild – and we had only just arrived! What I hadn't realised at the time was that someone was putting vodka in my beer and so I was getting drunk very quickly. At one point I went and sat next to this girl in a polka-dot dress and I was thinking that she was right fit but I couldn't talk, I really couldn't. So I thought, I've got to get out of here before I collapse or something. So I got into this taxi but I couldn't remember where the hotel was and I was starting to feel sick and the taxi driver was jabbering away at me in Spanish; I was in a right mess. So I summoned up all of my Spanish and said, 'Momento. Marina Hotel' and so off we went and the taxi driver found the Marina Hotel and dropped me off so I paid him and got out, thinking that I had finally had a slice of luck. I saw Gordon Smith walking out of the front door of the hotel so I knew I had the right place. I stopped 'Smudge' and he said, 'What are you doing Big Man?'

'Oh Smudge, I just want ma bed,' I said. So I went into the hotel and walked up to reception and told them that I was Mr Young but I that couldn't remember my room number. But they couldn't find me on their records and keep saying, 'No Meester Young' and I'm going 'Yeeesss Mr Young!' Eventually I gave up and ran out after Gordon Smith. I caught him up and said, 'Smudge, they won't give me my key.'

He looked at me a bit odd and said, 'I'm not fuckin' surprised'.

'Why?' I asked.

He grinned and said, 'It's not our fuckin' hotel that's why! Our is next door'. Now quite what he was doing in that hotel … I wouldn't like to say. He later became president of the Scottish Football Association of course. He could also play the piano really well; he would just sit down at a piano, any piano that might be in a hotel foyer or something, and go straight into Elton John's 'Your Song'. I used to think, you bastard. I was so jealous of that kind of talent. That is one my regrets in life, never having piano lessons. So anyway, I made it to my bed and I was up for training on time the next morning. We didn't have a blast like that every night, but my word did we ever go for it on that first night. And later on the bastards admitted to putting vodka in my drinks. The most amazing thing that happened on that trip however was that big Joe Corrigan (all 6ft 7in of him) got mugged in Alessandro's night club and had his watch stolen! I mean, Joe Corrigan! There must have been about a hundred guys in the gang that mugged him.

On the third day we had a game against Real Madrid and we trained in the morning in preparation for the game that night. I was just walking back to the coach to take us back to the hotel when I felt my back start to feel a bit sore. I hadn't had a kick on it or hurt it during training but as I got on the coach it started to bother me. So I asked Mike Yaxley (the most useless physio that I ever worked with) to have a look at it and he just told me to go to bed and see how it was after I had rested it. When I got up it was no better but I wasn't going to miss the game – not against Real Madrid; they had Santiana and Uli Stieleke playing for them and I really wanted to turn out against them, especially Stieleke (he was hard as nails, he would kick his Granny). So I got warmed up as best I could with a massage and so forth and in truth, I shouldn't have played. Madrid didn't score until the 85th minute but what a goal when it did come. I can't remember who took the corner but what a finish. You have to imagine a straight line drawn from the far post to the six-yard line and then make it a square; this is called the POMO position by the F.A. coaching personnel. It stands for position of maximum opportunity and that is where Santiana was standing. The corner went over Steve Foster's head and Santiana jumped about 2ft off the ground; it looked as if he was going to head it but he didn't, he chested the ball and as he came down, the ball came with him. He shaped to volley it but Fossie moved to block it. But Santiana didn't volley it, he dragged it to his left, and made to hit it as Corrigan dived to block it, but then he dragged it back and side-footed it into the net with his right foot. This all takes place in the little six yard space (the POMO) and I just stood and applauded him because it was the best goal I had seen in my life. I think Jimmy Case starting applauding as well. We lost the game 1–0 and we gave a decent account of ourselves, but the next day I was back home in England in Haywards Heath Hospital having manipulation under general anaesthetic to try and sort my back out. The first game was just around the corner at home to Chelsea and I was desperate to play – and play I did. I scored but Kerry Dixon equalised in the second half and it finished 1–1 and then I was straight back into hospital. This time they put a little television screen up so they could see my spine, they put local anaesthetic into the spine and then a longer needle into the space between two vertebrae where there was a nerve, they connected that up to an electric current and they cauterised the nerve between lumbar vertebrae one, two and three. I can remember them telling me that I wouldn't be able to drive, and so I asked Karen to drive and take me home. When I tried to stand up though I realised why I wouldn't be able to drive: my legs felt like rubber; I could hardly stand up straight! Poor Karen had to bring the car round.

I didn't realise until I looked recently that my goal return at Brighton was pretty decent; I got 12 goals in 26 matches and I really enjoyed my time at Brighton. The supporters were still recovering from losing the F.A. Cup Final to Manchester United in 1983 (this was the game when Gordon Smith should have won the cup for Brighton with a late chance when he was one-on-one with Gary Bailey) and the whole euphoria of the day and the occasion. I'm not saying that Brighton isn't a proper football club, but in Brighton the football was viewed as part of the entertainment industry. The football they tried to play reflected that and if the fans weren't being entertained then they got at the players and the manager. At Brighton we played with a lot of freedom, there were no restrictions, we were allowed to make our own decisions on the pitch and we had the players with the right experience to do that. I'm thinking of international players like Corrigan, Ryan, Grealish and experienced lads like Jimmy Case and Steve Foster. The football was very enjoyable there and never more so than when Jimmy Case and I were playing together; I loved playing with Jimmy. He was very quiet and has a hearing aid because he doesn't hear too well. I remember we finished training one day and headed off to Woody's and then on to the gentlemen's club as usual for a game of pool and then everyone started to drift away. By 10 in the evening there are only about six of us left. (Bear in mind that we didn't have mobile phones back then so you couldn't phone up to let anyone know you were going to be late.) So I got home and Karen asked me where I had been so I told her and then she asked me if Jimmy had been with us because Larna had been on the phone asking if we knew where he was. I told her not to worry because he left same time as me and would probably be home any time soon. So the next day Jimmy is nowhere to be seen and nobody knows where he is. So there is a little bit of panic around and nobody has a clue where he has gone until the following morning at training when Jimmy saunters in, whistling and acting as if nothing is wrong. So I asked him, 'Jim, where the fuck have you been?'

He looks at me and says, 'What do you mean?'

I said, 'Jim, nobody knows where you have been, we've been panicking.'

Then he smiles and goes, 'Ha! The Avenue.'

I'm like, 'The Avenue? What Avenue?'

To which he says, 'The fucking Avenue de Champs Elysee!' Then he tells us how, after we all went our separate ways that night that he fancied going to Paris! So he went up to Gatwick and jumped on a plane to Paris. He showed us the stamp in his passport to prove it – he had gone to Paris for a day just because he could and he fancied it. On the pitch he was different class though. I once saw him on the receiving end of a dreadful challenge when a guy (I forget who) tried to get the ball of him and put his studs down the back of his calf and Achilles – which really bloody hurts – and Jim just let the ball roll away and turned on this guy and (through gritted teeth) said, 'Don't you ever, ever fucking do that to me again!' Then he turned and went after the ball and got it back before it went out. I watched this going on and the guy was shitting himself. That is the only time I have really seen one professional footballer genuinely scared of another because Jimmy could be a hard bastard and really knew how to look after himself. He used to do about 200 sit ups every days after training and he would wear one of those polystyrene bags that you get from the dry cleaners when he did them.

He got me into it as well. He liked to shoot as well; I don't mean just at the goal, I mean taking a gun on to the South Downs and shooting rabbits and so forth. I remember we were in a Chinese restaurant one night with Tony Grealish and Pip (his wife) along with Jimmy and Larna and we were sitting near the kitchen which had those swing doors – saloon doors you would call them. We had ordered the crispy duck and the waiter was coming through the swing doors with the duck on a platter held up in the air and he tripped, the tray went in the air and the duck slid off. But before it hit the floor Jim draws out an imaginary shotgun and shoots the duck to the sound of 'Badoom!' and then says 'Got it!' He had a fantastic sense of humour did Jim. He would often turn off his hearing aid when Chris Cattlin was giving his team talks, Cattlin would be going 'Jim. Jim!' and Jim would be sat there miles away and eventually he might look up and smile and go, 'Wha?' and this would drive Cattlin mad, he would be shouting 'Have you got that bloody hearing aid turned off again?' But Jim didn't care.

That season with Brighton was enjoyable on the pitch because we played good football, even the 'keeper was told to give the ball to the full backs if possible and not kick it long, we passed the ball well and that suited my game because I had a decent touch. Jimmy Case and I got on very well because he appreciated getting a decent ball back and getting it early. We had a good routine at corners that got us a few goals that season as well. Eric Young joined Stevie Foster during the season from Crystal Palace and when we were out we would tell people that we were brothers; same Mum but different Dads! We also had a young Dutch lad called Hans Kray and he really loved to tackle – but every tackle was off the ground or sliding, shoving and kicking! Off the pitch he was a real gentle giant, a lovely lad. He wouldn't survive in the modern game because the whole game has been cleaned up and players like Hans would be sent off every single week.

The reason I mention Hans is that we had a Christmas do at a small restaurant in Brighton and the theme was fancy dress.

Well, I went as 'Jim'll Jinx It' from the old Russ Abbott character that was very loosely based on Jimmy Saville. My hair was all orange and I was all kilted up of course. I remember Jimmy Case went as a scuba diver with the full wet suit and flippers and oxygen tank; Gordon Smith went as Ronald Reagan; Joe Corrigan went as the fairy off the Christmas tree in a little tutu; and Tony Grealish went as Wee Willie Winkie. You could only get away with this in Brighton because anything goes down there. If you had seen us walking through the streets you would understand why I say that. I can still see Jimmy Case pouring wine down his snorkel! Now Hans Kray came as Frank Bruno and this meant he had to black himself up completely and he looked a sight. When it came to him doing a turn he got up on the table and said, 'Hush, we musht be quiet.' Then he gave us a version of 'Tulips from Amsterdam' only his version was 'Bruno from Amsterdam' and he got the biggest round of applause all night. This epitomised the fun we had at that club and we were such pals. This was more on a social scale and this was different to what we had at Leicester City where the camaraderie was more intense; we would have killed for each other.

One match that sticks in my mind was the final game of the season in May 1984 when Brighton flew up to Newcastle to play at St James' Park. It was Kevin Keegan's last match for them and there was a lot of fuss and attention on Kevin because of this and I think we lost 4–2, but I had a great day. I know that Chris Waddle chipped big Joe Corrigan and that I set up Terry Connor and Gerry Ryan for goals. I spent a lot of time at right-back trying to retrieve the ball and tackling back, doing all the stuff that I shouldn't have been doing. Jock Wallace would have kicked my arse for it! After the game we went back to Teeside Airport and we were preparing to fly home. We got to know some of the British Caledonian stewardesses quite well because they all lived in Brighton and all went out to the same wine bars and clubs that the players went to. Anyway, when we got on the plane there was a crowd of us that always sat near the back: Steve Foster, Tony Grealish, Big Joe, and Jimmy Case. So Cattlin gets on and starts making silly comments at us. We knew we had lost but we had played well and the season was now over so he should have left it alone. As he truned around and walked back down the plane Steve Foster piped up and said 'Er, Chris [because nobody called him 'Boss' or 'Gaffer']the only reason we are all sitting at the back of the plane is because I have never seen one of these fucking things reverse into a mountain, alright!'

Unfortunately Jimmy Melia was sacked quite early in the season and Chris Cattlin took over. I never got on with him, especially after he did the dirty on me. Tony Grealish once said to me that he couldn't understand why I didn't get on with Cattlin because he really rated me. The truth was that I never rated Cattlin and there were two big reasons why. The first involved Joe Corrigan. He told him that he wanted to give the younger goalkeepers a chance. Now that would be alright if he didn't then go and sign Frank Worthington as an additional striker. So where is the policy of playing younger players now? Frank was ten years older than me, so it was clearly a case of double standards. What Joe did (and tried to persuade me to do as well) was to get sick notes from his doctor which meant he couldn't train or play. His attitude was that he had two years left on his contract and he reckoned he could stick it out and see off Cattlin; he used to say 'He will go before I do!' and he meant it. Joe would come into training every morning, get changed and go out for the running and warm-ups and then pull up and say, 'Nope, can't do it. Still too painful' and that would be it for the day. I didn't go so far as to miss training but for the first time in my career I wasn't trying my hardest. I really didn't want to play for Cattlin and I had the opportunity in the local newspaper to go into print about it and I gave Cattlin 'pelters'. I was very demotivated at that time and by the start of the next season I was still having back problems, which is why I only played 26 games that first season.

Now when Frank arrived we were just about to go on a preseason trip to Ireland as part of the transfer deal that brought Stephen Penney to the club. This was arranged at short notice and I was told that the squad would all be going to Ireland. On the Thursday before we left Karen had driven up to Leicester to pick up Wesley and Jordan to spend the weekend with us and they had arrived in Brighton. I then had to go home and tell them that I had to go to Ireland and that I wouldn't be around so they had to go back to Leicester. That absolutely tore the guts out of me, honestly, I never been so upset as I was that night. When I saw Karen and the boys off on the train the next morning and watched them walk down the platform holding Karen's hands I had tears running down my face, I was crying my eyes out. I was gutted. So I went into training and to find out the travel details for the trip and there was a squad posted on the notice board for the Ireland trip and my name wasn't on it. So I went straight into his office and I was ready to strangle the bastard. I have never been closer to doing someone some serious harm than I was with Cattlin that day. I shouted, 'What the fuck are you playing at?' and I explained about having my children down and so on and said 'You could have fuckin' told me, you should have let me know. You could have sorted this out ages ago but you gave me the impression that I was part of the squad going to Ireland, you c*nt!' I hardly ever use that word but I was so angry. In fact Tony Grealish heard the row and came in to see what was happening. Not only did my kids come down to see me on a wasted journey but I had to disappoint them and put them on the next train back to Leicester which was even more painful.

After that I always said that if I ever won a pile of money I would buy a Rolls Royce and drive the bloody thing straight into his rock shop on Brighton seafront! I wanted to smash the windows in and it *had* to be a Rolls. I still wanted to play for Brighton because I loved it down there, but I just couldn't play for that twat Cattlin. Joe Corrigan stayed on and stuck to his guns and saw Cattlin off – good for him but I couldn't do that, I had to get away. I have no idea where Cattlin went after that and I really don't care. I wouldn't piss on him if he was on fire! I have to say that I very rarely fall out with people the way I did that man because what he did wasn't just personal, it was intentional. The decision to leave Brighton was made harder by the fact that we had finally got ourselves a house. It had taken a while and we had been in hotels for months but we finally got a deposit down on a new build in Peacehaven and by the time it was finished months had passed. The garden was a mess because it was full of building materials that get left behind, and so my Mum and Dad came down to stay for a while and helped to sort it all out. My Dad would be out there at eight every morning with a rotavator and he sorted it out a treat. But within two weeks of that I had to phone him up and tell him that I had some bad news and that I was moving to Notts County. When he asked why it was bad news I said that we would have to sell the house (the house that he had just helped us get sorted). Looking back now I didn't have to sell the house of course, I could have rented it but I didn't have such a business head on me back then. With the signing-on fee from Notts County I could have bought another house.

8

TIED UP IN NOTTS

Jack Dunnett, the Notts County Chairman and Larry Lloyd (who was manager at the time) came down to Brighton to see me and we agreed salary and terms very quickly, so signing for Notts County was a fairly straightforward affair. Unfortunately Larry didn't last long; we didn't have a great start to the season and he got the heave-ho a few games in. This meant that Jimmy Sirrell took over as Notts County manager (not for the first time or the last as it turned out) but he was already at Notts County as General Manager. Jimmy was in charge for a short while until Richie Barker was appointed a month later. Unfortunately Richie was sacked the following April and so Jimmy took over again for two more seasons.

Poor Larry was disappointed to get the sack but he couldn't really complain. He called a spade a spade did Larry, and he didn't care if he upset you. This meant that his man-management skills left a bit to be desired. All the players respected him for what he achieved at Liverpool and Nottingham Forest as a player but the team wasn't settled or stable under Larry.

Now Richie Barker was a legend, and I don't mean in a good way. I recall one particular training session on The Embankment (alongside the River Trent) which we also called 'Dog Shit Park' by the way. It was eleven versus eleven and I remember Seamus McDonagh rolled it out to Aki Laatenaan (the Finnish full back) and he gave it to David Hunt who gave it back to him, on to Charlie MacParland, he knocked it up to me up front and I laid it back for Mark Goodwin. He played the next runner in (probably Rachied Harkouk) and suddenly Richie barker says, 'Whoa, whoa lads! Hang on a minute. Take the ball back, Seamus get the ball. Back-four, push up. You three up the front – Youngy, Fash, Harkouk – one of you three try and get a flick on. Seamus, hit it long and if it goes for a goal kick we will settle for that.

So I'm thinking, did I hear that last bit quite right? 'We'll what?' I shouted.

Barker said, 'If it goes for a goal kick then we'll settle for that'.

'Settle for that?' I replied. 'We've just kept possession and knocked it around nicely and if we do that then they can't get the ball from us.'

'No no,' he said, 'we'll play percentages, if they have a goal kick then it's as far away from our goal as it can be'.

At that point I took my bib off and told him 'You can get somebody else to do that because I'm not playing that way' and I walked back to the ground. About two or three minutes later Seamus McDonagh followed me in and he was laughing and saying 'Fuck that! I'm not playing that way, bloody long ball game!' and not long after that Barker was sacked. I'm not saying that it was player power that got rid of him, but it must have contributed. We had good ball players in that team and we didn't need to be playing a long-ball game. It was an insult to my intelligence as a player and an insult to the rest of the players who were a talented group. We had Dave Watson at centre half for instance (We used to call him Sherlock – Elementary my dear Watson) and we had Steve Sims, Clark and Pedro Richards at full backs, Mark Goodwin, Ian Macparland, David Hunt, Dean Yates, Justin Fashnau, and Rachid Harkouk. Not a bad side.

Anyway, Jimmy came back into manage the side again and he brought a strange culture to the club; the football was serious but not that serious. The supporters would support you whether you won or not and they were a good set of supporters – even if they were small in numbers. The ground however was a different matter. I watched a clip on Youtube recently that showed how quickly the fire took hold at Bradford and burnt down the stand in the Bradford fire disaster of 1987. That could just as easily have been Meadow Lane, it was an accident waiting to happen with the big old wooden stands. But I enjoyed my time at Notts County and although it wasn't an outstanding time in my career it was still a good club that tried to play good football, and I have good memories even though my best days were behind me by then. Rachid Harkouk was a loose cannon though; he is Algerian and could be a bit hot-headed and headstrong. He was incredibly quick and strong and he struck a great ball and he definitely underachieved. I know he represented his country but he could have played top-flight football for many years if he had really wanted to.

I also played with big Justin Fashanu of course and what a waste of talent and life that was. but what a lovely, great man he was. Where do I start to discuss Fash? There were signs even then that things were troubling him and he wasn't always a happy, content person. But he was always kind and compassionate and had time for you. We all knew he was a devout Christian but he didn't bring that to the training ground or the dressing room, and he didn't preach or try and convert anyone at all. The rumours that he brought his Bible into training simply weren't true. Ironically, the women all loved Fash; he was very softly spoken and very handsome, an absolutely superb physical specimen and whenever we all went out the women would flock round him. On one occasion we came off after a game and we were in the dressing room and I had Wesley and Jordan with me, sitting beside me. At that moment Fash came out of the showers with a towel over his shoulders but he was stark bollock naked with his magnificent body on show. Now Jordan would have been four or five at the time and when he caught sight of Fash he froze in his seat. He was right next to me and I could feel him tense up. He was staring at Fash and edging tight into me and as Fash came towards me (he was getting changed on the other side of me to where Jordan was sitting). Jordan couldn't take his eyes off of Fash – who is still naked with his todger all over the place – and by this time Jordan had hold of my arm and was clinging on to me. Then as Fash sat down Jordan leaned across me and touched his arm as if he trying to wipe some paint off. He thought Fash was a white man painted black because he had never seen anyone like Fash before.

There was another Notts County legend that I didn't play with but got to know through ex-players' charity matches – Brian Stubbs. Big 'Stubbsy' played at the back in the same side as Dave Needham. Now he is the only player I have ever met who could light a fag after a game, go into the shower, have his shower and come out after with the fag still dry and lit! He would be in the shower with the fag between the fingers of one hand and washing his hair with the other, pausing to have a drag and then carry on washing his hair. Genius! There was another Notts County legend that I didn't play with but got to know and that was Brian Kilcline – Killer! He would occasionally come out with us because he was still good mates with some of the players, especially Rachid Harkouk.

One night we were out in a local pub and the drink was flowing as usual. By the way, I wouldn't want to give the impression that all footballers were raging alcoholics back then, but we used to socialise a lot and the pubs and clubs were where we did this. It didn't happen every day of the week but it was more prevalent then, whereas today that sort of culture is frowned upon. Anyway, it was a Christmas night out and we were playing a drinking game with Sambuca, which is poured into shot glasses with a coffee bean on the top. The idea is to light the Sambuca and down the flaming drink (literally) in one go. Well, we decided that the coffee bean was too much and might get in the way so we dispensed with the bean but lit the drink all the same. The drink was supposed to be lined up on the bar, the 'participant' had to grab the glass, blow the flame out and then drink it down in one. I abstained because it didn't look like my idea of fun, but Killer and Rachid and Pedro Richards were up for it. Rachid and Pedro did the challenge and then it was Killer's turn. He bent down over the drink but didn't blow the flame out properly so when he lifted the glass to his lips the Sambuca (still alight) went everywhere and set fire to his beard – whoosh! It was bloody funny.

As managers go Jimmy was different to anyone else I played under and completely unique, but he did pay me a huge compliment once. Mark Goodwin told me about this because he moved to Notts County whilst I was still at Leicester. When Notts County played Leicester, Jimmy would say, 'If you keep the boy Young quiet then Leicester City don't play' and then was a really nice thing to say. I've never forgotten that. Jim was fond of running and used to go on runs around the Embankment and across the bridges with his kagoul on with the hood up and the cords pulled tight round his head, so all you could see was a little bit of his face, his eyes and nose sticking out. He used to wear really tight tracksuit bottoms on skinny legs and huge running shoes and he was all different colours, a bit like a marathon running tramp! He would get back to the ground and he would be pouring with sweat. then his gear would come off and he would lie in the big bath, completely immersed with the hot water covering his old, knobbly body and he would be there for about twenty minutes moving his legs up and down whilst he was in there, almost like he was doing a breaststroke kick. One time I walked in and I hadn't realised he was in the bath and I said, 'Oh! Morning Gaffer.

He said, 'Five fucking kilos!'

I went, 'Eh? What did you say?'

So he said it again, 'Five fucking kilos.'

I'm like, 'I'm sorry Gaffer, I'm not with you.' He then explained that he could lose five kilos in this bath by doing this exercise. I finished up and went back out to the dressing room and said to the lads, 'The Gaffer's losing it lads'. Then I explained what was happening in the bath and then sent one of the other lads into see if he said the same thing to him. So in went David Hunt and said, 'Morning Gaffer!' and back came the answer, 'Six fucking kilos' and the more lads went in the more numbers of kilos he said. He really was losing it. But the thing is, we loved him for his eccentricities and his appearance with that big nose and the big tusk (tooth) at the front.

I remember we were at the training ground at Highfields and Jimmy turned up one day with a golf club and a load of balls and a bit of green matting. So he gets the club and the balls and he says 'Gather round' and with just his left hand he tries to chip a golf ball two or three yards. Not the most difficult thing to do I'll admit. So he chips these golf balls in succession off of the mat and they go about four or five yards away and after he has done this with about a dozen balls he changes hands and uses just his right hand to do the same thing and chip these golf balls a few yards until he finished. Then he got the bag and put all the balls back in the bag and he turned to us and said 'Practice makes fucking perfect lads' and that was it. That was a lesson! The thing was you were so shocked and all looking at each other that you didn't dare laugh because you knew that Jimmy was serious. Another day he brought a bag of footballs over his shoulder and walked across to a pitch about 75 yards away from where we were training, he put them down on the penalty spot and took a run up and he hit it. The ball barely hit the net but he still punched the air and shouted 'Yes!' Then he did it again and again until he hasdtaken about ten penalties and each time he jumped and punched the air, even if it took half an hour to cross the line. After the last one he ran behind the goal to an imaginary crowd shouting 'Yes Jimmy, yes!!' But he was great Jim. He loved his red wine and he loved the ladies as well. He was a real gentleman and would always be complimenting the ladies at the club, 'Hello my dear, don't you look lovely today'. He was eccentric alright, but in a way that we all loved him for it. We never laughed at him or were never unkind to him because he was genuine in what he did. Even when he was sitting up in the television gantry at Meadow Lane shouting instructions down to Ian MacParland when we were having a practice match 'Charleee! Charleee! Hit the fucking chalk'. In other words, get wide.

We weren't too bad on the pitch at that time and my personal highlight was scoring the winner past Peter Shilton in the County Cup final at the City Ground. We won 1–0 and that gave our fans the bragging rights for a while in the city.

Another of the lovely characters at Notts County was the physio, John Short, who was a big Geordie man. Big bald head, 6ft 3in, big lion of a guy, but he was a bit deaf. Anyway, it was early in the season and I had an ankle injury thanks to a shocking tackle from Tony Mowbray on my debut against Middlesbrough and I was receiving treatment. That day Tony Francis from Central News had turned up to do a piece with me and I asked him if he fancied recording the interview in the treatment room whilst John was seeing to my ankle. So that was what we did and I said to John, 'Come on Big John, get yersel' on the telly.'

He said, 'Eh? Telly? What telly?'

'No, not a telly, Central television, they're going to do an interview,' I said. Tony Francis told me what they were going to ask me and John began the treatment with the ultrasound device whilst the interview was being recorded. Then it was three, two, one, go and the first question to me was, 'So Alan, how is the injury progressing?'

I said, 'Well Tony, it was a nasty challenge by Mowbray and the injury hasn't healed as quickly as I hoped it would, in fact it has been slow progress.' Just as I said that I noticed that the ultrasound machine wasn't switched on and John hadn't noticed so I added, 'To be honest with you, the injury would heal much quicker if John would switch that bloody ultrasound machine on!'

At this point Tony Francis creased up laughing and I was laughing and John looked up and went, 'Eh?'

Sadly there wasn't a happy ending for poor John Short. He retired and we all had a night for him at the Meadow Club. We made a presentation to him and his wife and he died the very next day. That was tragic because they were going to emigrate to Australia to be with family soon after. I can still remember going in for training the next day and someone asking if I had heard the news about John; I didn't believe it because it just seemed so unfair. It was awful. John's replacement was an ex-Navy man called Davy who smoked continuously on his pipe and he was very much a believer in shifting and manipulating rather than using machines – he was unbelievable. I had a cricked neck once and so he told me to lay face down on the bed and he moved my head in each direction until it was as far as I could stand it. Then he told me to relax and he grabbed my head by my jaw and the top of the head and before I knew it – bam! He jerked the head to the right and I was on the ceiling at this point shouting 'What have ye fucking done?' and he didn't answer. Instead he did it again in the opposite direction – bam! And once I had calmed down I realised that I wasn't in pain any more. Sorted! Two minutes later I was like a fucking owl and looking in all directions. He was very good with the deep massage and manipulations and he was strong as well; only 5ft 2in but built like a brick shit house! I have a theory that this was part of a preventative medicine policy by the club – the players were too frightened to admit that they were injured because that would mean a trip to see Davy. A lad could have a leg fractured in three places but he would still be saying 'No. I'm fine. Nothing wrong with me boss!'

Davy served the club well, especially under Neil Warnock. I liked Neil and I think Neil almost offered me a job at Notts County on the coaching staff. I was doing the Community Programme at the time and he asked me to go with him to a function at the Victoria Centre. I think he wasn't as confident in those days and he didn't really fancy it. He asked me if I liked my job and, of course, I did because I had worked hard and I was three years into it by then. I think maybe he was fishing to see if I fancied getting involved in the professional side of the game again. Brian Little had a similar conversation with me when he was at Leicester. I had played in a testimonial match with a load of ex-players and the 'keeper cleared the ball up to the halfway line. I took the ball on my right thigh and then on to my left foot in one movement and volleyed it straight back and it only just cleared the bar. It was a lovely piece of skill, even if I do say so myself, and I looked across at Brian Little and I must have caught his eye. Afterwards he caught up with me and asked about my role at Notts County with the Community Programme and he also asked me if I enjoyed it. I think I missed out on both of those opportunities to really push my case for getting back into coaching in the professional game.

Towards the end of my second season at Notts County I started to struggle with the knee and groin injuries, which were manageable but clearly getting worse and I was spending more and more time on the treatment table. Then I made a daft move which I regret to this day and I signed for Rochdale. It came about because Notts County wanted to sign a lad called Davie Thompson from Rochdale and nobody had any money, so they asked me if I would consider being part of a swap deal and stupidly I agreed. It was the worst place I have ever played football at and it was my last professional club.

9

THE
LAST POST

I don't know what possessed me to go to Rochdale. The swap deal wasn't dependent on me agreeing as far as I know so I had a choice in the matter

Vic Halom at Rochdale persuaded me to move on again to Spotland, which is a lovely little ground now but at the time it was the most horrendous place I had ever been in my life. I have nothing against the people of Rochdale or the club, but it really was a bad move for me. Most of the players were bit parts and I didn't really fit into the squad or the style of play – which was terrible by the way. The whole place was a shambles; the pitch was covered in shale, they had manky gates and no supporters and it was all summed up by the fact that they were sponsored by a local garden centre.

The only good thing that happened in Rochdale was my youngest son, Kyle, was born there. The pitch was awful, the training was awful, the changing rooms leaked and there was only one toilet in the corner of the dressing room for the whole team and that absolutely stank! As it turned out Vic Halom knew fuck all about management, he hadn't a fucking clue.

When I was at Oldham and we played together I used to do a lot of his running and probably extended his career by a couple of years as a result. We got on alright-back then but I ended up hating him when I was at Rochdale. One of the reasons was the 'missing' five grand which was agreed with Tommy Cannon, the club chairman, during my negotiations and Vic knew this. He was there when it was agreed. If I ever brought it up to Vic he would just say 'What five grand? I don't know what you are talking about'. I hate liars and he was a liar.

I didn't enjoy my football at Rochdale at all. We were put into a hotel in the Derbyshire Hills in a place called Hayfield, it was called the Lantern Pike and it was run by a guy called Barry (who looked like a Bee Gee incidentally) and his wife who was very attractive but a complete psycho. She was always pissed and really scary. Now I had agreed this amount with Tommy Cannon as a relocation fee so that I could afford a deposit on a new house. But when we realised that it wasn't going to happen we took on another mortgage and let the house in Nottingham. Well I bought a new house in an area that wasn't the best and my neighbour had an Irish Wolfhound that was huge and the smells that came out of his front door were dreadful.

Anyway, Vic Halom didn't last long and Eddie Gray took over with Jimmy Lumsden as his assistant. Funnily enough Eddie Gray and Jimmy Lumsden became good pals of mine. I had never had that kind of familiarity with the manager before, but I was one of the senior pros by now and that made a difference to them and they treated me differently. Now Eddie would join in the five-a-sides and he still had that touch and control and some of the tricks. That caused a bit of resentment amongst some of the players because they had never had that level of skill or vision. They had only ever played at lower league level and the more they resented it the more we took the piss and that led to a few scuffles. Eddie and Jimmy tried to get that team playing football but it wasn't appreciated by the crowd.

Big John Bramall ('Brammy') was at centre half; he was a good lad to have around and he now works for the Professional Footballers Association. John Seaseman ('Cheddar') was a player who was batting further down the order than he should have done; I felt he could have played at a higher level with his ability. Derek Parlane was the other player that I built a strong friendship with along with his girlfriend at the time, Julie. Now Derek gave me the idea for Kyle's name; we were sitting in a Chinese restaurant in Manchester and Julie was ready to pop with the new baby and Derek pointed out that Kyle was a good name because Clint Eastwood's son was called Kyle. Well I liked it straight away because of the Scottish connection and it is a word that means 'opening' as in Kyle of Lochalsh. The other thing I remember about that night was Derek talking to the waiter; Derek had played for Hong Kong Rangers and he knew a bit of Chinese and he spoke to the waiter and said something like 'Yu lee lung la mohai' and the Chinese waiter looked horrified and ran off. I asked him what he had said and Derek grinned and said 'Your mother sucks sweaty cocks'. He had my sense of humour alright.

It was Eddie Gray that told me that my career was over. It's strange, most ex-professionals will be able to tell you their last ever professional game but I can't remember it at all and I don't care to. The standard of football and the facilities at the time were terrible. There was no malice between us when he said it, and he was absolutely right. I was playing in too much pain, I wasn't training properly and so this meant my fitness levels were dropping rapidly and retiring was the sensible thing to do. After I did, I had my contract at Rochdale signed up to the end of the season because there were only a few months left and that gave me a couple of thousand pounds. And that was it! I didn't know what to do at that point but I remember I was very sad and also very scared. We had just had my third son, Kyle, and I was worried about paying the bills, so I went and signed on. That was an horrific experience. It is for anyone who has to sign on when they're unemployed, but if Rochdale wasn't the most salubrious place in England then the dole office in Rochdale takes it down another level. It wasn't like the job centres that exist nowadays; this was a grotty office with everyone sitting chuffing away on their fags and it was horrific. I was there (an ex-professional footballer) to ask for money and they didn't give me any because I had my pay-off money which I declared. They told me to come back when that money ran out in July and looking back I wish I had lied about it!

I thought there was some money coming in from the flat that we let out in Nottingham. Unfortunately the guy who moved in wasn't paying the rent. By the time I got back from Rochdale to Leicester the building society was threatening to repossess the property because there was £2,000 outstanding in mortgage payments. I was also paying a mortgage in Rochdale at the time. So I had to sell the property in Rochdale and then try and get the occupants out of my Nottingham home. In the meantime I had been in touch with the P.F.A. and they paid the building society the money owed in mortgage arrears so that I wouldn't lose it. So I went and fetched my pal Barry Stretton from Leicester and he brought his best pal – a baseball bat! We knocked on the door but there was no reply. Next, I went to the police station in West Bridgford and let them know that there was a family living in my house illegally and what would they do about it. They didn't want to know because they said it was a civil case and they wouldn't get involved unless there had been a criminal act or violence or damage. So I let them know that I was about to commit a criminal act and lots of violence if this guy and his family didn't move out immediately. I walked out of the police station and by the time me and Barry got to my house there were two police cars already there! I remember a policewoman went to the door and spoke to them and they said that they would be out in two hours. Sure enough, when we all came back in two hours they had gone. When I went in the whole house was a complete mess. I remember thinking that my house had been raped. There was shit on the walls, the heads of the taps were all missing, the carpets were filthy, the couch was ripped. It was an unbelievable sight and the house was uninhabitable at that point, which really upset me because I loved that house and it was in an exclusive part of Nottingham called Turney's Quay. It was situated on a little triangle of land between the River Trent and the canal, but I couldn't live there anymore, so we sold it and eventually bought a new place in Nottingham.

I hung around in Rochdale for a while whilst I worked out what to do. I had a mortgage and a house to sell in Rochdale and a house that we were renting in Nottingham. Eventually we sold the house in Rochdale and came back to Leicester and stayed with Karen's parents for a while. Karen and I eventually managed to buy a house in Nottingham and only then did I settle back into the area properly and that was when I got the job at the indoor cricket centre in Thurmaston.

Before the job came up at the Indoor Cricket Centre I worked for a guy called Steve Powell (former Derby County player) who was managing Shepshed Charterhouse and they were funded by Maurice Clayton who owned Shepshed Textiles. I played for Shepshed for fifty quid a game but, more importantly, Maurice offered me a job driving one of his vans making deliveries around the Midlands. At this point I was living at Karen's Mum and Dad's in Wigston and then we rented a place back in Leicester. We had an Asian couple living next door who made the most fantastic curries and I used to love Diwali because the smells were amazing. Whilst I was driving vans for Maurice I remember I had a fear of being recognised; I am sure that if someone had asked me 'Are you Alan Young?' I would have said no. I felt at the time maybe I was letting people down by becoming what I was and not staying in the game as I should have done. I didn't have a pot to piss in to be honest and maybe I was a bit embarrassed about that.

I hadn't quit playing completely and as well as playing for Shepshed I also had a spell with Ilkeston Town. It was there that I had another frightening injury. I was playing for Ilkeston as a favour to a friend of Karen's whose brother ran Ilkeston Town (I know his name was Carl but that's all I remember). In fact, I was playing centre half alongside Kenny Burns for a while. We played away at Sutton Miners Welfare on this occasion (a real glamour tie that one!) and although this was a far lower level than I was used to I still had the winning mentality and instincts. So a ball was played up to me and I knew that if I could get a flick on then it would put 'Wiggy' (Wiggington) in on goal. I wasn't in a very good position to protect myself but I still ran into a position to head it and as I jumped up I was absolutely 'beasted' by the big centre half and his knee hit me in the ribs on the back right-hand side of my ribcage. I knew straight away that it was serious because I couldn't get my breath and I was taking very short gasps and each gasp gave me a blinding pain. So I had to go off but at Ilkeston Town there wasn't much by way of medical help. Now when I played professionally there was always medical help to sort you out if you needed it but here I was at Ilkeston, in real bother and there was nothing. I eventually went off in an ambulance (still in my football kit) to Sutton General Hospital (that's Sutton-in-Ashfield near to Mansfield) where I had an x-ray and was told that I had fractured two ribs. They also said that they hadn't done any further damage i.e they hadn't punctured anything. Broken ribs are left alone to heal themselves so I was sent home but I don't remember how I got home, or when I got home. What I do know was that I slept in the armchair in the lounge because I couldn't think about going up to bed. I had a large whiskey to try and help me sleep but it was a fitful night and by the morning I was rasping and had real difficulty breathing or talking. Karen went and fetched Mike (our next-door neighbour) who took me to the Queen's Medical Centre in Nottingham. I went to reception there and did my best to get the words out to explain what had happened. She must have understood because the next thing I know there are doctors appearing out of nowhere and a consultant who seemed to take charge. They told me that I was going to be admitted and (stupidly) I was trying to argue with him because I didn't want to be admitted. I was hoping I would be sent home with painkillers. That seems really daft now given what the diagnosis was. I only realised how serious it was when this lovely consultant (I wish I could remember his name) leaned across and said to me, very quietly, 'You can go home Alan but promise me that when your lung fully collapses – which it will – then you will be back into hospital in one minute. Because that is all the time you will have!' At that point I realised that this was for real and I looked at him and said 'Show me the menu'. They had to do a procedure called a pneumothorax and I still have a scar where they cut between your ribs and put a plastic tube down into the bottom of the lung to drain the fluid out into a big bell jar which I had to carry around with me for quite a while.

The way the procedure works is that the doctor puts the tube down into the lung, it all gets taped up and then they x-ray it to check that the tube is in the right place. After the first attempt they found that it wasn't in the right place so off it all came and they reinserted the tube and guess what? It was in the wrong place again! So I'm lying on this bed, on my side, waiting for this doctor to have another go and as he came around I reached out and grabbed his tie and pulled him close and said 'Get it fuckin' right this time!' And he did! So I was in hospital for about a week and as I mentioned, I had to carry this bell jar around with me and I could see the fluid and shit going into the jar. I had to keep it below my heart which I managed to do successfully for most of the time, but I got into trouble when I went to the toilet on one occasion. I was sitting on the toilet with the jar on the floor which was fine and when I finished I lifted the jar up before I stood up and this was the mistake because I lifted it too high and all the fluid came flying back up the tube because I had lifted it above my heart. I could feel this fluid and crap all going back in, it was pretty scary but the nurse just called me a silly twat! It was quickly sorted when I got back into bed. Whilst I was in hospital Phil Stant (ex-Notts County) came to see me and the bastard kept making me laugh and every time I laughed it hurt like hell.

Eventually I got a job at the ICP (Indoor Cricket Pavilion) in Thurmaston near Leicester. I saw it advertised and went for it but funnily enough John Wile (ex-West brom) was on the board of directors; it was an Australian company run by Chas Dale and his two brothers. So I went for an interview in Solihull for the job of Assistant Manager at the ICP where they had another establishment the same as the one in Thurmaston. There I met John Wile amongst others and I got the job! It was alright as it turned out and I got to know the job and got to know my new colleagues which included a girl in the admin team by the name of Jo Chamberlain. She played for the England Women's Cricket team and I really hit it off with her; we worked really well together and I am still in touch with her to this day. Only recently I did a presentation for her husband, Kevin, and his under-14 side. If ever I own a business she will be the first person I employ.

Anyway, I got into the job and to be honest it wasn't going that great as an indoor cricket facility. But me having had a bit of history with Leicester City meant that I was getting in business a lot easier than the manager of the place and as far as I was concerned, he wasn't trying. Eventually he got the push and they put me in charge because I was the one trying to bring in more businesss and coming up with new ideas and he was just treading water. The way it was run was really designed for serious cricketers with organised divisions and the majority of the patrons were Asians, who took playing very seriously and who wanted to win everything. They didn't have any (what I would call) social leagues i.e playing for fun. I would be visiting work places and factories around Leicester and inviting teams down for a social game. I wanted to let them enjoy themselves and then encourage them to sign up. So, we had the likes of Thorn Lighting playing against ASDA, it was mixed gender and usually a great night. People stayed for a few pints afterwards and a bit of a buffet. Figures started to rise and there were more teams signing up and this meant that profits were on the up, the bar takings doubled and the place was just a lot busier and more active. And then I started to wonder if we couldn't make better use of the space we had in the actual playing area. The set up was two indoor cricket areas that were totally enclosed with very taut netting. In between these two playing areas was a space that was partly enclosed by the indoor cricket areas and I managed to persuade one of the ICP Directors to let me try and put an extra piece of netting over the top to create a four-a-side football court with goals at either end. I told him that if he let me do that then I would fill the place with footballers.

Well, it worked a treat. As it turned out four-a-side was enough but we had teams of eight with rolling subs on and off, twenty minutes a game, proper referees; from 10 o'clock on a Sunday morning until 10.30 on Sunday night we had four teams in action at any one time. On the back of this success they asked me to visit Coventry, Solihull and Wolverhampton where they had the other indoor cricket centre. They wanted me to show them what to do to replicate the Thurmaston success by introducing football into the cricket set up. So I did this and it went very well. Then one day the directors paid us a visit – they visited about often once a week – to see how things were and tell you what you weren't doing it right (as they nearly always did!). On this occasion I asked to speak to them and I ran through the success that we had been having with the increased revenue, increased bar takings, and the increased visitor numbers. I told them we had staged charity events with celebrities taking part like Farouk Engineer, Gary Lineker, and Willie Thorne and the directors loved this. I was lucky that I was still known in the area and that helped me a bit when I was asking for favours and people were very kind. The management all wanted to be associated with this type of publicity but when I had finished stating my case and explaining what I had done for IPC I asked them for a pay rise in recognition of the effort I had put in. They didn't want to know; they said I was on a suitable salary for my position and what I was being paid was ample. I disagreed and said that I should have a wage rise for what I had done for them, but they said again that what I was being paid was for fair for the job I was doing. At that point I said, 'That's where you have got it wrong because I fuckin' resign!' and I walked out.

They were on the phone to me later that day and offered me a £1,000 pay rise. I told them that I wouldn't go back if they offered me a £10,000 pay rise after the way they treated me. I shouldn't have even had to ask for more money after the job I had done for them, they should have been coming to me offering me a bonus and a pay rise and improved terms. But they didn't and I stood by my decision to walk out on principle because that's the way I am. So it was another career change and this time I was back in Nottingham which was good news for me because I had been travelling from Nottingham to Thurmaston every day to work. Then out of the blue I got a phone call from Neil Hook who was secretary of Notts County – I knew Neil from my time playing at the club – and he asked me to come into have a chat. The reason he wanted to chat was because there was something starting up called The Community Programme in Professional Football and it was being piloted in the North-west at Bolton, Bury, Rochdale, Burnley and Blackburn. So I went into see Neil and he explained what was happening and also admitted that he didn't really understand the scheme or how to get it started and would I be interested in giving it a go. The answer was a big 'Yes'.

10

COMMUNITY CHEST

When I started the Community Programme at Notts County there wasn't much money on the table. There was £7,500 from the scheme itself but Notts County topped it up with another £2,500 to make a £10,000-a-year salary. It still wasn't much to be honest but I said yes which made me the Community Football Development Officer and I was housed in a Portakabin in the car park off of the old wooden stand at Meadow Lane and I had a desk, a bag of footballs, an old filing cabinet, some training bibs, some discs and a telephone. And that's where I went to work every day and I went in and sat there on my first day and I didn't know what to do. I didn't have a 'Scooby' if I'm honest! But the whole Community Programme was still finding its feet back then and very much in its infancy, which is amazing when you think that it is now a multi-million pound industry. Back then (and still today) every club was striving to get an ex-player involved in the Community Programme because it helped to raise the profile of the scheme and it meant that people were more likely to pay attention when we were trying to get them interested. It is fair to say that a lot of people didn't really know what the whole Community Programme was trying to achieve back then, but after a while I understood what was happening and what the goals were. It was basically this: the P.F.A. was trying to clean up football and it was doing this by trying to encourage more women, children and disadvantaged people to get involved in football. This meant the clubs reaching out into the community to bring the community to the football club and the football club to the community. It meant using additional staff drawn from unemployed people, but the crazy thing about this, as I said, was that you had to have been unemployed for at least six months before you were eligible to get on the course. I was recruiting people (coaches and helpers) from the local job centre and there was a real mixed bag of ability and enthusiasm. What I had to do was turn them into qualified coaches so that they could go on and contribute to the community scheme and, at the same time, develop some sort of career for themselves. The P.F.A. body that was supporting and funding this project was the Footballers Further Education and Vocational Training Society (FFE & VTS) and it was headed by a guy called Roger Reid who was very helpful, even though I was a bit suspicious and defensive when he first used to come and visit to see what we were doing. I thought he was coming to find fault but he wasn't, exactly the opposite in fact. Richard Finney was my area manager and he would come and see us as well. As well as the money from the P.F.A. we also had money coming in from the soccer schools that we ran in the holidays as well as Saturday morning coaching sessions. We were always struggling but we still had to keep pretty tight accounts of the money spent and received.

The club (Notts County) were a little bit suspicious of the scheme when it first started, maybe because they didn't really understand it and what we were trying to achieve. I would often get called into speak to the chairman (Derek Pavis) or the manager (Mick Walker) to explain why a certain character that they didn't recognise was wearing a club tracksuit or hanging around the ground. I would have to explain that they were part of the Notts County Community Programme and therefore part of the club. This changed when Neil Warnock was manager and he was brilliant. Very supportive. He would allow me to take any of the first team squad that I wanted to help out with a presentation at the soccer schools for example. I can't speak highly enough of Neil Warnock and although he has cultivated a certain media image, he is a smashing guy and would do anything for you. Neil and his assistant, Mick Jones, took the trouble to get to know all of my staff on the scheme and took a genuine interest in what I was doing.

I remember the very first school we went to was Fernwood Primary School in Hucknall. I went there on my own and ran a session for an hour and then came back again and I sat there and thought – is that my job? Is this what I do now? It wasn't just schools of course, but from those humble beginnings that was where I started. After a while I started to run sessions in association with the local job centres and they would send me all sorts! This meant a different approach. As well as the football side of it I also had to get involved in something called Training for Work (TFW) and became qualified to run a TFW course for these unemployed folk that I was looking after. The stupid thing about the scheme was that you had to be unemployed for six months before you could be part of it. Anyway, we managed to get some sponsorship which meant that we could get better kit and proper tracksuits and so on, but the club was still very suspicious of the whole thing and they seemed to think I was making thousands and not giving any of it to them.

I would take these people on and let's be honest here, some were good, some were not so good and some I would have poured petrol on and set alight! It was very hard work some days but we also had some great success stories. There were three lads in particular: Joe Edwards, Dalton Powell and Norris Carlisle-Stewart. We had some good laughs with them but the reason for them being on the course was to get them some qualifications and hopefully, some employment. We managed to get them a bronze lifeguard's award and an F.A. Preliminary coaching badge, as well as a first-aid qualification. People received these qualifications through the Training and Enterprise Council (TEC) and some people (like Joe, Dalton and Norris) really went for it and loved this opportunity but some couldn't be bothered and didn't turn up after the first week. That was the way it was. Eventually I went back to the job centre and the TEC and asked them to stop sending me just anybody because it was obvious that they were being paid by numbers. The more referrals they made, the more they got paid but that didn't help me because I would have to interview these guys and fill out their forms (which was very time consuming) and most wouldn't show the next time. So I thought bollocks to this and I let the Job Centre and TEC know that if they sent anymore like that then I was sending them straight back.

Eventually the three boys were helping me with the interviews and this was part of their development and growing maturity. Soon we started to get a decent bunch and some of the characters are still very clear in the memory like Little John. He was about forty-odd years old; not the sharpest tool in the shed and a real 'harem scarem' little chap. He was a lovely guy and always smartly dressed and well-liked by everybody. The three boys (Norris, Dalton and Joe) and I went back to Fernwood School in Hucknall and on the way there in the minibus there was a commotion in the back. A lad called Bruce (who was a bit camp, strawberry blond and an incessant talker) got a smack in the face and when we arrived I looked in the back and his nose is all over his face and I'm thinking – 'Oh for crying out fuckin' loud!' Joe was looking a bit guilty so I said, 'Joe, was that you?'

He said, 'I'm sorry Al but he was getting on my fucking tits.' Joe had just smacked him one. Unfortunately Joe ended up in prison later, but I helped him with a couple of references to help him when he was released. He lost his way a bit but he's ok now.

Dalton was a superb athlete and he looked incredible at 6ft 4in and his muscles had muscles! Now I had seen how quickly Dalton could run and this helped me to take twenty quid off of Neil Warnock one day. Kevin Bartlett was playing for Notts County at the time and he was quick and everyone knew it (including Neil Warnock obviously) and I was chatting about Dalton's sprinting ability and when I said 'He'll beat Bartlett.'

Neil's reaction was 'What? Nobody will beat Bartlett Al', and this quickly became a twenty pound bet. Neil couldn't see how his fastest player was going to be beaten by one of my lads who helped run the Community Scheme.

I remember saying to Neil, 'Tell you what, Bartlett can start on the edge of the penalty area and Dalton will start on the goal line, he can have an eighteen yard start.'

By now Neil Warnock is thinking he is about to get the easiest twenty quid of his life and so he agrees but says, 'Fuck off Al, he'll never do it!' So all the players are out watching on the pitch and it is down to Dennis Pettit, the physio, to start the race with a clap of his hands. Well, Dalton sailed past him and he was passed him by the time they reached the halfway line! Now everyone is interested in Dalton and they're all saying 'Fuck me, how quick is he?' and I had to calm them all down and said 'Aye, he's quick but If you put a ball at his feet he will fall over it'.

One of the main objectives of the scheme was to bring football into the community so that youngsters and (in particular) disadvantaged kids could take part and enjoy the football. One such success story centred on a lad called Marky. He had brain damage as a child and so he had speech problems and he couldn't walk properly, but he was a cracking lad with a marvellous family supporting him. His wee brother was called Tom and they both came along to a soccer school that we ran at West Bridgford Comprehensive. They came along with their mother who said that she wasn't too sure how Marky was going to get on, but we reassured her that we would take care of the boys and give her a call if there were any problems that we couldn't handle (we had contact numbers for all of the kids on the soccer school). So in came Marky and he was hard to ignore, what with the noises he was making. This caused the other kids to be a bit stand-offish. Especially his younger brother Tom, who was walking about 50 yards behind looking very embarrassed by the whole thing. So at the end of the first day I spoke to their Mum and told her my concerns about Tom rather than Marky, and suggested how we could get past this stigma that Tom was clearly feeling. On the second morning all the kids came in and Tom was lagging behind again so I thought, ok, let's do something about this now. I called everyone together and I went and stood with Marky and said, 'We've got a pretty special guy with us today, he was with us yesterday and his name's Marky. He's my pal and he wants to be pals with every one of you. Now the thing is about Marky is that he is a wee bit special, he's not like all of you but that's what makes him special, because he's got something that you haven't. Now we have to look after him and he needs a wee bit of help so let's all do it eh?' On the third day we had a penalty competition and I called Marky across to go in goal and he loved the fact that I chose him for this. Then someone gave him his goalkeeping gloves and he was chuffed with that as well. Anyway, the kicks started and Marky managed to save one and the place erupted; the kids went mental. That was the only he saved mind you, every single one went in! But that didn't matter, he was accepted then and he was first picked the next time they were choosing teams for five-a-side, even though Marky didn't always realise that you had to change ends at half time! Now the kids were encouraging him and passing the ball to him and if there was a penalty then they wanted Marky to take it and it was so different compared to the first day. Then on the Thursday, Tom walked into the session holding Marky's hand as if to say, 'That's my big brother.' He looked genuinely proud of him. What a turnaround!

In terms of achievement and satisfaction nothing can ever compare to scoring a goal, but what I achieved that week at West Bridgford with Marky and Tom gives me a huge amount of satisfaction and pride and all the other similar achievements during the whole of the Community Programme at Notts County. We won awards for our achievements and we were in the top five in the country in terms of quality of delivery i.e the number of kids we were contacting and the diversity of kids we were including. I have a letter from the (then) Prime Minister congratulating us on our achievements in taking the programme to drug prevention teams in high-risk areas.

The team I worked with had a great 'can do' attitude and pitch in and help out with anything. On one occasion there was a bad spell of winter weather and the Meadow Lane pitch was covered in snow, but Derek Pavis needed the game to go ahead so he could get the money in. So, my community team and I cancelled the sessions we had scheduled for that day and Karen helped by phoning around to let everybody

10 DOWNING STREET
LONDON SW1A 2AA

THE PRIME MINISTER

I was delighted to hear about the success of the drugs prevention initiative at Notts County Football Club and to use the scheme as an example of excellence in my speech on 9 September 1994.

The kind of work you are doing with the Professional Footballers Association to draw youngsters into football training schemes and away from the temptation of drugs is tremendously important. I commend your achievement and hope others will follow your example.

John Major

September 1994

know whilst we were all out on the pitch with shovels. I got battered on the head with a shovel and had to go to hospital to have the cut stitched. When I eventually got back Pavis called me into his office to thank me (and my team) for the help in clearing the pitch. He said it was a marvellous effort and gave me twenty quid. I started to laugh and said,

'What? We've been nearly eight hours clearing the pitch in the freezing cold, I've been to casualty and all you can offer is twenty quid! Stick it up your arse … er … Mr Chairman.' He started laughing as well and I went on 'All of my staff are through there freezing their balls off trying to get warm right now. Why don't you go and thank them personally and give them twenty quid. Each!' And to his credit he did. To be fair to Derek Pavis, once he understood what the Community Programme was all about he was very supportive and helpful, as was a director called John Mountney. He got it from the start (and his wife Daphne) and they accepted us. Everyone else was wondering who this bunch of scruffs and toerags were wandering round the ground.

Part of the programme was a bronze medallion life-saving certificate and we did this at West Bridgford Comprehensive where there was an elderly, female swimming instructor. She was a small, diminutive lady and she looked a bit odd next to these lads who were ripped and tall. Norris wasn't too keen to do the qualification and when I pushed him he told me why. He said, 'I don't like swimming Al, black people can't swim very well. It's the density of our bones'. I looked at him and he went on, 'How many black people have you seen win Olympic swimming medals? None!'

I said, 'But you learned to swim when the crocodiles were chasing you in the jungle didn't you' and he laughed but he said it again and when I asked around it turned out to be essentially true. I can still remember them messing this swimming instructor around and having a laugh at her expense, but it was funny one day when they were doing the missing persons drill. In this drill you had to hit the alarm, get someone to call an ambulance, clear the pool, and then you had to find the missing person which was a mannequin.

Once you had found it you had to perform CPR on the mannequin; this last bit was really important to show that you could do the CPR. On this occasion it was Joe's turn to do the drill so someone came running through and shouted 'Help! I can't find my little brother.' Straightaway Joe hits the alarm and tells someone to call an ambulance and then gets on the tannoy and gets everyone out of the pool. He then begins the process of finding the imaginary missing child and people are checking the changing rooms and the pool itself and so on. There is no sign of the mannequin at this point and Joe is walking around. Then he spotted the mannequin and this was the point when he would have to do CPR. So he says, 'It's okay everybody, we've found the missing child ... and he's fine!' And we are falling about laughing and poor Joe is laughing knowing full well that he won't get away with it.

Following on from the life-saving awards is a less amusing tale. I was doing a presentation about the TEC programme to the commercial department of the local government office and I am trying to help them understand what the programme was and how they could contribute with things like facilities hire and the benefits that they can get from it. So we held the meeting at the football club as part of a big open day and we had a meal and so forth and I was explaining to everyone in my speech about all of the work that the Community Programme was now doing. I said how we received over 3,000 kids a week; ran disabled football matches and coaching; women's football; after-school coaching; Saturday coaching; birthday parties; and initiatives with the drug prevention team. We had achieved so much in a relatively short space of time and I was trying to get this across. I had some trainees with me to help make the point, they were sitting with me looking very smart in their tracksuits, and I told the story of the life-saving awards and how black people aren't good swimmers because of the bone density. Anyway, one woman in the audience reported me to her council and alleged that I had been discriminating against black people. So the Nottinghamshire Council contacted Derek Pavis (the Chairman of Notts County) who then pulled me to ask what fuck was going on. I explained to him that I was merely repeating what Norris had said to me and that it was actually true. So I went back to my office and I took the three lads back up to Derek's office with me and asked them to explain to Derek Pavis in no uncertain terms, 'Norris, explain to Mr Pavis about black people and swimming.'

'They can't,' Norris said.

'Tell Mr Pavis why,' I said.

'It's the bone density,' he said.

'And tell Mr Pavis about black Olympic swimming medallists,' I said.

'There aren't any because we can't swim very well,' he replied.

'Right then Derek, get back on to the council and explain what you have just heard.'

And sure enough we received an apology from the lady concerned and she may have even lost her job. It just shows what that left-wing attitude can do; we could have lost everything we had achieved because of one person and her stupid attitude. Fair play to Derek Pavis, he backed me on that one. The Allardyce issue was another matter but more of that later.

As things progressed with the Community Programme we started to get more recognition and raised our profile, and then the club started to recognise what we were doing. When it started they just thought it was some sort of strange money-making machine and they didn't really get the whole concept of the Community Programme. It was a programme of football-related activities for everyone, from any walk of life, but I suppose it tended to concentrate on those that were less fortunate and less privileged to start with. But as time went on and we gained more resources we started to run soccer schools. On the back of this I got a phone call from Neil Hook one day (he is sadly no longer with us). He was the club secretary at Notts County and he got straight to the point and said 'Do you have your full F.A. coaching badge?'

I said that I did and he came straight back with, 'Good! You are now the Director of our Centre For Excellence.' It turns out that he was at a meeting with the Football Association and it was a requirement that Notts County had to have a director in place to oversee and run the Centre for Excellence. They had to name someone at this meeting and I fitted the bill. My first move was to combine the Community Programme and the Centre for Excellence; I wanted to get people in, get them a basic coaching qualification, some first aid training and other leisure-related stuff. I knew this amalgamation would help us to get them on board. The recruitment policy for the Community Programme had become stricter and we were getting people who were more reliable – they turned up on time, they looked smart, they represented the club very well and they wore the club tracksuit. All of this helped build a stronger association with the club. I was able to appoint a lieutenant, a guy called Graham Moran. He took over when I packed it in and he eventually went to Nottingham Forest (still is today I believe) but he was a right turncoat as I will explain later. Because we were out seeing loads of kids in the community and visiting schools, we tried to make sure we did the community thing, but also kept an eye out for kids that stood out. I would always instruct the coaches and helpers to look out for any kid that did a trick or had real pace or did something that made him stand out – and if they also had a smile on their face – then they were to get the kid's details. They would then explain that there would soon be trials for under-9s, 10s, 11s and under-12s and then get the permission of the headmaster or someone in authority. Once we got the details of the best kids then we would contact them all individually and invite them to Wilford Sports Centre for trials with Notts County. At the very first set of trials for under-10s we had nearly 200 kids, so we gave each kid a sticky label with a number on and set them into four-a-side teams over all the pitches. We had about twenty pitches with matches going on and we sent the staff round with clipboards to see if there were any players that caught their eye. We swapped the teams around so they would all play against other teams and it worked very well and it was also a good social occasion; all of the Mums and Dads were there and I deliberately got amongst them and explained what we were trying to do and how we were going to do it. I also explained the rules and the need for discipline and if their son wanted to be part of the club and he was good enough, then we would be glad to have them. All of this helped to get everything off on a good footing but, of course, not all of the ones we took were good enough to make it through the entire youth system. So we needed to keep finding good players at secondary schools in addition to the primary schools that we had started with. This we did and pretty soon we had 120 kids in the Notts County Centre for Excellence and I knew every single one by name. I also knew their parents or grandparents that would bring them along every Tuesday and Thursday evening at the Wilford Sports Centre and then to play on a Sunday morning. They had the official Notts County home and away kits and training kit as well as sweatshirts and waterproofs and official tracksuits for match days. I've still got pictures of every single child in the Notts County development programme in their kits looking smart as paint. I was very proud of that because we had good players. We had lads such as Jermaine Pennant, Leon Best and Will Hoskins. (They were all the same age as my lad Kyle but unfortunately he was thrown out when he was fifteen, but I wasn't there at the time and that still rankles with me.) But to see those names playing at under-10 when you know you have something special is a great feeling and we knew we would have to do something to keep hold of them. By the time you get them to under-16 level then you have known them for five years, so you are bound to feel some attachment to them. But this could lead to the hardest part of the job and that was to tell some of them that they weren't being kept on, and that they weren't going to get a scholarship. I hated doing that to them but to be fair when we signed new, young players and they started on the programme I would say to the parents, 'We will do our best for your son but we make no promises whatsoever'. If you make false promises then you will end up in trouble further down the line because their expectations are too high.

We got the best kids into our scheme at Notts County and bear in mind we were competing with Nottingham Forest. The reason we managed to get the best kids was because we were the underdogs and we had to try that much harder and we had developed a programme that was better than Forest's; our programme was fantastic and everyone knew it, but we had to be good or the best kids would have naturally drifted to Nottingham Forest being the bigger club with the higher profile. As part of the scheme I would work very closely with a guy called John Gaunt. John ran the youth team and I have a lot to thank him for; he was a delight to work with.

Unfortunately for him he lost his job as youth team coach and I was asked by the chairman (Derek Pavis) and the chief executive, a guy called Geoff Davey, to take up the role. This gave me the opportunity to get back into professional football and I was desperate to grab this; don't get me wrong, I loved the Community Programme and I met some lovely people and some inspiring people. I am proud to say that I got some people out of the shit and back into the mainstream community and into proper jobs, in fact, I know two or three of them who are still coaching in America today. I am immensely proud of the whole Community Programme success at Notts County and I know that I made it work by being dedicated and working every hour God sent, if I had been given the opportunity, I could have done the same at Chesterfield.

Despite all of this it was the prospect of involvement in the professional game again that meant I took the youth team job at Notts County without any hesitation.

11

BIG SAM AND THE EXIT DOOR

I made a good start to the new role at the club. Howard Kendall was managing the first team but he left and the club was managerless for a while. During this time Mark Smith and I were asked to form a temporary, caretaker management team but it only lasted or a few weeks and then Sam Allardyce was appointed. Initially I was quite happy with this appointment; I remembered Sam as a player and we had had a few ups and downs on the pitch, in fact, the dirty bastard used to kick lumps out of me whenever we played against each other. I remember a game at Burnden Park, the ball was played up to me and I was just about to chest it when he knocked me over and walked all over my back. I had his stud marks all up my back for a while afterwards and that was Sam – he couldn't play but he could kick people. So in came Sam and I welcomed him and just got on with my job, but maybe I should have realised that the writing was on the wall from very early on. He hadn't been there long when he called me into see him. Now for some reason I hadn't signed a contract and he would have known that of course, so when I went into see him and

Derek Pavis and Geoff Davey, I knew that something was up. Sam started by telling me that they were reviewing everyone's salaries and contracts and went on to say that he needed every penny he could find to spend on new players. Then came the killer statement, 'I see you're on seventeen thousand. I am going to reduce that to twelve thousand.'

'You can't do that! That's very unfair Sam,' I said.

Then his exact words to me were, 'There's plenty of other people out there would love your job Youngy.' I thought immediately that he was trying to get me to walk and that showed me what it would be like working for him. But I didn't walk – I got my head down and got on with my job. I put the bullshit to the back of my mind and thought if I do my job well then there is nothing they can do. I also believed (wrongly as it turned out) that I had the backing of Derek Pavis. Maybe I did have his support for a while, but I certainly didn't when Sam eventually shafted me. So I got on with my job and the youth team was going well; we had some decent kids and we got Jermaine Pennant through to a first team debut. He was the one that we looked after more than most because we knew that he would be an asset to the club. In fact, the achievement in getting Pennant through the system was remarkable. He was a handful when we got him from an area of Nottingham called the Meadows and he was always playing truant and getting into trouble. His Dad was involved in drugs and was also in trouble, so I felt that Jermaine was either going to be a football player or he was going to jail. I remember seeing him as a nine year old at a session on Victoria Embankment and he was pretty useful then and by the time he was about thirteen we decided we needed to give him more supervision and keep a closer eye on him. So we approached the school and worked out a timetable whereby he came to us Tuesdays and Thursdays and he went to school as usual on Mondays, Wednesdays and Fridays. I told Jermaine this arrangement and basically laid it on the line and said that if he failed to show at school on any of the days he was supposed to then we would drop him and there would be no going back. However, I promised him if he could stick to the days we said until half-term, turn up, work hard, get his head down at school then I would go and see his headmaster and tell him that we wanted to swap the days around so that he came to us for three days and school for two days. Now he really liked that idea and he responded to it. I used to go and pick him up from his house (he didn't live far from me) and we bought him a blazer to wear so that he looked like a professional footballer in the making. That wasn't easy for him because there was a lot of name calling and nonsense that he had to put up with, but he handled it.

When I next went to speak to his headmaster he told me that Jermaine had been a model pupil and a great role model. So we swapped his days around and now we had him for three days a week. The last thing we had to do was get him away from his home environment, and so I asked John Gaunt (who looked after the kids in a club lodge) and he had room so that was that. So Jermaine went and stayed with the rest of the lads from the youth team and it wasn't easy because he got a lot of teasing about being the 'Golden Boy' and 'Son of Youngy', but they respected his football and what he could do on the pitch. He made his youth team debut when he was fourteen, away at Shrewsbury on a dry, bumpy pitch. With fifteen minutes to go our 'keeper launched it long because there was nothing on. Jermaine was just over the halfway line and I could him looking over his shoulder, moving towards the defender, looking up at the ball; he half-spun and half-shielded the defender and allowed the ball to bounce over his head and he was away. It was just him and the 'keeper. The ball bounced high again and as it came down, he jumped as high as he could in the air and he side-foot volleyed the ball over the 'keeper's head and into the net. It was a magnificent goal and a brilliant indication of what was coming. I asked him afterwards what he thought at the time and he said, 'Well I could see the defender was struggling already and all I had to do was lean on him and he would miss because he was already out of position. I had already looked at the 'keeper and I knew how to beat him but I knew I had to jump to meet the ball or I wouldn't have had time to get the ball down and the 'keeper would have been on me so I had to go up and meet it'. That last bit was what really impressed me and convinced me that we had something really special in Jermaine Pennant, it was genius to work all that out. After that he changed a bit and started to shirk his duties (basic cleaning duties around the stadium) and he learned the hard way that you don't let your teammates down like that. The lads would take him to the boot room and turn the light off and paste him and he soon got the message. All Jermaine wanted to do was play football, but there was also some hard work to be done and he had to do his share and the lads made sure he understood that. Sam Allardyce gave him his full debut at Sheffield United in the League Cup but he never made a first team appearance at Meadow Lane because Allardyce cashed in and sold him to Arsenal. Leading up to that deal we played Arsenal in the F.A. Youth Cup at Highbury. I deliberately kept Jermaine on the bench because I didn't want Arsenal to see him, although, they would have known about him already I suspect. Anyway, it was 1–1 when they had a lad sent off with half an hour to go and I got a message from Sam from the stand that I had to put Jermaine on. So I did and he absolutely ripped the Arsenal full-back to shreds for the last twenty minutes. There is no doubt that football was Jermaine's saviour and there are a number of other lads that we helped along the way through the Notts County youth scheme: Kris Commons, Will Hoskins and Leon Best.

Sam wanted everything done 'just so' at the training ground and when I look back I can see that nothing ever pleased him. He would find fault and complain about anything I did, but I deliberately made sure that if he asked me to do something then I did it and did it well. I worked hard for him, I really did; I would be in at eight in the morning and often wouldn't leave until six and I was still the Director for the Centre for Excellence, so that was Tuesday nights taken up and Mondays and Wednesdays. I was also still helping with the Community Programme. This often meant that I would be busy on Saturdays and Sundays with fixtures and this all added up to a very long working week. Despite the reduced wages that Sam had put me on I still totally loved the job and this meant that when the fateful day arrived it was very hard to take.

On top of this my relationship with Karen was less than perfect but, I thought, it wasn't beyond repair. All sorts of things had been happening, but one incident stays with me to this day and it happened when we had been having yet another argument and it was the one and only time I raised my hand and I slapped her on the back of the head. I am not proud of what I did, in fact, I am deeply ashamed and at the end of the argument I got in the car and drove to her parents and told them that I had hit Karen; that's how ashamed I was. Well, all hell broke loose then. She was an only child and even though I had always had a great relationship with her Mum and Dad they were always going to side with their little girl and protect her. Unfortunately Karen didn't help this situation by telling them some stuff that they didn't need to know, and she ought not to have told them. This painted a poor picture of me and suddenly I was the evil one. This couldn't be further from the truth; I am a nice guy and a great father and I was never unfaithful to Karen, I never even looked at another woman. In fact, Karen had been going out and staying out a lot more but she never told her parents this. This was causing us a few problems and it was then that I started to drink a bit, more through boredom and then fear about the future. I can also remember her Father putting a big bed sheet up outside my bedroom window and on it he had painted 'Alan Young is a wife beater'. Imagine that! Her Mother – Dot – said to me, 'If I see you standing in the street I will mow you down.' It was awful. Then her Dad topped it off when he turned up at Notts County with a load of bin liners full of my clothes and I got a call back from training and when I got back to the ground her Dad (Colin) was in Sam's office. I have no idea what was said between the two of them, but Sam was saying stuff like, 'This isn't right Alan, this can't go on.' This was just before I got the sack, so it is possible her Dad contributed to me losing my job. What did her Dad think he was doing? Why is it ok for someone to march into my employers like that because I upset his daughter? It's nothing to do with Notts County – it certainly wasn't affecting my work but I am sure that Colin contributed to my sacking.

Sam didn't give a shit about me though. Now someone like Jock Wallace would be round at my house to 'smell' if there was a problem and to see how he could help. But Jock was a better human being than him because Sam didn't try to support or help me in any way he simply said, 'fuck off!' To this day I have to say that there are not very many people that I don't like because I am a decent person with very high morals, but I wouldn't bat an eyelid if Sam dropped down dead tomorrow because that bastard ruined my life. Everything went in an instant because of a decision he made. I get really annoyed when I see him taking top jobs and getting paid millions in pay-offs when he gets the sack and then talking on the television like he is some sort of expert, because he isn't. The final insult came when I found out that I was replaced by a guy called Gary Brazil who had done Sam a favour. He gave him the youth team role and he eventually became manager when Sam moved on in 1999. All of that makes me think that my sacking was concocted so that Gary Brazil could be brought into the club. I think if I had stayed at Notts County then there would have come a time when I would have been offered the manager's job. I had been there ten years and people knew me inside-out; and my knowledge of the game was very good and I had my UEFA 'A' coaching qualifications by then. I know you have to be philosophical about this and say that this is the hand I have been dealt and make the best of it, but on this occasion I can't and I will never, ever forgive Sam Allardyce. Even my kids hate him because they know all about him and if they see him on the television, they turn him off!

When the end did come it was still a shock. I remember getting the phone call one Friday morning towards the end of the season and Sam said, 'Al, I need you to come up to my office.' I knew straight away what was coming. I was preparing for the Midland Youth Floodlit Cup Final that night at Molineux against Wolves so I had to leave that and when I walked into Sam's office Ian Moat, the secretary, was with him (he was a right little snake as well!) and I said, 'You wanted to see me'

'Aye. I'm going to have to let you go' That was it, straight in. 'You what?'

'I'm going to let you go.'

The feeling of dread and disappointment and sadness that hits you at that moment is hard to describe but it totally overwhelms you and I took a moment before I said 'Why?'

'Because you treat the kids too much like the first team.'

So I had a wee think about that for a moment and said, 'What's wrong with that?'

'You train at the same time as the first team; they get the same food as the first team at the training ground.'

'What am I meant to do? Let them starve? Of course I have them training at the same time as the first team because I want them to get a feel for the professional game as early as possible so that they are better prepared when you get them Sam. Isn't that what you want?'

This was really important to me because I had seen too many very talented kids develop to first team standard and then come apart because they couldn't handle the step up to the first team dressing room and everything that goes with it. It is a big move for a youngster and I wanted to prepare them as far as I could and if that meant that they trained and ate and associated with the first team then so be it. I wanted to build strong characters as well as good footballers. But Sam didn't see it that way, he just said, 'Nah, I'm not having that.'

So I said 'Is that it? Can I still run the Centre for Excellence?'

'Nah. No way. Are you still driving the minibus?'

'Yes, I am.'

'Give the keys in at reception.'

'Is that it?'

'Yeah!'

So I walked out of his door, out of the gates and out of Notts County and then walked back across Lady Bay Bridge over the River Trent and then walked home. I walked in and said to Karen 'I've just been sacked' and that was the start of a series of events that changed my life.

It was the first time I'd been sacked in twenty five years in football and then in walks Sam and thinks he can treat everybody like shit. The timing was perfect for him because he had won promotion for Notts County sometime in April so he was 'all powerful' if you like, and he could do anything he wanted. He could've told the chairman to piss off and got away with it. That was why nobody contested it and stood up to him; they should have said, 'You can't sack Alan Young, he's been here ten years working all the hours God sends, clearing snow off the pitches, winning awards for the Community Programme, receiving letters of commendation from the Prime Minister and national bodies for the work with the drug prevention scheme in Nottingham. He took the scheme from a Portakabin to a nationally recognised project.'

But nobody did. Maybe Sam saw me as a threat, maybe not, but it was really hard for me to understand why he did what he did. This led to all sorts of problems beginning with my relationship with Karen. We had been having problems as I have already said and it was made worse when I began to hang around the house a lot more. that was a massive change from the hours that I had been working and so me and Karen started to argue more and that moved on to arguing in front of the kids and eventually we split up. Karen's Mum and Dad became heavily involved as well and that didn't help to be honest, because I had nobody to turn to. All of my family was back in Scotland and I felt completely alone because my work had been my life along with Karen and the kids. When all of those things disappeared very quickly then I became very down and very lonely. I was still in love with Karen and it was breaking my heart when she took the kids and left and the house (a beautiful Edwardian house on Edward Road in Nottingham) was put up for sale and that saddened me greatly.

In the midst of all of this the phone rang one day and it was Neil Hook who was at Chesterfield. He was working for a chairman by the name of Norton Lee and he wanted to know if I wanted to be the new Youth Development Officer. The youth team was a shambles but I went and met Norton Lee and one or two other board members and they were all local businessmen, shopkeepers and so on. Only Norton Lee fell into the category of 'millionaire' and he was a miserable bastard but I took the job anyway. John Duncan was manager at the time and Kevin Randall was his assistant. There were some decent players at the club: Jason Lee and Steve Blatherwick from Nottingham Forest, Paul Holland ('Dutch') was there and he went on to manage Mansfield Town. They had just had the F.A. Cup semi-final against Middlesbrough at Old Trafford where they had basically won the game but were denied by a poor decision where a goal was disallowed when it had clearly crossed the line. So it was a buoyant club and John Duncan was doing a good job even though some of his methods were questionable, and I was happy to join them, even though they gave me the smallest of offices to work from. I concentrated on the youth team first of all and had a good look at what I had inherited.

The problem at Chesterfield was that they usually picked up the lads that weren't wanted by Nottingham Forest and Derby and Sheffield Wednesday and the like, so the team were not the best. There was definitely not another Jermaine Pennant waiting in the wings that's for sure, so I went back to Notts County and picked up some of the kids that had been released at sixteen there and basically got kicked out after I had left; lads like Timmy Hogg. They were better than what we had at Chesterfield and it gave some lads another chance. I then wanted to get something started similar to the system that I had at Notts County with the trials, but this meant getting some staff to help me. That was difficult because I wasn't actually running the Community Programme, Nicky Law was doing that. The same Nicky Law that used to batter me when he played for Barnsley, but he and I became great pals and he gave me a hand to set up the trials and some of the youth team lads helped out as well. But the overall quality of the kids was poor to be honest. I knew it would be a long time before we had a good dozen or so under-10s that we could nurture through to youth-team standard but I was determined to give it a go and I managed to get sponsors and tracksuits, as I had at Notts County, and once again the kids looked smart as paint. Even though a lot of them weren't that gifted, they represented the club really well. I was also working really hard at this stage and putting in about eighty to ninety hours a week; I had the Centre for Excellence in the evenings on Tuesdays and Thursdays; Monday and Wednesdays with the women's team; and of course the youth team every day, as well as fixtures at the weekend. You might be with the youth team at Carlisle on Saturday and then away at Stockport with the kids on Sunday. So that was an entire weekend wiped out. I'm not sure what I did Fridays … maybe I slept! It was really hard work.

At this time the first team wasn't doing very well and there was a lot of talk about the club being sold which was a bit unsettling, but I carried on and did my job as usual. It was then that the chairman came and watched his first youth team match. We beat Wrexham who were a decent side themselves. Now the chairman loved it and could see what was going on and liked what he saw I think. Despite this, he didn't seem to take to me and in fact, he actually seemed to turn against me after a while.

We would have meetings with the chairman every Friday where he wanted to know everything that was going on – I think they refer to this as an autocratic management style! Poor John Duncan was forever being told to prune his staff and he would reply with something like, 'I can't prune any more staff chairman. I've done all the pruning I can, I can't prune prunes!' He would always come to me last and ask what I had been doing and I always made sure that he had a weekly report from me detailing exactly what I had done. One week he started on me during the weekly meeting and pointed at me and said, 'You! Don't park in the front car park. You can park round the back; the first team need those spaces'. That was fine with me, I didn't complain and I used the car park at the back of the stadium. By then I some space under the stand had been converted into some new offices for me and a guy called Jonathan Pepper to use. Now Jonathan's father was a director and he was there to help me.

The next thing that the chairman did was to try and get me using time sheets. I had never used time sheets in my life and I wasn't ready to start. But he wanted to know where I was every minute of the day and what I was doing. I pointed out that everything he needed to know was in my weekly reports which were very detailed by now. So he challenged me and said, 'It says here that on Monday last week you came in at 8 o'clock. You didn't do anything of the sort.' He was banging his finger on the table and shouting, 'That's a fucking lie because you don't get into this football club before me. I'm first here!'

At this point I am aware of John Duncan to the side of me and I can see that he is about to explode laughing and I said, 'I did come in early, in fact it was half past seven'

But he won't back down and he goes on ,'You are a fucking liar and do you know how I know you weren't in before me? Because your car wasn't in the fucking car park.'

So I said, 'I know it wasn't in the car park and do you know why? Because three weeks ago you told me to park in the back fucking car park!' He didn't like that at all because he had been shown up. But I kept working hard and eventually the club was sold but (rumour had it) that it was bought by a guy who borrowed the money from Norton Lee. The new guy didn't want to be the hatchet man when he took over. He didn't want to come in and start sacking people straight away, so Norton Lee did it for him before the sale went through. I remember walking into the board room with John Duncan and Kevin Randall, where Norton Lee was waiting. There were three envelopes on the table and Lee said, 'There you go. Read them and fuck off!' John and Kevin went into the manager's office to open theirs but I opened mine in the corridor and the letter used words like '…after a final warning…' which was nonsense. There had been no warnings at any stage.

So I was a bit sad to be leaving and the players were as well. It was a good dressing room and I was accepted by the players because I was an ex-professional. I could walk into the dressing rooms and feel part of it. There were some great, decent lads there; journeyman footballers like David Reeves and Tony Carrs who were genuine lads and not thinking that they were superstars. John had let me take some of the first team training sessions and I had absolutely loved it. I would tell the groundsman that John had said I had to train on the main pitch (even though he hadn't) and I would give them great training sessions and try out some new stuff which John didn't always like. John Duncan had some strange ideas about the way the game should be played at times; he used to say, 'Don't get outside of the game'. This meant that players were always inside the ball and the midfielders didn't go past the front men. I never argued with him about this, but to me he was turning over some fundamental principles of the game. Chesterfield was a funny place and I had a wee cottage on the Mansfield Road in a village just outside the town. We would drink in the Shoulder of Mutton which was run by lovely people, and on Sundays we would go there after our games at the Centre of Excellence with the Mums and Dads. It was friendly and kept everyone together and created a community spirit. I think the other reason I was sad to leave Chesterfield was because it was occupying my mind and my days at a time when I really needed to be busy. It stopped me thinking too much about the split with Karen and the kids.

By that time the split with Karen was permanent and the house had been sold in Nottingham and I was pretty low. I remember I got really legless one night in Nottingham and I was walking across one of the bridges over the Trent and I sat in one of the small recesses on the bridge with my legs over the side and thought to myself to just topple in and put an end to it. I was laughing to myself but it wasn't happy laughter it was a sad laugh; I was devastated at the time. I was staying in our house on Edward Road and travelling back from Chesterfield when I first got the role there and every night when I got home something would be gone; it might be the settee or the lovely old pine kitchen table that we had but piece by piece, Karen was emptying the house. I wasn't seeing the kids at the time either, I didn't know where they were. Eventually I was allowed to see them now and again and I could take them back to my place in Chesterfield but that was horrible as well, when I picked them up there would be screaming and shouting in the street. It was the stuff of nightmares.

Karen was my best friend; I didn't need anybody else, she was everything I ever wanted and in an instant she was gone. I loved her more than anything else in my life apart from my children. We had some great times and then everything was gone. Kids – gone! I was a fucking wreck at that time and I couldn't understand why someone could do that to me. I wasn't totally happy at Chesterfield if I'm honest but I worked so hard because when I was working I didn't have to think about the problems elsewhere in my life.

So I was sitting on Trent Bridge with my legs over the side and all sorts of thoughts are going through my head. I am not sure how fine the dividing line is between thinking about suicide and actually doing it and we will never know because the people who do it can't come back to tell us. I remember a Scottish girl came by whilst I was staring into the water and she asked if I was alright. I said I was fine and then I found out she was from Inverness and she asked the killer question: 'You're not thinking about going in there are you?'

'Well I was but I'm not now. Now that you've come along I'll be alright.' I stopped thinking about suicide when she came by and started to talk to me. We walked for a while and eventually she went off home and I went back to my house on Edward Road. I never got her name and I have no idea to this day what would have happened if she hadn't come along. I think it takes a strange kind of courage to take your own life. I would be tested again later on.

12

KAREN NUMBER 2 AND THE BLACK DOG

I met Karen Hespin during my time at Chesterfield. It was in the pub one evening when I spotted a very attractive girl. I should never have got together with her because, although my relationship with Karen Towers was over, I was still grieving for her and still hurting. It was doomed from the start to be honest. She had been in physically and mentally abusive relationships and she had her own problems to deal with and she was still with a guy when I met her. She was a quiet girl from Knaresborough, who was quietly spoken and she also had two kids (Jade and Tom). We just sort of gave it a go and she fell hopelessly in love with me and I don't know if I felt the same because I was missing Karen and Kyle and Sophie so much. But she was a decent girl and I know that I helped her get over her own issues over the six or seven years that we were together; I did her the world of good. It is fair to say that she recovered whilst she was with me, not just because of me, but I was very supportive. I went along to some of her counselling sessions and her counsellor pulled me aside one day and said that Karen was scared to death that I was going to leave her and that was her biggest problem. She was a very attractive girl but also incredibly insecure, for example, we were walking around Linacre Woods (a beautiful location to the west of Chesterfield itself) and as we came to the reservoirs she said, 'If me and Sophie both fell in the lake who would you save first?' And I knew at that moment that something wasn't quite right. And then when I didn't give her the answer she wanted she got really upset. Despite this I tried really hard with Karen Hespin and moved in with her because at this point I had lost my job at Chesterfield and I was cutting steel in a factory in Sheffield for a living. At one point I moved in with her Mum in Knaresborough and slept up in the attic bedroom. All the time I was thinking that if we could just get a place of our own then everything would be alright and so we bought a semi-detached cottage in a lovely village called Ferrensby in North Yorkshire. We had an extension built and some other improvements made and it was a great house to live in. It was far enough out of the city to enjoy some peace and quiet if you didn't mind being woken by the cows in the morning; we backed on to a big old barn from the farm next door! Unfortunately we weren't alright and the longer the relationship went on the more I realised that we were poles apart. Anyway, Karen started to go out on her own a lot and I am thinking that this was history repeating itself and so I got hold of her phone one day and heard a message from another guy and this was starting to make me insecure as well.

At least I had managed to get some work back in football at this point and that helped me I suppose. I was working for Leeds United and doing a bit for the Community Programme and driving all over the place to cover the ground that they needed me to. Unfortunately I lost my driving licence and that caused me some serious problems. I remember exactly what happened and I wish I could turn the clock back but I can't; it was F.A. Cup semi-final day and I told Karen that I was going up to the pub in Boroughbridge (the next village, only a few miles away) to have a few pints and watch the game but that I'd leave the car at the pub and collect it in the morning. So I did and met up with a guy called Adie Shaw (who I replaced as youth team manager at Chesterfield when Adie went to York) and we had a good time and it got a bit outrageous, so I said to Karen to come up and meet us and join the fun. The plan was that she would drive home but halfway home on these quiet country lanes she said that she felt ill. So I swapped places with her and drove the last bit of the journey. We were about a quarter of a mile from home when we passed our local and (as it turns out) there had been a sixteenth birthday party in the function room at the pub and there had been a bit of noise and complaints so the police had turned up. Just as I went past the police car, having dealt with everything, pulled out behind me. I was just about to turn into my driveway when the blue light went on and that was it. I was breathalysed, taken to Harrogate Police Station (where I spent the night) and eventually banned for eighteen months and fined £350. That was a real kick in the bollocks but it was entirely my fault; I should never have got behind the wheel of the car. That seemed to be the point at which we both realised that the relationship was effectively over; it was just an existence to be honest and we both slept in separate rooms from then on.

I must pay credit to the staff at Leeds United at this point. I went in on the Monday and explained to Mick Ferguson and Rick Passmore and told them that I had been breathalysed and I would lose my licence. They didn't judge me or condone what I had done and I could tell they didn't like it but they stuck by me and they gave me a work partner called Tina Reeves.

Never mind the pancakes, what about the
van in the background? At a Holiday Inn in 1980.

Young, Alan.

Not long before the Blue Army joined me on the pitch
... Leyton Orient away in May 1980 ... Champions!

With my mentor, Andy Lochhead, at his
house in Burnley, September 2011.

This is the birth of the book with my son, Kyle, at the Little Chef on the A46
north of Leicester.

Probably the best header I've ever scored. Southampton at home in the FA Cup 3rd round, January 1982.

Alex Stepney on his knees, Martin Buchan looks on in despair as my diving header at Old Trafford flies in, October 1974.

Jock Wallace's tartan army: McLeicester!

Leicester Town Hall Square, May 1980, se
me and 'Ted' acknowledging our fantasti
supporters.

The culmination of a long, hard but
successful season with a great manager and
fantastic teammates.

Town Hall Square, May 1980 – Youngy start the wave!

Finley and Archie, my two grandsons who I don't see often enough.

My very first love, Fiona.

I'm not happy with this picture, Jock should be in the middle! Not a bad squad though eh?

With 'Knocker' at Notts County. Not everyone's cup of tea but we got on fine … still do.

With the Notts County community kids at Wembley for the play-off final in 1991. Very proud day for our Community Programme.

Why have I got a green shirt on John? The Shrewsbury FA Cup quarter final, March 1982.

Why the hell did I ever sign for Rochdale? Shit manager, holes in the roof. What more can I say?

My little girl Sophie. She's twenty-one this year but she's still my little girl!

With Karen; Kyle and Sophie's mum. She's pretty huh?

My youngest son, Kyle, wearing my Scotland cap. He had more ability in his little toe than I ever had in my whole body.

The very lovely Dot Smith … I still miss 'wee Nissie' to this day.

I got too many injuries at Brighton but still finished with 13 goals from 26 games. Not too shabby huh?

My two eldest boys, Jordan and Wesley, at our lovely house in Oadby in 1981. Jordan was born in Leicester.

Gary and Michelle's wedding reception at The Hinckley Island Hotel. Who is that handsome bastard in the middle?

Peakey, Kevin Mac, Smelrose, Linkener and wee Stewarty Hamill in Torremolinos…
get that top off Kev it's a 100°f for Christ's sake!

Torremolinos again but there is a new signing with a purple bikini top on. Hope she's not a striker!

Kirkcaldy High
School, some of the best days of my life
but looking very dodgy?

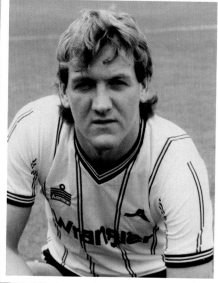

Notts County. I had more success
off the pitch than on it. A lovely
club with some lovely people.

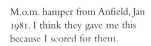

M.o.m. hamper from Anfield, Jan
1981. I think they gave me this
because I scored for them.

Final whistle v Charlton after securing promotion. Orient away next Saturday for the title.

Boundary Park, Oldham v Preston, in my early professional days ... do you think it went in?

The ball that got me my move to Filbert Street. A hat-trick v City was enough for Jock to sign me. Feb 1979 ... my Dad still has that ball.

Old Trafford, 1974. Scotland Schoolboys v England Schoolboys sees me back row, second left. I think the barbers must have been on strike in Scotland!

Look out Family Stand, here I come! Left foot volley puts us one nil up in our 2–1 win over Charlton. Promoted!

Ron and Ella, AKA Mum and Dad in my Dad's precious back garden. Is that nearly a smile Mum?

My two wonderful sisters, Lyn and Karen … where would I be now without your love and support?

Apart from my Father there is no man closer to God than this man. Irreplaceable.

My marriage to Julie in Oldham in 1977 I think … it was a long time ago! Does anyone recognise my best man?

Take a good look at this photograph folk it was very rare for me to smile during a match.

Tina was a little lass and a 'ginger' as well and she lived quite close to me, so she would pick me up and we would work together and she would drive me everywhere. I will be forever grateful to Tina; she was about eighteen at the time and I loved her like a daughter and we are still in touch today. She always had a smile, was always pleased to see you and one of the nicest people I have ever met in my life. I suppose I had been doing a good job for them and instead of knee-jerking, the staff at Leeds thought about it and considered how they could help me out. I paid them back with the biggest and best soccer schools for Leeds United in Harrogate and Knaresborough and it turned into a great experience for me. I started up some satellite centres where the best kids would attend regular training for a while and it was up to me to find players and to recommend them for professional scholarships. Some of them are still playing professional football today.

My personal life was a mess at this stage, so I couldn't stay around and I quit the Leeds job thinking that a fresh start would be the answer. Going back to Scotland was one of the options available to me. Living in Ferrensby was perfect; a lovely little village that was just far enough out of Knaresborough to get some peace and quiet so it made it very difficult for me to leave and move back to Scotland. I remember that Jordan (my eldest son) drove me to Scotland in my Mondeo because my brother had offered to buy it off me whilst I was banned, and said he would give it back to me when the ban was up. That was a great idea so Jordan and I drove up to Scotland and caught the bus back; the drive was hours and hours. Unfortunately my brother allowed his daughter to drive my car and she trashed it, so I never got it back. That was typical of my brother. That short trip back made me think that moving back to Scotland permanently would be the right thing to do.

I was convinced that I would be able to get work in football at one of the Scottish professional clubs and so I left Karen Hespin and went back and stayed with my brother at his place for a while, thinking that I would soon be back in work.

I met my old girlfriend, Fiona, from my time in Kirkcaldy and we started to see each other again and I could feel myself falling in love with her again, but I knew that I didn't have anything to bring to the table. I had a whole load of problems that I was trying to deal with and this included psychological problems and self-esteem issues. I was putting on an act for everyone to try and give the impression that I was alright but I wasn't. I was fucked. The biggest problem was not having any work; I wrote to every club in Scotland and asked for a job. I had a strong CV with my experience and qualifications but I got fuck all. I had one reply from East Fife from the chairman who asked me to go and meet him. I rang the club to arrange this and was told that he was on holiday, so I left a message for him to call me when he got back. He didn't call so I phoned back but was repeatedly told that he wasn't available and he never called me back. So, I just gave up on that one. But that was it. One reply from every club in Scotland! It was a case of who you know not what you know. I had to try and find work though so I got application forms to work in a call centre, filled it in and tore it up. I couldn't do that and by this time I was getting very down and depressed and the 'black dog' was starting to follow me around.

Well, the honeymoon period (about two weeks) at my brother's place was fine but I soon realised that I had to get a place of my own. We just didn't get on and eventually I moved into a caravan that he kept at Loch Lomond. That was also meant to be for a short while, but I was there for eighteen months. Unfortunately that was when the serious drinking started.

It was just lager at first because I had never been a spirits drinker, but by the time the drink took control then I was into stuff like Jack Daniels. The problem was I didn't know anyone; I was totally on my own and so drinking passed the time and made me feel better for a while. I was still in touch with Karen and I kept phoning her and asking her to come up and she did make the trip one time, but that just made us realise that we were miles apart. The other problem was that I didn't really have a social life. All of my friends from the game were back in England and all of my old mates from school were around but I didn't know anything about them anymore. Karen Towers was my mate, my pal, and I had always thought that we would be together into retirement and old age, so I didn't think I needed anyone else. Suddenly there was nobody I could call up to go for a pint with me and drinking alone isn't a good idea as I found out. So instead of two or three pints with your mates in the evening, it was three or four cans in the afternoon and a few vodkas at night and then to bed, wake up and start again.

I never really understood the meaning of the expression 'stir crazy' until I was on my own in that caravan. It Isn't just the isolation that causes the problem, it's also knowing that you have a problem and that the problem won't go away and it isn't going to get any better in the foreseeable future, in fact, you can't actually see a future. Now Loch Lomond is a beautiful place but not when it rains! When it rains it has its own special cloud and it always seemed to be right above my caravan and the sound it made was the sound of 1,000 demented hammers on my roof. Money-wise all I seemed to be doing was buying booze and there was a thing called Glen Vodka that was dead cheap; it was raw as hell but it did the job. I had to walk six or seven miles into Alexandria to get my dole. So I could have the money to buy this stuff, but the walk there and the walk back in the pouring rain was miserable and most of the time I couldn't even remember the journey, I was just numb. I wasn't eating very well either; when the money ran out I would live on fried bread for days on end. And when the bread and the money ran out then I would starve until the next dole cheque. Most of the time I was on my own and I had day after day to keep myself amused and it was tough – that was the start of the big decline. My knee, which had been a mess for a while, was really starting to scream at me by then and so the drink was helping me to self-medicate my pain. A drink became two, became three, became four and so on.

My brother told me that he wanted to sell the caravan, so I had to get out and I moved out and into a place at No.68 Balfour Street which was just around the corner from where my Mum and Dad were living. I got it thanks to my sisters spotting it and dragging me round to see it. Now I didn't have much in the way of possessions (mostly clothes) but that all went missing when my brother cleared my stuff out. My new flat was ok I suppose; it was empty so I would need furniture and the kitchen was tiny, but it was enough for me. I went to a place called Methel to sort out the terms for rental and so on and I had to warn them that my credit rating would be rotten, so my sister helped me out with the deposit and the first month's rent. The renting company were appreciative of my honesty and the fact that I had guarantors and so I got the flat. My sisters then spotted a sofa bed for sale in the local paper and got that for me (I've still got it actually) and whilst they were in the guy's house getting the sofa bed they made him an offer for a two-seater leather settee and he parted with that too. Great stuff! I managed to get hold of some other essential furniture and I was sorted. Some of the details of my move into the new flat on Balfour Street are vague, and I also have no recollection of getting my stuff up from Ferrensby. At this stage my drinking was getting progressively worse and days became weeks, became months, became years. I really can't remember much from that awful time. What I do remember is that my sisters (Karen and Lyn) took care of me and did everything basically; they are fantastic, absolute diamonds. Karen is seven years younger than me and when I left to go to Oldham at eighteen Karen was eleven and I didn't really know much about her back then. We had never really done anything together in our lives and so we set about rediscovering each other and the area we grew up in. I would borrow Dad's car and we would drive all over Fife and spend hours at a time together. Lyn didn't come with us very often; Lyn is a few years older than me and so my relationship with her is different. We knew each other better when I was younger. Lyn is the sensible, level-headed one in the family; Karen is a bit more scatter-brained. Lyn is totally devoted to her own family and has kids of her own now.

I have the greatest respect for my Mum and Dad; I admire the way my Dad copes with everything that life has thrown at him and especially for the way my Mum raised the five of us in a tenement with very little money at times. I only wish my elder brother could have turned out better, but then four out of five isn't bad Mum! I used to get on great with him and we had some great times together. I can remember some great New Years at his place, but sadly I remember him for lying to me and deceiving me now. We were in the caravan together one Saturday afternoon when he was back from the oil rigs (where he worked) and we were betting on the horses. He had a Ladbrokes account and I didn't so we agreed that we would share the winnings that afternoon. There was a horse called Hurricane Alan running at 10–1 and he put a grand

each way on it. That meant about three grand in winnings.
The next one we picked was a horse called I'm So Lucky and
he put a grand on that one too and it came flying in at good
odds as well. That same afternoon Dunfermline were playing
at Dundee and they had to win or they were relegated.
Now they had just asked Jim Leishman (the legendary Jim
Leishman by the way) to take over the side on a caretaker
basis for the final few matches having sacked the incumbent
manager. Jim was on the board of directors and stepped in and
turned the club's fortunes around with a handful of games left.
They had a really difficult trip to Dundee and the odds were
5–2 against the win for Dunfermline. I said to my brother
that he had to get something on that and so he put two grand
on. Now he knows about as much about football as I know
about nuclear physics (which isn't much) but he followed my
tip and put the money on. We had a few drinks and forgot
all about the results and the bet and it was only the next
morning when we went to the shops to get the paper that
we saw that Dunfermline had won 1–0, goal scored in the
89th minute. We had won five grand! So the whole day had
brought in about £11,000 and, despite our agreement that we
would split the winnings, I never saw a penny of it. It wasn't
physically in his hand it was in his Ladbrokes account and
that's where it stayed. He never said a word to me about it and
I didn't challenge him because I didn't want to cause a row,
even though we had shaken hands on it. Where I come from
you don't let people down when you shake hands on a deal.
That was the start of the fall out between me and my brother
and it didn't help when I would hear about him coming back
from the oil rigs and going into his local and throwing money
round like confetti and buying everyone drinks and giving
out duty-free fags. He would say that they were 'real people'

when in fact they were just a bunch of hangers-on who were getting something for nothing. That didn't bother him though because it made him feel good to be the big 'I am' in his local pub. He has no friends and his job doesn't help that being in charge of an oil rig. He could have helped Mum and Dad more than he did as well; not just financially but physically as well. He hardly ever went to visit them and when I was back for five years I saw them in that time more than had in the previous thirty-six years. My sisters don't like the situation and want me to make up with him, but I have told them that he has to come to me first, I'm not the one in the wrong and I will go to my grave before I make up with that twat. If my brother was to come and apologise to me then I might think about but not until. Bear in mind that I was living on benefits at the time and when I moved into Balfour Street I had barely enough money to pay my gas and electric bills and buy food. I haven't bought clothes for years now which is why you only ever see me in a Leicester City tracksuit!

The move to Balfour Street was fine for a while and I guess it was another honeymoon period and it was great having my family around me and being able to get together and have a few drinks with them, but it was only temporary. The thing I remember most about Balfour Street was how bloody cold it was. I didn't have enough money to keep feeding the meter and heat the place the way I needed to, so I used to stay under a quilt or a massive coat that I used to have. There were also a whole load or mice in the house in the winter and I woke up one morning and there was one of the wee buggers running all over my bed. This just made me reluctant to go to bed because when it went quiet all I could hear was the mice scrabbling around in the traps that the Environmental Agency had put down. At times it was just as lonely in Balfour Street as it had been at Loch Lomond in the caravan; my Dad would pop in at about 9.30 in the morning and ask if I fancied coming over to the bookies for a bet and I would usually say 'no' as I was skint. That was it then, I wouldn't usually see anyone else for the rest of the day and that suited me fine. Some days I didn't even see my Dad because I would leave the curtains closed and Dad would see that as a sign that I was still in bed. Even if I wasn't, I would do this just to be alone. Even if Dad was banging on the door I would ignore it. I think my family knew about my troubles, but they rarely said anything. Occasionally when I saw them one of them would stuff a £20 note into my hand but all I would do was get home and go straight round to the off-licence and stock up on booze and get hammered. I would wake up the next morning and see how I felt and decide if I wanted to see anyone that day. If the answer was 'no' then it was straight to the fridge and open a can of lager. My body clock was dictated by the booze and so I slept around my boozing sessions, but even when I couldn't drink because the money had run out I still wouldn't do anything. I just lay on my bed, not wanting to see anyone and would eventually get up and open the curtains to let the world in. I had never experienced anything like this so I didn't know how to deal with it. I really needed help.

I went to my GP at one point and told him how I was feeling and about the depression and he was pretty good. He told me to set myself a target and that was to get my driving licence back and I tried again and again and eventually I was given my licence back for a year, but then they took it away again when I was reviewed. So that was another body blow I could have done without.

There was still no work and I even applied for jobs back in England: there was a job back at South Notts College and a community football job at Peterborough that I should have got. Phil Stant was looking out for me and doing his best to find job opportunities and Phil Turner was helping me as well, back in Nottingham. In fact, Phil became indispensible when I eventually moved back to Nottingham and without him I wouldn't have managed. Another job came up at Notts County and it was the Community Scheme Director's job again and it was available because Graham Moran was leaving. I phoned Graham and asked him straight if he would have any problem with me applying for the position and he said he didn't. So I applied for the post in writing and I got a letter back from Steve Hill (another guy I gave a job to) and the letter basically said, 'Thank you for your application but we have had to reject your application because we received your letter a day after the closing date for the role.' I had only seen the job advertised a day before the closing date. I was livid and especially after all I had done for them but I think there was a feeling of: can't have him back, too popular, knows too much! I founded that scheme in 1991 and so I felt really bloody upset about that rejection. More so because I gave Graham a job ten years earlier when he really needed one. Another job that came up was the youth team manager's job at Notts County when Ian McParland was first team manager there. So I phoned Ian up and told him that I really wanted that job. I was basically asking him for a lifeline, but he went on about how many people had applied and then finished off with, 'I'll have to see' and I never heard back from him. They gave the job to Mick Leonard, his best pal.

In Scotland I was starting to apply for jobs as a social worker or care worker but I wasn't getting anywhere and most of the time I wasn't even getting responses. I would get these surges of enthusiasm where I would go after jobs with a bit of optimism and drive, but it would soon get beaten out of you and that was when I would lose heart and 'medicate' myself and disappear for a while. I was still on benefits at this stage, of course, and the pain in my knee was getting worse. It was a relief when my GP finally gave me a referral to start me on the road to getting a knee replacement. I also went to my GP to ask for help with the drinking and he referred me to some psychoanalysts who were a fucking joke. No use to me whatsoever and I was playing them off one another. I don't believe that sort of medical professional can help someone like me (as I was) with a serious drink problem. I think you have to do it yourself; you have got to want to make that change yourself. But I wasn't at that stage yet and one of the worst episodes began with me waking up at about seven thirty in the morning and the first thing I did was go to the fridge and get a beer, and then another, and another. As the morning went on I decided I had had enough and at some point I walked out of the house and set off for the big pier near to Kirkcaldy. I didn't even close the front door; I didn't need to because I wasn't coming back. I have this very vivid memory that I was ready to call it day and take my own life. We used to fish off of the big pier at the Firth of Forth when we were boys and it was well out to sea – if you jump in there you're not coming back out and I thought, that'll do for me. I remember I was bouncing off of walls as I walked down towards the big pier and I remember my knee was really hurting. The further I went the harder it got and I started to think that I wouldn't make it, it was too far. So I went into the graveyard on Abbotts Hall Road and sat down. It was nine in the morning and pissing down with rain but there I was and I fell asleep. The next thing I know there is a policeman prodding me and telling me to get up

'Hello son, what are ye doing here?'

'Fuck off!'

'Alright, that's enough.'

'I haven't committed any offence have I?'

'No son, nothing … apart from telling me to fuck off.' (So I thought, oh well, at least he's got a sense of humour)

And I found out later that I had phoned Karen Hespin but I have no recollection of that at all. Apparently I said to her, 'I helped you didn't I? I really, really helped you didn't I?'

She said, 'Yes, you did.'

And all I could say was, 'Alright then, see ya', and then I hung up. And I was crying as well. After that she phoned the police and they managed to trace me using my mobile phone signal. She had worked out that I was about to do something stupid and that made her call the police. After they picked me up I wasn't making any sense, they went through my phone and found my sister's number (Karen, my eldest sister) and contacted her and she came down with her husband, Andy, and they took me home. Even then as they were dropping me off I asked to borrow some money so I could get some beers!

On another occasion (although I have no recollection of this) I phoned Karen at one in the morning and asked her to tell my kids that I loved them and I had a pile of pills next to me that I was planning on taking to finish it all off. Anyway, within minutes the police were banging on the door and I let them in and they came in with my sister, Karen, (who was bloody furious by the way) and they saw that I hadn't done anything and left and took the whiskey and pills with them.

Despite all of this my sisters never once told me that I was drinking too much. I have to admit that I was good at keeping people away from me; I would never have visitors and I kept my bedroom curtains permanently drawn and, if I was drinking, I kept my living room curtains closed and the front door locked. If anyone came to the door I just ignored it.

Then the phone would go and I would ignore that too. If I did let anyone in (like my Mum and Dad) I would hide all the cans out of sight.

Occasionally my youngest kids would come and see me (Kyle and Sophie) and of course I would put on a good show for them, but I was still in a bad way and the drink had really taken hold. My Mum and Dad would pay for them to fly up from East Midlands Airport and I would ask a friend to give me a lift to the airport so I could meet them. The truth was that I didn't really want to see them because from the moment they arrived I was counting down to the awful moment when I would have to say goodbye to them. That was hell on Earth. I didn't need an excuse to drink but my circumstances were giving me plenty of reasons to go on another bender. My two older boys, Wesley and Jordan, had no idea about my problems because they were busy with their careers and families.

Then Sophie called me one day and she was really upset; her Mum and new partner had decided to move to Basel and had told Sophie that the house in England was being rented out so she couldn't stay there. I mean what a thing to do your daughter, they were kicking her out and she ended up sleeping at friends' houses on the settee. I was very grateful at the time for the Orange Mobile deal where you could talk for an hour for twenty pence and Sophie and I would time it so that we hung up at fifty nine minutes and then redial and get another twenty pence worth. There were a lot of tears spent during those calls because Sophie was so unhappy. I remember one time I called and her mobile was answered by some guy and I said, 'Who's that?'

'Who's that?' he replied. and

So, I said, 'That's my daughter's phone.' It turns out he had found it and it was miles from anywhere. So I called the police and the Nottinghamshire Police referred it to the Kirkcaldy Police and an officer came round and took a description from me and a photograph. Anyway, she eventually phoned me from a friend's phone and I went ballistic at her. Anyway it turned out that she was going to a concert at Newstead Abbey which is north of Nottingham but the phone was found ten miles south of Nottingham close to her friend's house where she was staying. The whole thing was sorted out in about two hours, but I was shitting myself.

I would talk to her constantly at that time because she was so desperately unhappy. We would always talk after she finished school and I would always talk to her if she was walking home late at night from the bus stop to where she was staying and we wouldn't hang up until she was back safely. I had tried to persuade her to come to Scotland and live with me but I knew deep down that that wouldn't work because she needed to be near to her friends and I knew she would still have the same problems if she lived in Scotland. The alternative was that I moved back to England to be near to her. When I made the decision to move back to Nottingham, that was the moment that the light came on again and the drinking stopped and I had a purpose, a focus, a mission if you like. I went straight round to my Mum and Dad and told them, 'I'm going back to England!' and I asked them for any help they could manage. I called Wes and Jordan in Rochdale and they had a big works van and were ready to move me back down as soon as I was ready. So all I needed to do now was to find somewhere to live in England. I started to get some help looking in England, and began trying to get a deposit together. The most important thing was that I had a new purpose. I didn't quit drinking entirely, but I had was some control. I might only have one or two pints instead of a twenty-four hour drinking session. Suddenly I was more active, going for walks and visiting my sisters and this all helped beating the drink. To help the process of getting back to Nottingham I phoned Phil Turner (I called him Skip) the former Notts County and Leicester City player. I don't think Phil will mind me saying this but I know he had a drink problem and he had been in a similar situation to me when he split up from his wife Rachel. Anyway, we met up when I came down to Peterborough for the community football job interview and we chose to meet in one of the little cafés that we knew. We sat down and we were so in tune with each other and the problems that we had both had, that we were finishing each other's sentences when we talked about it. He had also been on the edge and been to the darkest of places. I also contacted Gary Lund (who was another teammate at Notts County) and he and Phil Turner started to find flats for me to look at and then I contacted the P.F.A. and they helped me out with the deposit for the flat that I liked. Then Wesley, Jordan and a mate called 'Jacko', helped me to move in. They drove up from Rochdale on the Friday night, we packed the van on Saturday morning and drove down to Nottingham. They drove away and left Scotland behind again! I had my Dad's old car which he had given me when he got his new one and I followed them back down. When we got to my new flat they nearly killed me; the flat was on the fourth floor and I hadn't told them that bit so they went mental! But everyone who helped me get back was brilliant and my sisters came through for me again; they got together with Mum and gave me just short of £1,000 to help me move in. We had a chinese that night and a few beers and that was it. Mind you I was awfully house proud in my new 'luxury penthouse' and I spent the rest of the evening panicking that one of the boys would spill something on my new carpet! It didn't really matter of course, because I was back!

Without Sophie's phone call I have no idea what would have happened to me or if I would have ever stopped the downward spiral I was on. I would have been a shambling alcoholic somewhere on the streets and at some point the drink would have killed me.

I had visions of being back down in Nottingham within two months but it took me a year. In that year Sophie got herself sorted out anyway; she lived with Karen's parent for a while and then she went to Basel and saw the place and eventually moved out there. She is now working in a nursery and has settled in very well. We still speak regularly on the phone and she sounds as if she is having a good time and she is a beautiful girl. I'm very proud of her and she will always be my girl. When she was born it was a such happy time for me and the experience in the birthing pool will stay with me forever. She was a lovely, peaceful baby and hardly ever cried. As she got older it was always me that she called for in the night if she was scared or couldn't sleep and I would hear her feet padding across the landing as she came to our room. I had a really strong bond with Sophie and I missed her terribly when I was working at Chesterfield. I think that was one of the reasons that I didn't really enjoy my time there, even though I worked very hard. It became really hard when I did get some time with Sophie and had to pick her up from Karen's house. Karen had moved a bloke in by then and the wounds were still raw. There was one stupid episode when I went to pick Kyle and Sophie up to go up to Scotland for the New Year. When I got there Karen decided that they weren't going.

I would drive back to Chesterfield from Leicester after dropping the kids off and I would be in tears and this went on for weeks and weeks. I would drive away from Karen's house and I can still remember looking in the rear-view mirror and seeing the kids bawling their hearts out. That was really tough. All of that got taken away – the chance to be a proper Dad to them. I also lost the chance to be there for Kyle when he was playing football at the Notts County Academy. I am not sure he always wanted me watching him play, but I made sure that I treated all the kids the same. There was no special treatment for Kyle, but when I wasn't there I couldn't look out for him and I think he suffered a bit because of that and he was eventually released. I wanted so much to be there for him but I wasn't allowed to be and it was at a time when he could have really done with some support. But once I was back in Nottingham I found out that Kyle wanted to come back from Switzerland. So I originally wanted to come back for Sophie, but by the time I got back it was Kyle that I helped out and he came to live with me. He has been a great help and although we argue occasionally I love him to bits.

Kyle hasn't had a great life; he's been shipped all over the place as the family has been on the move between England, Belgium, Denmark, Germany and Switzerland, so I'm pleased that I can offer him a bit of stability and he's been with me for about 2½ years. He has been a real help, helping me get about whilst I am waiting for my knee to get sorted.

13

THE ENDLESS LOVE AFFAIR WITH LEICESTER

By the time I moved back to Nottingham I had got control of the drinking and I could go for days or weeks without having or needing a drink. Now I wasn't drinking to forget things or help me get to sleep, I was drinking on social occasions when I was with friends and family. The drink was no longer a dependant thing!

Part of my rehabilitation and a return to normality has been a chance to revisit old places around Leicester and the biggest element of that has been Leicester City – The Walkers Stadium (now The King Power Stadium). Of course this is the first time Kyle has experienced all of this and he goes everywhere with me. That might mean a question and answer session with the fans some evenings. I like that as it gives him a chance to hear about my playing career and experience some of the good days through the fans comments and questions. Bear in mind that he was born in the same year that I retired, so he knew nothing of me as a professional footballer until I moved back to Nottingham and started to revisit the football places and people that I knew thirty years before. It has been a real insight for him. He is daft about Liverpool but he is proud to wear his Leicester City tracksuit when he attends coaching sessions and he loves watching matches at Leicester City; he helps me get around when I am commentating on BBC Radio Leicester and when a goal goes in I can hear him shouting behind me and jumping in the air. This is great for me because I have hardly ever been to football matches with my lads.

Funnily enough my journey back to Leicester started at Bobby Smith's funeral when Steve Walsh and I were sitting in the back pews comparing knee injuries and scars from surgery. At the wake we got chatting about his radio work with Radio Leicester and he asked what I was up to. So I told him I was thinking about moving back to England and I promised to give him a call when I did and so the plan was that I would get in touch when I got settled again in The Midlands. Before that happened I was asked by the lads from *The Fox* (The Leicester City Fanzine) to do an interview with them which I did in June 2010. When they found out that I was basically unemployed and available for work they made a few phone calls and one of the guys that they contacted was Geoff Peters, who now works for Talk Sport Radio – he was someone I worked with previously. He put me on to Radio Leicester and I was invited to summarise at a Leicester match early on in the 2010/11 season. They quite liked what I did and I got invited back for another match and another and then I was asked to sign up for the remainder of the season with the help of Dean Eldredge at Soar Media.

Apparently the listener figures have increased since I started to cover the matches, so I must be doing something right and the great thing is that I love doing it. I am also helped by the fact that I have a very distinctive accent and so folk immediately recognise me and remember me. There are a number of people that have helped me along the way including: Justin Bourne; Ian Stringer; Martin Ballard; Charles Dagnall; and John Sinclair; all from radio Leicester. It is great to work with these guys and they have all been very supportive and kind. I have built up a rapport with Ian Stringer (the main match commentator) and we have a good routine going now on match days; I know what time to go and sit at the microphone, I know which are the good grounds and bad grounds for commentary positions (Burnely, by the way, is a nightmare. You need to be a mountaineer to reach your position there!) and generally the new grounds are superb for the media and they have been a pleasure to work in. It is so refreshing to see so many good stadia and facilities since I retired from playing and even smaller clubs like Doncaster have a stadium to be proud of.

It's not always easy to sit behind the microphone though. Take Leicester's match at Ipswich as an example. This was played in December in a blizzard from start to finish and I was having to summarise on the biggest load of nonsense that was going on in front of me. It was a farce, but the Sky television cameras were there and that must have influenced the referee as did Roy Keane (the Ipswich manager at the time) but that match should never have been played. If the match had been tied at 0–0 at half time then it would have been easy for the referee to call it off but once Ipswich went 3–0 up then there was no way that the game was going to be abandoned. There was also no consideration given to the spectators who had to get home after the game; the longer the game went on, the worse the roads were getting and the journey back to Leicester was frightening.

I try and bring a touch of optimism to the occasion and I am a born optimistic. If a situation seems hopeless for Leicester I will be the one reminding everyone that one goal can change a game completely and try and focus on the positives. I am also very honest and I won't hold back from criticising individual players. There was a young left-back called Patrick van Arnholt on loan from Chelsea in 2011 and he had bags of talent, but he was prone to mistakes. Leicester were 2–0 up at home in this particular game with Barnsley and he went on a forward run. He beat the opposing right-back and set himself up for a cross but then decided to try and nutmeg another player and lost the ball. The play moved very quickly to the other end and Barnsley scored to bring the score to 2–1. I said at the time that if I was his manager he would get such a bollocking for being so stupid and letting his team down like that. From cruising at 2–0 Leicester were suddenly at 2–1 and the shape of the game had changed. He wouldn't have done that if the score had been 0–0, so why do it when you are winning comfortably? That could have cost the game just because of a bit of piss taking and I hate that.

The flip side of that is when we win with a late goal; and Martyn Waghorn did just that when Leicester beat Bristol City in the same season. Martyn smashed the ball into the roof of the net in the 4th minute of stoppage time to win the game and I went mad because I know what that feels like. I scored in the last minute when I played for Leicester against Notts County and it was a brilliant feeling because you know you have won the game then – it's all over! I still have a photo of me lying on the floor with Pedro Richards standing over me saying, you spawny bastard! I still have the mindset of the professional footballer and I will describe the state of the match as if I was still playing. If Leicester are 2–1 down and it is late in the game I will not be doom and gloom, I will be saying, 'Come on, we can still get something from this.' My overall aim is to bring the game into the house or workplace or car, wherever folk are listening in. The only problem I have is that I have to try and be controlled and calm when Leicester score and let Ian Stringer be the one that goes mad so that he can use his commentary for a 'clip' on future programmes. I have to sit back and the voice of reason and analyse what just happened; that is very difficult for me because I still care passionately about the team. I would like to think that I have helped him understand the game better and he is certainly better and more knowledgeable than when I started working with him. Conversely, I have learned a lot about live broadcasting and the technicalities of outside broadcasting (e.g. which button to press on my microphone if I'm going to sneeze on air!). I have also learned that there are certain things you cannot say on the radio. Last season during one match we reached half-time and Leicester hadn't been very impressive and Ian asked me, 'So what will the manager be saying in the dressing right now Alan?'

'Well Ian, he will be giving out the biggest bollocking to that players and quite right too,' I said.

Charles Dagnall stepped in (from the studio) and said, 'That was rollocking that Alan said there listeners … er … yes … rollocking) and when we went off air.

I turned to Ian and said, 'What? What's wrong?' I was convinced I had said 'rollocking' but Ian was telling me it was 'bollocking' and then Geoff Peters walked along from his seat and told me that he heard it and it was definitely 'bollocking'. Fortunately it didn't cost me my job and they saw the funny side!

I think the key to being a decent summariser is firstly, having the right words. You have to be able to speak and say what you mean and have the words to get your message across. Secondly you have to understand the game and have some football intelligence and I have been helped by having done my

UEFA 'A' coaching qualification which helps me to understand the tactical side of the game. Thirdly, don't over-complicate things, just try and paint a picture for listeners and keep it simple.

I love Jeff Stelling and what he does with Sky Soccer Saturday, he is a great example of how to do it right. I would love to do that programme and if you fuck Phil Thompson off and give me his chair then I will make the viewers laugh alright. Gary Newbon is another example of a man doing his job very well, no matter what the sport. On the other hand when it is done badly it can be painful to watch and Iain Dowie is a living example of that. Terrible! Chris Coleman is another one that sends me to sleep and whenever Sam Allardyce tries to use words with more than four letters in them then he is in trouble. You can have highly knowledgeable individuals who just sound wrong on television or radio and David Pleat is in this category; I think it's his voice, it just grates with me. I remember a strange incident concerning David Pleat when I enquired about the youth team coach's job at Leicester. I phoned up and spoke to him and he asked for me to apply in writing and I did that and followed it up with a phone call to let him know that I was applying and to let him know how keen I was. He then let me know that he wasn't surprised that I had phoned back and that I was the only one that had. He also said that there were a lot of applicants but he would look at my letter the next day. So I phoned him back the next day (the third time now) and I really emphasised how badly I wanted the job. So he told me to meet him at Houghton-on-the-Hill (in east Leicestershire) where there was a youth team match going on the following evening. So I drove over and there he was with Gordon Lee and it is really strange what happened, or more to the point, what didn't happen! They could see me so they knew I was there and I thought I would leave it until half-time and maybe then they would come over – but they didn't. And at full time they got in their car and left without saying a word to me. To this day I don't know why, but needless to say I didn't get the job. Maybe I should have phoned up again, but I suppose actions speak louder than words.

I actually believe that I am good on the radio, but I don't know what to do to get on and move to a higher level. My hope is that I will still be on Radio Leicester if they achieve promotion to the Premier League and I can summarise at Anfield and Old Trafford and so on. If not then I would want to move on to better things, but that would mean being totally impartial and leaving aside my passion for Leicester City and I'm not sure I could do that very easily. Would I be as good if I had to be impartial? On the other hand, I love watching football, any football. I will stop to watch an under-10s match if I see one, and I can bring a knowledge and insight to listeners with my experience as a player and as a qualified coach. I am not interested in statistics and signing on dates and fees and so on, what I can do is help folk understand what is happening in the match. I suppose I am not a football supporter but I am a supporter of football.

My dream job would be summarising at the World Cup when Scotland win the final. I don't think I would keep my job more than ten minutes of that game; I wouldn't be able to contain myself! The truth is that I don't know where this will lead, but I do know how much fun I'm having and I love the buzz of match days again. Even the regulars on the row in front of my commentary position, who bring me cakes and chocolate and always have a chat, are part of my match-day experience.

Because of my work with Radio Leicester I have become more well known around Leicestershire (and beyond) and I get asked to attend presentation ceremonies or prize-giving days at various schools and organisations and one of the first such occasions after I moved back to the area came when I was asked to hand out the prizes at Ashmere School.

I felt so proud to be there and be part of the presentation day. There were a lot of photographs taken that night and John Sinclair's wife, Kim, took some great shots and I stuck them up on my Facebook page and the response was great. As a result I was asked to do more of the same for other organisations. It's just giving out a few medals and stuff but it means something to them and I take pride in the fact that I have been asked. Even though they hardly know me, it doesn't stop them giving me a lovely ovation and making me feel incredibly welcome. All of this has helped me to feel part of the community in this part of the Midlands again. I get a buzz from working with kids and I always have, especially less-privileged kids and I remember when I finished working at Leeds United I had the chance to work at a place called Henshaws. This is a college for kids with all manner of conditions and challenges, but I used to be (and still am) in awe of the courage and attitude of some of these kids. I never got over the way one young boy lived his life in a wheelchair when he was blind, deaf and couldn't speak. How does he communicate? How does he tell his carers what he wants for his lunch or anything else that he needs? But he did and it was amazing; they used a system called Makaton. Makaton uses speech as well as gesture, facial expression, eye contact and body language. It is a language programme which is based on a selected list of everyday words, such as *Daddy*, *Door*, *Fall* and *In*. The amazing thing is that kids of three or four years old are able to learn this language even though they are (for example) deaf and blind. I had such admiration for the people that taught this system to young kids, they were so skilled and patient.

There was one kid at the centre called Nick who was autistic and blind since birth, and one of the biggest things I have ever achieved in my life was to get Nick to jump into a swimming pool. It took me weeks and weeks; he always walked in down the ramp and I was working for ages to try and get him to tuck his knees in and jump into the water to make a huge splash. But he did it eventually and I was so proud of him. Nick also had an extraordinary talent that I have never witnessed in anyone else. He had a 'perfect musical ear' and he could sit and listen to any music (Elvis, Rachmaninov, Elton John, anything …) and he would then go and sit at a piano and play it note perfect. Astonishing!

But you know it's funny, wherever you go there is always someone who wants to bring you down. I nearly lost my job at Henshaws because a girl reported me when I took two lads swimming and you were only supposed to go swimming with one-on-one supervision. Now I knew that the manager of the swimming facility was present at the pool and he had seen me and said it was ok to take both lads in. So when we finished one of them was alright to make his own way back to the dining hall for tea at 5 o'clock and the other one was on tea duties and had to get back to the house, so I took him back. This girl (Sarah was her name) saw me with the two lads and assumed that I had been swimming with the two of them and she went and reported me. This meant that I had to explain to myself and I was really pissed off because this was outside my working hours which finished at 4 o'clock anyway. But I wanted so much to help these guys that I was always willing to put in the extra hours, either before or after my shift, and I knew how much they enjoyed it. There was another incident that got to me that didn't have to be turned into an incident. Without even trying I was in trouble again. Now, every kid when they in their teens has a nickname, don't they? Well these guys were no different and I gave a lad called Chris Gold the nickname of 'Goldilocks' which he loved and so did all the other boys. But one lad named John Cornes came to me a bit upset because he still didn't have a nickname and Chris did. So I told him not to worry and that I hadn't thought of a nickname for him yet. So whilst I am having fun with the kids doing all this stuff, someone objected again and I found myself in front of the principal. Now I knew that worse things were going on at the college than me giving the guys nicknames but I was so annoyed by the fact that I was on my second 'strike' (three and I was out) that I gave him my resignation and walked away.

14

TEAMMATES

My days at Oldham were a wee bit different to the rest of my career because I went through that phase of maturing and making that transition into the first team – growing up if you like. When I did make the step up and was allowed into the first team dressing room it was Les Chapman and Alan Groves who I spent the most time with. They became my best friends at the club; they were flamboyant characters, full of laughter and great fun to be around. Les was twenty-eight and I thought that was bloody ancient! They were great to me; always picking me up and giving me lifts home and we would always be out in a nightclub together after an away game. Funnily enough Alan didn't drink so he was always driving. I remember being absolutely stunned when I heard that he had died. I had been out with Alan for the evening and the next morning I got a phone call from my (then) mother-in-law and she told me that Alan had died. I said 'Alan? Alan who?'

'Alan Groves.'

'Don't be daft, I was out with him last night, you must have the wrong name.'

But it was true and he had died in the night from a massive heart attack. Doc Hollis, the Oldham club doctor said that his heart had literally exploded. That scared me because he was twenty-nine years of age. There was a stage, when I was about forty, that about three or four players died. This unsettled me and made me think about my own mortality.

But 'Gus' was having a bad time as well then with the authorities because he was dating a fifteen year old girl called Debbie. People were after him for trying to get her out of school and the press were hammering him as well. None of this was helping his stress levels. After Alan's death it was Les Chapman that married Debbie and had a couple of baby girls. Les is now kit man at Manchester City.

I think because I was so young when I joined the whole squad seemed very old and experienced; I am thinking of players like Maurice Whittle, Dick Mulvaney, Paul Edwards and Ian Wood, and, of course, 'big' Andy Lochhead. Not only did they seem old but they were all big and strong; they were massive men to a young lad like me. My time at Oldham gives me a lot of happy memories and it was a great club to start my professional career, even though the ground was shite, the training facilities were shite and the equipment was shite. Oh, and you had to wash your own training kit. We would put the kit in the drying room overnight to dry and the next morning it would be stiff as a board; you could hold one of your socks by the toe and it would stay upright on its own! We didn't worry too much I suppose, and I didn't realise until I arrived at Leicester how different it could be in terms of facilities and the way players were looked after. The other big difference was the age of the players; they were nearly all the same age as me. I found out later that the Gaffer wanted young, fit hungry men. He liked you to be early to mid-twenties, married, and settled with a couple of kids. He liked all that. My big pal at Leicester City was, of course, Martin Henderson. We had grown-up together as kids. It was Martin who made that first phone call after the F.A. Cup tie and the hat-trick and told me that the Gaffer fancied me and maybe I should give him a ring. He went on to explain that the Gaffer couldn't ring me because that was illegal, but he knew that my contract was up at the end of the season. Anyway, Jock did ring me eventually and the conversation was a bit strange: 'Dinnae tell a soul about this, nobody knows I am calling ye and we need to keep it that way. But I want ye, get yersel' doon here. When's yer contract up?'

'In June.'

'Have they offered you another one?'

'Aye, for another year.'

'Fer fuck's sake! Get doon here.'

'But I'm still – '

'Don't worry aboot that. Freedom of contract is coming so don't worry aboot it. We will take care of everything; just get yersel' doon tae Leicester.'

And that was it. It was a particularly close group of players at Leicester and that was Me, Eddie Kelly, Martin Henderson and Bobby Smith. Trying to get in and join us was Ian Wilson and Paddy Byrne; occasionally we would let them in … and then sometimes we wouldn't.

Then there was Larry May and John O'Neill. Now 'Jonjo' could hand out a bollocking. He seemed a very quiet lad most of the time and he was a very good footballer. I liken him to Jamie Carragher; he wasn't quick but he read the game well and he never got caught, and he was hard as nails. I was very wary of John because he didn't take prisoners, even in training, and many's the time (in that lovely soft Irish accent) that he told me to feck off, or he would call me a big soft Scottish twat!

The Gaffer loved him; he had a lot of time for John. However, I have one thing to say about 'Jonjo': It was his fault that I got knocked out cold when we played the famous game against Shrewsbury Town. He misread the through ball and he flicked it on back towards me and it wasn't firm enough so I had to collect it and if I didn't get it then McNally was in on goal. Being the big, brave bastard that I am, I got you out of jail. He owes me one and I think he should send me one of those lovely bottles of wine that he deals in these days.

Larry didn't like his nickname; he was called 'Dage', which was short for Dago! I think Wallington gave him that nickname. Big Larry was good enough to play for England; he could jump really high, he was great in the air and he was tough when it was needed too. He was decent on the ball as well and scored a few goals. But I would get really annoyed when he was always told to attack the key areas at set-pieces. They would try and pick him out, and I would be thinking, 'I can do that! Why won't Jock let me attack those balls into the box?' I remember Larry was invited to play in Cyrille Regis's testimonial match and it was Cyrille that wanted a black XI versus a white XI and Larry was invited to play for the black XI and he refused. He said he wasn't black. He would be out getting a tan when we went away together to somewhere hot.

Tommy Williams was another one that was quiet but could be hard when it was called for. And occasionally he would surprise everyone and have you laughing in the dressing room when he ripped the piss out of someone. His nickname was 'Biled Ham', which is a Scottish version of 'Tam'. Likewise Mark Goodwin. 'Goody' was a journeyman, a fetch-and-carry player and he was always tracking up and down between the penalty areas and could be invaluable in certain teams and

I don't think he got the credit he deserved for the work he put in. I was at Notts County with 'Goody' as well and he did exactly the same job there.

I must say I was sorry to see wee Dennis Rofe leave so soon. He went to Chelsea before the end of the promotion season and I'm not sure why. I loved 'Sid'. He was a great club captain; he had bags of experience and a superb demeanour about him. He was tough and he had legs like a snooker table. I loved that cockney accent of his and the first thing he would say at training every morning was 'Awroight big boy?' He was good for morale was Dennis.

So was Eddie Kelly (nickname 'Ned' or 'Ted'). He was the funniest of the lot and he could find a joke in any situation. It really annoyed me when he laughed on the pitch because that was a serious time and place for me; I didn't see anything funny during a match. I would grab him and ask him 'What the fuck is so funny Ted?' but he didn't care and he would carry on chatting to opponents or referees as if he didn't have a care in the world. But he was very influential on and off the pitch and a natural leader; he would lead us from pub to pub and club to club! I remember being amazed when he left the club just after we had won promotion in 1980. The thing is, he was twenty-nine and looking for a few quid in the bank and maybe he thought that last move would do it for him, so he signed for Notts County and I don't blame him for that. I can only assume that the deal he was offered at Notts County was better than anything he had been offered at Leicester. What I do know is that we missed him. At the training ground, in the dressing room and, especially, on the pitch. We missed that steadying influence and that valuable experience. He would shite on for the entire match and he was always demanding the ball. However, he accepted responsibility as well as reading the game, setting things up and slowing things down when it was needed. He had it all and he could have played for Barcelona with that kind of vision. His absence was one of the reasons we missed out and got relegated.

Andy Peake was one of 'Jock's babes' as they were known. He was bold and brash as a youngster and his nickname was 'Nelson' (Piquet). He was very composed, elegant and upright on the pitch when he ran. If a tackle was needed then he wasn't shy – he could be an assassin! He really liked a tackle did Andy. He was a nice boy and when my younger sister (Karen) came to Leicester to see us play one time, she absolutely fell in love with him. Whenever I see her she will always say, 'The one regret of my life is that I didn't marry Andy Peake'. I'm not sure Andy knew about this! Andy had an incredible shot on him as well, but I don't recall him ever practicing his distance shooting at all. He was encouraged to take free kicks, but he didn't always get a chance because Eddie and Bobby Smith were always fighting for the ball at free kicks.

Now 'Nizzie' (Bobby Smith) had enough dead-ball opportunities as the club's penalty taker (we called him Nizzie because his middle name was Nesbit). If they had let me take the penalties I would have had about 30 goals in that promotion season. Nizzie and I had a bet of thirty quid on who would be top goalscorer that season (a tidy sum back then) but it didn't affect your game, and I carried on being selfless in front of goal. Now Bobby was also a ladies' man and I don't think Dot (his wife) will mind me saying that. He was always the little laughing cavalier with his dark, curly hair and he had a great sense of humour. It was a very sad day when he left us.

Other lads like Stevie Lynex were very quiet, but absolutely great to play with. He was nicknamed Charlie Chan because he had an oriental look about him. He was so direct and you knew when the ball was coming in. As a centre forward playing with your back to goal, you might get the ball from Tommy Williams coming up from full-back. You'd get hold of it around about the 18-yard line and then were looking for a midfield player. Stevie was very good at running the full back away and then checking back; I would take a touch and give it to him, he would have a touch and he knew then that you had to get a position in the box and he was very good at keeping the ball long enough for you to get into position. He would just keep the ball moving slowly towards the full-back and keep him on the back foot, take a touch, then another, and another, all the time moving to the byline. Then he would release it and whip a cross in for me to attack the ball.

Mark Wallington ('Duke') was a real joker and a good captain. He didn't have to be forceful but he said things when they needed to be said, and he would occasionally try and inject a bit of humour into a situation. We might be defending a corner and he wouldn't scream at the full-back to get on a post, he might say 'Er, young Mr Williams, would you mind getting on your post please'. 'Duke' was alright; he liked a fag and the occasional treble vodka. I believe he is teaching up in Lincolnshire now and I heard someone say recently that he was generous and hospitable – well that's a turn up because he was a miserable bastard with his money when I played alongside him! Never first to the bar was 'Duke'.

Kevin MacDonald used to hate the nickname bestwoed upon him, 'Neck', because he had the longest neck in the world. He really hated it. We would be training or in the dressing room and all you had to say was 'Neck!' and he would be like, 'Fuck off wull ye'. He was very serious was Kevin and not the most social of players and I am sure he had a personality bypass operation before he came down from Inverness! He was a tough player though and very versatile, he even played centre-back a few times as I recall. Midfield was where he was at his best though and he could be very effective there. You would always rather have him in the team than play against him; he could pass a ball very well. Even though he wasn't the quickest of lads, he was a bit like Mark Draper in that he was good with the ball at his feet. In fact, he could run quicker with the ball at his feet than without it. He maybe should have scored a few more goals but he was good enough for Liverpool to come and buy him.

Now I have to mention Gary Lineker, 'Link'. We built up a very good relationship during our time together at Leicester. He was fresh into the game but the first thing you noticed about Gary was that he was quick. We knew that we had to get the ball up to the frontman, get hold of it, bring a midfield man into play and get Gary through on his way. Jock used to say 'Up, back and through' and he was good at keeping it simple like that. I know that I helped the early part of Gary's career; I looked after him and I took pressure off him and I took the hits because Gary couldn't play with his back to goal, he needed to be running on to the ball and using his pace. So if I was getting battered I didn't mind as long as we got a goal at the end of it. I know I was very good for Gary Lineker's career even though it wasn't always obvious to us that he was a star in the making. In fact, I even had some doubts if I'm honest because, occasionally, he would miss some chances that I thought he should have buried. I remember in the F.A. Cup semi-final against Tottenham and Gary was in on goal about three times. The first chance came when the ball was played up to me and I turned and all I could hear was Eddie Kelly screaming, 'Stick him in, stick him in!' and so I bent a ball inside the full-back (Chris

Hughton I think) and Link was in but he hit it straight at Ray Clemence's chest. Soon after he was in on goal again but he was brought down and it was a free kick. Today, of course, it would be a straight red. At the time I remember thinking, for fucks sake, put one in will you. If one of those had gone in then it would have been a very different game and maybe a very different outcome. Gary would miss a few back then and a lot of it was down to naivety and decision making and just the inexperience of youth. To be brutally honest, I resented him being in the side to begin with because he had replaced my best mate, Martin Henderson.

Martin would be left out for Gary; remember I had been playing alongside Martin (on and off) since we were about five or six years old. We knew each other's game so well. I remember a goal at Leeds United away when the ball was played into Martin and he dummied it and it came through to me and I knew he was going to that, I just knew he was going to dummy it before he received the pass. So, he spun off the defender, I played it behind the defender and he was on it – bang! Goal! We won 2–1 and that was the winner. We actually laughed about how well it had worked and we both knew that the goal was made in Kirkcaldy! Three points, thank you very much, back down the M1, fuck off Leeds! Martin was better than he looked; he was quick over 20-30m and he was incredibly big and strong, but he didn't have the natural football intelligence that some players have and maybe that stopped him going further and playing more games in the top flight. Technically he was excellent – he could ping a ball 50 yards and land it on a sixpence. He could do things in training that would have us in awe, but he couldn't take it on to the pitch in a match and I'm not sure why. Maybe it was a confidence thing because he was in and out the side at times.

Pat Byrne gave us all problems because we couldn't understand a bloody word he said. He loved the ball at his feet and he loved to dribble, but he wouldn't get his head up and that used to drive me insane. I would get furious with him, but you had to be careful with Pat because he could be a feisty one. I remember the time when he took on Eddie May, the youth team coach, who was a big bear of a guy and it was over nothing more than a bit of criticism during training. Pat reared up and was in Eddie's face saying, 'What did you fuckin' say? Eh? What did you fuckin say?' Pat was in there swinging punches and he caught Eddie a beauty and then we are all in there trying to pull them apart. But Pat could be a clever player and he could surprise you as well; the goal he scored at Anfield in the famous 2–1 win was a good example. The ball was played into the far post and I got up and got my arm across Ray Clemence, probably fouled him in fact, and got the knock down for Pat who side-footed it in and as the ball hit the net he turned away from goal and I could hear him laughing his head off. Extraordinary reaction for a player who has just scored in front of The Kop.

On a trip to Spain once he got hammered and passed out on his bed so we sneaked in and Mark Wallington shaved half of his moustache off. It was a good while before he found out the next day and he went mental because his missus (Mary) apparently really liked his moustache; he had to shave the rest off.

I recall a trip to Torremolinos which we had during a bad spell of weather in January and Jock took us all over there and told us he didn't want to see us for three days. He said we could do what we liked. We didn't need telling twice! We never left our rooms for three days; mine and Martin's room was the lounge, Eddie and Bobby's was the bar and Pat and Ian Wilson's was the toilet. We were playing drinking games along with fitness challenges and if anyone tried to sneak off for a sleep we would find them and drag them back. Occasionally we would get one of the young lads and send them out for another crate of San Miguel beers and chips! Inevitably we would also have a 'who can pull the ugliest bird competition'. There were nine of us taking part in that one, a tenner each in the hat. Some of the lads like Larry and 'Jonjo' and 'Duke' wouldn't do something like that, but there were still nine of us that would. And Bobby Smith won it – he pulled a blancmange! She must have been about 4ft high in her high heels and she looked like the Michelin man. She came down the stairs the next morning and we were all sat in reception a bit hungover and then gradually it dawned on us. We all looked at each other and started to snigger. He didn't take her to bed or anything, but he did have a few dances with her and that was enough to win Bobby the money. That type of team spirit does go out on to the pitch with you. We would stick together and look out for each other during matches and personally, I hated to see a teammate get hurt. The tackle that Tony Galvin made on Tommy Williams when he broke his leg in the F.A. Cup semi-final was a coward's tackle, a shocking thing to do. He had tried to take me out at a corner earlier in the game and he landed on top of me as we both fell and he hit me with his elbow, right in my chest. If you watch the footage of the game then you will see that I take ages to recover. Galvin was a bastard like that.

I suppose I never really bothered whether my teammates liked me or not but now, I know that they did because if I ever see any of them it is never just a handshake, it's a big man-hug and a real 'great to see you' hug and we still have that bond that we had when we played together. I'll give you another example; during the famous game against Shrewsbury, before the incident where I was knocked unconscious, just after I first went in goal I went for a high ball and thought I had lost it, but I recovered and grabbed it and then Chic Bates (who had done Mark Wallington) tried to 'do' me. Well, lads like Tommy Williams, Larry May, John O'Neill, who wouldn't normally lose it on the pitch, they had him by the throat in the back of the net in front of The Kop. I was watching this thinking that normally I would be in there as well, kicking shit out of Bates, but now I had the green jersey on and so I just kept out of it and held on to the ball! At the time I didn't really think about it because the game was going on, but later on I was really chuffed that they looked out for me.

We would look out for the young lads coming in as well: Derek Strickland, little David Buchanan, 'Buck', and Paul Friar, 'Tuck',who once squared up to Big Joe Jordan during a game at Filbert Street against Man United. Tuck went in with a pretty strong tackle in front of the East Stand and sends Joe flying. So Joe got up and got hold of Tuck's shirt. He looked him straight in the eye and before he could say anything, Tuck said, 'What are you fucking looking at?' Brave lad! At that time Paul Friar was sharing the left-back spot with Norman Leet who was one of the worst players I ever played with. I think Jock put him in because he had a long throw-in, other than that he was an imposter.

Peter Welsh, 'Welshy', was a lad who had weight and fitness problems and never really established himself in the first team, but he was the best striker of a ball at the club in all the time I was there. He would also win any head tennis games that were going on in the gym at Belvoir Drive. I don't recall anybody ever beating him. We went to Watford once and Pete was playing and Jock was going round the dressing room reminding everyone of their duties and he got to Peter Welsh and he said, 'Now then Welshy, what are ye gonna do?'

Now poor Pete had a lisp and so we all fell about when he replied, 'I am going to mark Luther Blithett, Gaffer'.

A guy who arrived at Leicester at about the same time as me was Gregor Stevens from Glasgow Rangers. Now I am convinced that Gregor was a gnat's whisker from being a mass murderer. He was really frightening and he hardly said a word, but he would smash people on the pitch and then get up and walk away as if that was ok – that was his job! He was a decent player, don't get me wrong, but I remember the first time I played with him during the preseason tour to Sweden and there were opposition forwards that were genuinely frightened of him. They shirke challenges and let him have the ball. Jock got rid of him back to Scotland after a few weeks of the season because he realised that Gregor would be spending more time in the stands, suspended, than he would in the back-four.

During the promotion season of 1979/80 we had a very stable side and lots of players had 20+ appearances to their names and that consistency and familiarity helped to strengthen the bond between the players. I have to say that I never truly enjoyed my football as much after I left Leicester. The team spirit was never the same anywhere else that I went, and only the lads at Brighton even came close to having the same type of togetherness. I missed that team 'thing' so much and being around the lads. I missed Filbert Street and Belvoir Drive and nothing came close after I left.

I went to Sheffield United and at first it was ok, but after the honeymoon period was over I can honestly say that I never enjoyed my time there. I did ok I suppose; I scored on my debut, I scored a hat-trick against Boston United in the F.A. Cup, I played alongside a smashing centre forward called Keith Edwards and made a lot of friends. The best of these would have to be Tony Kenworthy and wherever you are Tony, get in touch. John McPhail was another great lad but we used to call him 'John 'McRail' because he got caught travelling from York to Sheffield on a forged rail pass! Kevin Arnott was a mate and so was Terry Curran, 'TC', who was probably the most frustrating player I have ever played with; he would lend you the ball occasionally, a bit like Martin O'Neill did when I was at Notts County. TC stayed with me at my little cottage '… just for a couple of nights Al, just until I can get my stuff moved up'. He stayed for two months and never paid me a penny in rent! I'm still waiting for that cheque in the post.

The best thing about my time at Sheffield was that I became good friends with Emlyn Hughes and we had some great times in the Rising Sun pub which was our local. Emlyn wanted to take me to Rotherham in a swap deal with Ronnie Moore, but there was no way I was going to go there. Although Sheffield is a lovely city with decent people and I enjoyed being in South Yorkshire it was the football club that made me unhappy.

The training schedules were awful. They were running for the sake of running and you ended up taking so much out that you had nothing left on match days. At Leicester City I came off the training ground wanting to do more, and Jock was a superb judge of that and he knew when enough was enough. At Sheffield United we were always bollocksed, even on a Friday when what you should be doing is light training, some ball work and maybe a five-a-side.

When I moved to Brighton, I loved Jimmy Melia and his girlfriend, Val, straightaway. They had not long come down from their F.A. Cup final appearance. That suited Jimmy because he was a flamboyant character, but a thoroughly nice guy. When Karen Towers and I met him in the Courtlands Hotel in Brighton we took to him immediately. During our discussions I asked Jimmy what he wanted me to do at Brighton and what my role would be. He said, 'I want you to play up front and look after Terry Connor, that's all. You looked after Lineker, now look after Connor'. And so I did. TC and I got on well, even though he could be a bit moody but he was a young lad in contrast to the rest of the squad at Brighton which contained a lot of experience. There was Joe Corrigan in goal who became a great friend and then you had some older lads like: Steve Foster; Steve Gatting; Tony Grealish; Jimmy Case; Danny Wilson; Gordon Smith; Chris Hutchins; Neil Smillie; and Gerry Ryan – seasoned internationals some of them. We all worked hard in training and it was there that Jimmy Case introduced me to a regime of 2–300 sit-ups after training every day with a plastic dry cleaning bag on. This would really make you sweat. Training was decent and we trained right next to the Goldstone Ground, unless we had to go indoors, in which case we would be at the university up the road.

They were good players and I had a good season there and if I hadn't got injured I would have had 25 to 30 goals; as it was I scored 13 in 26 appearances and that was a good return, but some persistent injury problems were starting and the worst one was my back which I did in a preseason game in Spain. The social side of the squad was superb and it was helped by the location. Brighton is a carefree place, a holiday resort and a place where people went to enjoy themselves, so whenever we all went out we would tap into this. I remember a guy called Marcus who always wore a cravat and always called me 'Dear boy …' That wasn't unusual in Brighton!

Steve Gatting was, of course, Mike Gatting's brother and possibly the slowest player I have ever played with; but he was good. He had a great left foot and he read the game very well.

Chris Hutchins was a good friend and I saw him the last time Ipswich played at Leicester and we laughed a lot and just picked up where we left off at Brighton.

I've talked about Jimmy Case elsewhere in this book and he a guy that you don't mess with and I am honoured to be able to say that he was a teammate.

Tony Grealish was a lovely fella and became a good friend but I couldn't say the same of Gordon Smith. Gordon was incredibly vain and he had to look immaculate all the time and although he spoke with a Scottish accent it was nothing like my Scottish accent! He was always destined for grander things and he eventually became President of the Scottish Football Association. I think he might be a football consultant at Rangers now.

Danny Wilson and Gerry Ryan were both quiet lads and both became good friends and so was Chris Ramsey who, I remember, had a load of bananas thrown at him when we played at West Ham and he did no more than pick one up and peel it and eat it, right in the middle of the game!

The social scene at Brighton was unique and there was a devil-may-care attitude when we all went out which was in stark contrast to Leicester. Although we had a lot of good times, there was always a line that we knew we shouldn't cross. At Brighton there wasn't, and this led to some amazing nights out. Apart from the injuries I really enjoyed my time there. I had some low points too though because I hadn't long been split up from Julie. In order to see the kids I would drive back up to Leicester once a fortnight, take them out somewhere and then after I'd dropped them home and drive all the way back again to Brighton. Every time I had to drop them off it would be a sad moment and that was tough. It was harder during the winter when the weather was bad because there isn't much you can do with two kids that are three years old and eighteen months old. There weren't the same options available that we have today. That took a lot out of me because they were my children and I had left them. I still wanted to do my best for them, but I had fallen in love with someone else.

My final few months at Brighton were spoilt when I fell out with Chris Cattlin, so I was pleased to get back up to Notts County. Larry Lloyd was the manager then and I agreed terms very quickly with Larry and the then chairman, Jack Dunnett. I stayed in the Westminster Hotel for a while with Karen and we then moved into a flat right on the river; we were on the seventh floor. When the wind blew you really knew about it! Martin O'Neill was a teammate back then and he was as intense then as he is now, but he had a wicked sense of humour and you had to be sharp to know whether or not he was winding you up. He had a bad knee injury that finished his career, which was a shame because he was great to have in your team. Even if you sometimes wondered when he was going to give you the ball. But he was a class player and there were a few others that were useful; Rachid Harkouk and Justin Fashanu ('Rash and Fash') to name but two. Charlie MacParland was a class act and we had Dave Watson and Steve Sims at the back, both very handy centre-halves, even though Steve only had half a knee and Watson (elementary my dear Watson)was also at the tail-end of his career. Funnily enough I used to love playing against Dave Watson and I think I scored every time we played against each other. Dave had a very domineering wife, which might surprise a few people!

We had Aki Laatenan and Tristan Benjamin 'Benji' at full backs, and David Hunt and Mark Goodwin, 'Goody', were in central midfield. Seamus McDonagh was in goals. It was a decent team and myself, Ian MacParland and Mick Leonard were probably what you would call, social secretaries.

My Notts County playing career didn't get off to the best start; I was injured in my first game at home to Middlesborough when Tony Mowbray clattered me and damaged my ankle in the process. I had an up-and-down season and I managed to score some goals in between being injured. I was also losing any pace that I had and we were going through managers as well, and so my time at Notts County became a job for me.

I have always admired the way that Martin O'Neill found a role for John Robertson when he was in management and that to me is being a true friend. I know that when he first took John on, he wasn't having the best time in his life and that is true friendship. So when I was in the midst of my darkest days in Scotland and the Youth Development job came up at Notts County I had hoped that my old friend, Ian MacParland, might help me out. I remember calling him and asking for a favour and letting me go for the job; I explained that I was out of work and he knew that it wasn't a gamble and he knew I could do that job with my eyes shut and I wouldn't let him down. Unfortunately he gave the job to his pal Mick Leonard at a time when I really needed a lift. That really chewed me up and it was on my mind for weeks and weeks afterwards. I felt so betrayed.

I think this is part of a wider trait in professional football whereby ex-players that are in management roles are afraid of losing their jobs and feel threatened particularly by people they know well. People who they know are capable of outdoing them. Mick Walker at Notts County was a great example of this; when he got the manager's job he went from, 'Good morning Alan' every day to being completely ignorant when he saw me. I remember going into see him when he first got the job and said, 'Mick, if there's anything I can do for you, anything at all to give you a hand, then just say the word.'

His reply was brief:, 'Yes Alan. I won't be needing your help.' I thought that a very poor reaction. He and Russell Slade became the managerial partnership at Notts County for a while, but it was never going to work because they didn't have the right-background or experience in professional football as players. Which meant that they weren't accepted easily in the dressing room. If things aren't going well then you need that link between the players and the manager; someone that knows professional footballers because they have been one. That is why Ian MacFarlane and Jock worked so well together; Ian would be able to sniff out a problem amongst the players (not that it happened very often at Leicester) and his background as a player meant that he was able to do that. Mick Walker missed a trick there because I hadn't long retired and I still knew most of the squad and I could have been that link for him.

15

THE
BAIRNS

I married Julie in 1977 in Oldham but I shouldn't have done. We were too young. Although, I got on really well with Marjorie and Gerrard (her Mum and step-father) it was never quite right. At Oldham I was just another player, but when I came to Leicester I was playing the best football of my career. I was a bit of a cult hero I suppose which meant that I was getting a lot more attention and I was in the spotlight a lot more. There was always something going on in Leicester and we had a great social circle; the Axe & Square in Countesthorpe became the centre of the universe for Leicester players. I didn't neglect my responsibilities at home but I did live life to the full. Now Julie was happy to be at home being a mother, but she never really got the social scene and didn't really want any part of it. After a while, if I was out having a good time, I really didn't want to go home and face Julie. This came to a head when we had lost a match at Arsenal. We got back to Leicester I called her and asked if she wanted to go out. She didn't of course, so I said that I was going out for a few pints with Peter Welsh and we ended up in a place called the Bali Hi and then off to Granny's with

Karen Towers in tow, and that was that. We started to see each other but we denied everything at first. However, by the time I left Leicester we were together. I remember going home and telling Julie that I had asked for a transfer and I told her that if a club made an offer for me then I going and leaving her and the kids. That must have been so hard for her and I know it was hard for the kids, especially Wesley. I've spoken to the kids about it and they don't really like to revisit that time and I've never really spoken to Julie about it, but at Jordan's wedding last year we were all there and everyone was fine. Julie did well out of the divorce, financially, and the boys are cool about it these days.

There is a unique thing about my four children; they were born in four different towns or cities and my eldest, Wesley, is left-handed and left-footed; Jordan is left-handed and right-footed; Kyle is right-handed and right-footed; and Sophie is left-footed and right-handed. So that's two right-and-rights, one left-and-right and one right-and-left. I think that's pretty unique!

I always used to joke about where all the kids were born; one in Oldham, one in Leicester, one in Rochdale and one in Nottingham. Then I would say that I wasn't sure about Brighton and Sheffield. Maybe one day a kid will come up to me and shout 'Daddy!'

Wesley Alan was born 12 July 1978 in Oldham on his Mum's twenty-first birthday, which was a lovely present for her. Being a good Protestant we all know what happens every year on July 12th! It's when all the pipes and whistles come out and the Orange Order raise their flags and go marching through the Catholic parts of Belfast and cause mayhem. He was also born a week before Louise Brown(the first test-tube baby) on the same ward. I remember going into see him before or after training because it was, literally, just across the road from where we used to train. He was in the birth canal a long time, so when he came out his head was misshapen and looked like one of those cartoon characters just after they have been hit on the head and the massive bump immediately pops up. I was quite worried for a while, but I was told to relax by the nurse and that it was quite normal. He was also jaundiced for a while and so he spent some time in an incubator with a little ultra-violet lamp inside to help the jaundice break down and clear from his bloodstream. It looked like he had his own sunbed! Despite the reassurances from the nurses, I was a first-time father and so I was panicking a bit. He was a lovely child, an easy baby. I loved him as a father always loves his first son. I can still remember phoning Scotland to let everybody know and I was absolutely bursting with pride. So we went home to our new house on Hayside and I was twenty-three years old and suddenly married with a son. I look back and think that it was only four years earlier that I was groping Fiona up the Grampian Gardens. By the way, Grampian Gardens is an address and not a part of Fiona's anatomy! It was scary believe me but I settled into fatherhood quickly and I have very clear memories of giving Wesley his bottle just before bedtime. Julie's parents, Marjorie and Gerrard, were terrific and very supportive during our time in Oldham. Gerrard was great company and very generous and we would often go out for a meal in places like Saddleworth and Delph. We had a favourite Italian restaurant called La Pergola and that was where we had the party after Wesley was christened. Gerry and I formed a sort of father-son relationship which I was missing having left my own Dad behind in Scotland. We would often just get together and go for a pint and I really enjoyed his company – a lovely guy. I think his relationship with Julie's

Mum didn't always run smoothly because I can remember him knocking on the door more than once and asking if he could stay the night! Gerry was still brilliant with me when Julie and I were breaking up, even when it had become clear that the marriage was over. We were in Leicester by this time and we had Jordan, but I remember meeting Gerry on a motorway and he said something that has stuck with me and it was good advice. He said, 'Alan, you have to think of yourself in a situation like this. You could go for years being the most miserable bastard on earth, we don't have long so be selfish and do what you need to do, just make sure you look after the kids'. For him to say that was a surprise; I expected him to want to punch my lights out. Very different to Karen Towers' Dad.

We moved to Leicester in 1979 and Jordan Lewis Blake was born 19 March 1980 in Leicester Royal Infirmary. That was a great time for me because we were having a great season and Jordan came along. I couldn't have been any happier.

He was a very long baby (about 22in I think) but he was also very poorly with Psoriasis (a skin condition) when he was a baby and he was in hospital when I made my return to the first team after my serious knee injury. After we played Southampton at home in the F.A. Cup I wanted to get away to see Jordan across the road at the Royal Infirmary, but I fell out with one or two journalists in the process and I know I shoved one of them. All they wanted to talk about was my 2 goals and I kept saying, 'Fuck that! My son's in hospital' So we fell out. I remember when I got there that night he was covered in coal tar and wrapped up in bandages. It was very upsetting because he was lying there, crying, and we couldn't pick him up to comfort him. He grew up to be a feisty little bugger and real devil-may-care attitude.

He had the cheekiest little face and I loved him to bits as well. He would do some daft things at times and I can still remember the time he wanted to be Superman. So he jumped out of the bedroom window and landed in the gateway between the back of the house and the garage. If the gate had been closed then Christ knows what would have happened; it was open thankfully, so he landed on the garden hose, which cushioned his fall. Normally I was tidy and would have rolled the hose up and put it away, but for some reason I didn't that day. It's just as well because it was better to land on the hose than on the concrete. He went to hospital and his only injury from the fall was a broken arm.

Jordan always had a funny way of walking and his son, Finlay, has the same walk. For a while we considered having his leg corrected but it didn't come to that in the end. When I moved to Nottingham and bought Edward Road it coincided with Jordan having a few problems at school; he was caught smoking and one or two other things when he was about fourteen. We had a few heart-to-heart sessions at the kitchen table and sorted it out in Nottingham. Jordan and Wesley were coming down to see us now that we were settled again and that was the first time all of the kids got to know each other. They got on really well and it has remained like that. There is a very strong bond between the four of them.

Jordan pulled off one of the best stunts I have ever seen when I managed to get tickets for him and Wesley to attend the P.F.A. Awards do in London. Now, we had a good table because Notts County had just won the division with a record points tally, and so Jordan had his chair back-to-back with Dennis Bergkamp. We were pretty sure that Bergkamp would win the Player of the Year, so I told Jordan to listen out and when they announced his name to stand up (because the cameras and the lights would all be on Bergkamp at that moment) and shake his hand quickly before he realised who he was. Well that is exactly what happened and there it was on the big screen and on the television coverage; Jordan got up and said, 'Well done Dennis' and shook his hand before he walked up to collect the award. Jordan was playing the footage in his pub for ages. Brilliant!

Later on he bumped into Dion Dublin in the gents and he came back to the table and said, 'Dad, he's huge!' Afterwards we all went back to the hotel. We were sitting around chatting and I remember Jordan was sitting on his own with his head down looking a bit tired. Then in walked John Mountney, the Notts County Director, who I had a lot of time for, and he said, 'Good evening boys, who is going to have a drink with me?' So a few of us said yes and he looked at Jordan and said, 'Jordan, will you have a drink?'

Jordan looked up and looked at Mr Mountney and then looked at me and said, 'Do you know what? This has been the best fucking night of my life. I'm going to bed Mr Mountney.'

It was tough for me and for Wesley and Jordan once Julie and I separated. I was a weekend Dad at that point and it felt as if I spent forever going to and from Leicester to Sheffield, Brighton or Nottingham. I would drive down and pick them up after the match finished on a Saturday and spend the rest of the weekend with them, but dropping them back home afterwards on a Sunday was traumatic at times; there were always tears. It used to break my heart some days and more so when we started to lose touch for a while. I think I was in Nottingham at the time and it was only when they were in their teens that we started to build a good relationship again. By this time Kyle and Sophie were on the scene and Jordan and Wesley were fabulous 'big brothers' to those two.

Kyle Alexander Kilby was born on 29 May 1987 whilst we were still in Rochdale and my playing career was coming to an end. Karen had a nightmare delivering Kyle; she was in labour for about twenty-four hours and I was writing down the timings between contractions. She was in a lot of pain and screaming in agony at one point, so I went to find someone to help but there was nobody to be seen at the nurses' station. I eventually found them all having a cup of tea in some side room and I went mental at them: 'My wife is in agony down the end of that corridor and you're sat having a cup of tea. Get down there and help her now!' And they did! They gave her an injection in her bum that didn't take very well so they had to do it again. To this day (I presume) she has a scar where the first injection failed. Maybe she'll let me have a look again someday!

Kyle eventually appeared and I was delighted that I had another boy. I only needed two more and I had a five-a-side team. I remember phoning Karen's parents to give them the good news and after I told them that we had a boy and said, 'Karen's had forty-six stitches.'

They said, 'What?'

Again I said, 'Forty-six stitches. It was a long labour'. Karen's Mum didn't believe me and made me go and check. It turns out it was four to six stitches! A little bit different. Kyle was another great baby; quiet, no bother, slept well. There was one sad aspect of Kyle's birth. Karen's nana was admitted to hospital, feeling poorly, just before Karen went into labour and she died about a week after Kyle was born. That was very sad because she never saw her great-grandson and Karen was very close to her nana.

Kyle was so quiet; we never knew he was there. They tried to tell me that Kyle had an 'abnormality' when he was born and it was nothing more than a small tab of skin in his ear. I argued with the nurse who weighed and assessed him and eventually persuaded her to remove the 'abnormality' comment from his chart. He got teased at school about it later in life though, and for a while it bothered him when he was a kid.

When Karen told me she was pregnant with Sophie we were in an Italian restaurant in Nottingham. It was a great pregnancy and Sophie Isabella came along very quickly. She was born 24 June 1992 in Nottingham, Queens Medical Centre; it was one of the most wonderful days of my life.

Karen's waters broke whilst she was at a neighbour's house and she staggered through our front door at Edward Road and told me what was happening. So we got into the car and practically flew to Queens Medical Centre. I had a little Peugeot 1.8 GTi at that time and it was rather quick, which was just as well that day. We had prebooked a water birth for Sophie and my duty was to get the water bath full. I was using a thermometer to make sure that the temperature was as close to thirty-six point two as possible (body temperature). So I was going hot-cold-hot-cold-hot-cold and trying to get the right temperature and all the time the nurse was saying, 'The baby is coming Mr Young.'

While I was saying, 'It's gonna have tae bloody wait, I'm not ready yet!'

Eventually Karen was in the bath and I was ready for a long night. I had brought the cool box with beer, food and champagne and I was prepared for anything. I had only just opened my first can when Sophie was born! That wasn't in the plan! But she was gorgeous; she had lots of lovely dark hair, her face was underwater; her eyes opened when she was still underwater. At this point I am saying 'Get her out, she'll drown.'

The midwife reassuringly said, 'She won't drown Mr Young, she's been underwater for nine months, she's used to it'.

Eventually they brought her up and she opened her lungs and had a good scream and she never screamed again as far as I know. She went on to Karen and I had my little girl and I was thrilled. In fact, none of my kids really cried, but Sophie was especialy placid. We would be hunting round the house looking for Sophie because she was so quiet and we would quite often find her sitting in an unused fireplace; there she would be sitting quietly, sucking her fingers. I adored my little girl. What man wouldn't adore his daughter? Bed times were the best because Sophie would fall asleep holding my ear with two of her own fingers in her mouth. She looked adorable and she would love me to tell her a story before she went to sleep; her favourite story was the one about Kyle-Pig, Jordan-Pig and Wesley-Pig! It was my version of the Three Little Pigs. They were precious times and I was so patient with Sophie. But for some reason Karen didn't seem to have as much time for her which I never understood because these are the most wonderful days of your life.

For two or three years life was pretty good until the marriage started to go wrong and my lovely kids were taken away from me. Sophie was about four then. To this day it hurts me deeply to think about it and how stupid it all was; Karen wanted her youth back and she was going out a lot with mates who were single women in their early twenties and they would be out partying to all hours and I just let it go.

When Karen told me she didn't love me anymore and we started to come apart it was Kyle and Sophie that suffered the most. I was very much on the straight and narrow at this time and I was staying at home and looking after the kids whilst she went out and chased her lost youth. I was really confused and upset by this behaviour and it was the start of the most horrendous time of my life because I still loved Karen with all of my heart and even today I wish that I was still with her. Unfortunately, I also had to contend with Karen's parents at this point as well. If Karen had shot me point-blank in the head with her Mum and Dad standing watching they would, on police questioning, deny that she had done it. That was how blind and stupid their loyalty to Karen was; she could do no wrong and that didn't help us one bit.

The break-up with Karen in 1998 coincided with a time in Kyle's life when he really needed support from me but he didn't get it. He was at the Notts County Centre for Excellence when I was the director there and he had all the support he needed, but after I got the sack and moved away from Nottingham I couldn't come and see him. I was working in Chesterfield at their Centre for Excellence and that was a massive time commitment, but I had to work; I needed to pay my bills and keep my career going. Sadly Kyle lost his way a bit and was released when he was fourteen, the same year as Leon Best. I would have to say that I haven't had nearly as much time with all of my kids than I would have liked but you are not always in control of your life and circumstances sometimes get beyond your control. Things are given to you and things are taken away and you have to make the best of what you are left with. I'm very proud to say that I have four fantastic kids and I love them all to bits.

I love my three boys dearly but the relationship I have with Sophie is different again – it is true what they say about the unique relationship between father and daughter. I would have done anything for Sophie and I have a message on my phone to this day that was sent by her that says, 'That message made me cry, I will keep that message for ever, I love you millions and more big Daddy, love you xxxx 4 eva'. That was on 15 March 2004. She was eleven years old then.

She was having problems at the time and there was a guy called Scott that was giving her a hard time as well; I hated him. Had I been there I am sure I would be in jail now because I would have done him some serious damage. I hated being apart from Sophie so much; it made things so much worse. In fact, that period when I lost Kyle and Sophie is one of my biggest regrets in life, even though there wasn't anything I could do about it.

After the initial trauma of the move to Switzerland, Sophie has settled down now and has made lots of friends and has got a decent job as an au-pair. It's more than that to be honest and she looks after kids in preschool. She misses her friends back home but she has made a new life for herself and she seems to be settled. She still calls me up to ask for advice occasionally and she is still my little girl; I'm very proud of her. I wish she was back here in Nottingham but we can't have everything.

My kids are all individuals but I see a bit of me in all of them, especially Kyle, who is very like me at times. I had a conversation with him a while ago about heroes and I mentioned that Peter Osgood was my hero once, but that he let me down and that my real hero is my Dad. At that point Kyle said, 'Funnily enough my hero is my Dad as well.' I was very moved by that. I often wonder how difficult it must have been for him to say that because he is very sensitive like me and if you cross him then you will know about it. He runs on a short fuse but he is a very loving and popular lad, and I happen to think he is very good looking. He is also very talented when it comes to sports and he has a natural ability that means he can do well at any sport that he turns his hand to. But if I have a criticism of him it is that he starts things and doesn't finish them, which is a shame because I believe he could have played sport professionally. Kyle came the closest to following me into a football career because Wes and Jordan are useless and they won't mind me telling them that. Wes played for Oadby Town during a time when he thought he was the new Franz Beckenbauer! Jordan's claim to fame occurred during a charity football tournament between Notts County, Chesterfield and Mansfield. I got the kids involved and Jordan went in goals and he did really well; he was unbeatable! Then a guy called Richard O'Kelly (who was with West Brom at the time) came across and asked me who the 'keeper was and when I told him it was my son Jordan he said (in his best Brummie accent) 'Chroist! We'll have to keep an oiye on 'im'. So afterwards I told Jordan that West Brom wanted to sign him and he loved that. Sometimes when we are all together and we've had a couple of beers Jordan will start up, 'Hey Dad, remember when West Brom wanted to sign me?'

Wes will be all over him and Kyle will be like, 'Shut up! Those goals were only 3ft high!' But we will still have to tell the story again.

My relationship with Wes and Jordan is now on a different footing, I think we all regard each other as pals and less of a father-son relationship. They can say what they like to me and they will get it back, they can take the piss out of me but they will always lose! We talk on the phone all the time and we have similar interests. I call Wesley, 'The Big Cheese' because he has been successful in business and is forever on his phone wheeling and dealing. Jordan now works in the business that his Mother and her partner run. They put up spray-painting booths for cars all over the country. Jordan is a very pragmatic sort of guy; nothing is a problem, everything can be solved and nothing fazes him. Both of them call Kyle 'Longshanks' because he is 6ft 6in tall.

It was Jordan that made me a granddad for the first time with Finlay. I have two grandsons now; Finlay Jordan Young and Archie Lawrence Young. Archie was born on 24 June (Sophie's birthday coincidentally) and he was one of the last babies to be born in the maternity unit in Rochdale (where Kyle and Finlay were also born) before it was closed down. When they brought Finlay down to see me at West Bridgford we went across to Bridgford Park and put Finlay (who was about eighteen months old) on to the swings and I thought, 'Christ, this is déjà-vu!' It was the first time I had seen one of my lads doing stuff with their kids that I had done with them. In this case it reminded me of my times at that same park with Kyle when he was little. That was a real 'wow' moment.

Looking back one of the things that irritates me most is the technology that is available today that wasn't around back then. If only I could have had a mobile phone with a camera or video on board to capture all of those lovely moments with my kids. I'm quite jealous of parents today who can carry a camcorder in their pockets or just grab their phones if something happens that they want to remember.

I don't have to worry about my kids so much anymore, although I do have concerns about Kyle some days and where he might end up and what career he might settle into. I don't have to worry about Sophie, she is grounded and sensible; I just worry for the poor sod that tries to marry her one day because he will have to get past me first! I would be a very proud father in church on her wedding day, but I won't give her away, I will say, 'Here you go son, you can borrow her for a wee while.' But I'm never giving her away! I've even got part of the father of the bride speech written already. It goes something like this, 'Allied carpets have been on the phone Sophie and they apologised for the delay in delivering your new carpets. It seems you won't be getting any carpets but you will be getting your under felt in the morning!'

I heard Gary Lineker's brother use that line at Gary's wedding. I suppose I have concerns that Sophie will remain in Switzerland if she marries and have kids and I might not get to see my grandchildren very often, but there isn't much I can do about that. As for Wesley, I suppose I worry that he will never get married; are you gay Wes? Well, are you? Only kidding.

16

BETTER
IN MY DAY

I went to a presentation last year for children with learning difficulties; it was for their prize-giving day and I was asked to help out. I was asked to say a few words beforehand and I chose to say:

Footballers nowadays are an interesting breed. There are some who do a lot of good work and genuinely want to give something back to the community in return for a very good salary, but you never hear about them. On the other hand there are some that are paid astronomical wages and they won't even stop to sign an autograph and I find that disgusting and even more so when you consider that some of the fans are working hard all week to earn enough money to go and watch their team at weekends and then out comes 'Billy Big Time' from the players' entrance and walks straight past them. He gets into his big, flash 4x4 motor with its blacked-out windows, and drives away without even a thought for the guy who just wants an autograph and a few words. That is one of the most worrying trends about today's game.

Even in the lower leagues there are players who are 'Billy Big Time' and you see them interviewed on Sky after a game and you think – for God's sake, just be yourself will you. Even in the semi-professional level like the Blue Square Premier you will find players earning upwards of £1,000 per week. My son Kyle is twenty-three and he goes out in Nottingham in the evening and he sees some of the professional footballers out for the night. Now someone like Steve Howard, who has a solid background, appreciates every single penny he earns from the game and although he might be two sheets to the wind and having a great time, he won't be giving it the big 'I am' . He will talk to anyone and welcome them into his company. On the other hand there are some of the young Nottingham Forest players taking themselves very seriously indeed and making sure they get noticed with bottles of Bollinger and flashing the cash.

One day the money could disappear from football. All it needs is for Sky to pull out and then who would come in and pay the same sort of money to broadcast the game? Players are horribly overvalued in the modern game and a lot of it is down to the amount of money flowing through the game now. I think that pound for pound, Kenny Dalglish was the best buy ever when Liverpool signed him from Celtic for £440,000. What a return they had on him! Compare that to someone like Ade Akinbiyi who cost Leicester City £5 million; surely Peter Taylor is a better judge of a player than that. The daft sums of money in the game have caused situations like that to occur and Akinbiyi isn't the only one.

As for wages; I've always said that if you are a plumber and you are working for Mr Jones who pays you £10,000 per year and Mr Brown, up the road, needs a plumber and offers you £15,000 per year then what are you going to do? You will take the higher wage for yourself, your family, a better lifestyle – anybody would and footballers are no different. I don't begrudge players getting as much as they can because if clubs and managers and chairmen are prepared to pay them stupid money then why on earth not take it. To think £200,000 per week is not so rare anymore but it is fucking ridiculous, but if some tosser of a club owner is prepared to put that sort of money into a player's bank account then he won't turn around and say, 'I'm sorry, I don't want that, it's too much'. He will take it and I defy anybody to say that they wouldn't do the same. What I don't always see is the players responding to these wages in terms of accountability, behaviour and responsibility and this is in contrast to my time when we would have written into our contracts that we would do a certain amount of charity work and spent time giving something back to local causes and charities. Players have all the power now and there are some worrying trends developing as a result. You see it all the time in the media, particularly during transfer windows, when players keep clubs hanging on and hanging on and managers dangling whilst they wait for an answer. Agents have a lot to answer for here; I never had an agent, and if I played in the modern game I wouldn't want one. I would want to be the one doing the negotiating and I don't want to be dealing via any intermediaries. I want to look my potential manager straight in the eye and get a feeling of whether or not that relationship is going to work. I want to get a feel for the club and whether they really want me; are they really selling the club to me. I think that is why Leicester lost out to Brighton two years ago when they went after Craig Mackail-

Smith from Peterborough – I think Gus Poyet grabbed him and made a big fuss of him and made him feel very wanted, which was in total contrast to Sven Goran Eriksson who thought that the player would naturally want to come to Leicester without him making any real effort.

Agents will talk to a lot of clubs at a time when they are in the process of selling 'their' player and they will play one off against the other in an attempt to get the best deal (and the best percentage of course) but they are not for me. As far as I am concerned they are the scourge of the modern game, they should be told to fuck off and leave the game alone. I realise that some players are not the brightest and maybe think that they need an agent, but the truth is that these players could use the P.F.A. for most of their requirements during transfer and contract discussions. We did fine for decades without the need for agents so why are they so important now and so needed (apparently). Decisions have been taken out of the hands of the players and a lot of stuff goes on without players being aware of what is happening, but I think it is dangerous when a player's affairs are being managed by a non-football person. I remember getting criticised during my last season as a player at Rochdale because I was earning £400 per week and some people thought it was obscene. I had been on £400 per week for five years – that was five years without a pay rise.

The irony is that players are paid more than ever today, but they play fewer games than we used to. I hear a lot of talk about the need for squad rotation and how tired players are, but this seems to be a luxury to me. Our best seasons at Leicester City were when we only used about sixteen players and we played on some horrendous pitches, we never flew to games and we quite often didn't stay overnight – we would turn up, play the game and go straight home. We just didn't need all the pampering that we see these days. But I would love to play in the modern game; the striker is now a protected species and overprotected by the referee. You can't touch forwards anymore and they have a much easier life as a result.

When players do get injured I am sure that they are rested far more readily, and clubs are less likely to patch them up and send them out. But they can do this because they have the luxury of bigger squads. And as for wearing hats and gloves during a match – I can imagine what Jock Wallace would have said. He wouldn't even let us wear tracksuit bottoms during training in the winter. He would say that we don't wear them on Saturday, so we don't wear them for training. He would let you wear them to keep warm afterwards or to keep warm when you are going to the training ground, but once training started off they came! I don't want to give the wrong impression about my life as a professional football because it was mostly fantastic. I loved playing, we just had lower expectations in terms of the rewards we would take home. I think the rewards that players earn these days are much better than we enjoyed (we didn't have decent pension plans for a start) and their lives are better all round in terms of the support and care that they enjoy as an accepted part of the modern game: the best travel; the best accommodation; the best advice on looking after yourself; the best food; best pitches; best kit; and best physiotherapy. When I played I had a can of lager after the game; John Mcvey was our only physio; Jock and Ian MacFarlane were the sum total of the coaching staff, and the accommodation was ok, but nothing to write home about.

I think there is more team spirit and less individuality when you get down the lower leagues; players are far more likely to regard each other as teammates and work for each other in the way that we used to at Leicester. I played with a guy that I hated (Jim Melrose) but we were on the pitch to do a job and if he was in a good scoring position then I would give him the ball. I wouldn't celebrate with him mind you! I look at the Premier League sides at the moment and I can't help but think that there are teams of individuals turning out and not 'teams' in the true sense of the word. It can be a strange place the football club dressing room; if you get it right then it doesn't matter how big the squad is, but you have to have the right balance and the right attitude throughout the squad.

I think players are too far from the supporters these days, certainly they are in the higher divisions and this is not a good thing. Fans keep your feet on the ground and give you a dose of reality sometimes. When I was playing I was always happy to talk to fans, but the one question that was always certain to get to me was, 'So what happened today then Al?'

My first response was always, 'Did you go to the game?' If they said no then I would tell them to fuck off because they hadn't earned the right to ask that question. If they said yes then I would usually say something like, 'Well you were there, you tell me. We lost two nil'. Alright, I was winding them up a bit, but we would always have a beer and a chat. There is a line that I don't let fans cross though. I understand that fans are passionate about their club and they get upset and angry sometimes, and I can handle that. What I object to is when supporters bring my family into it like they did after I left Oldham; the whole Chaddy End reckoned they had shagged my missus! I remember Wes and Jordan used to come and watch me when I was playing at Notts County (they were too young up until then) and if I was with them and someone started swearing when they were talking to me then I would jump on that. I think the whole fan culture changed after the Bradford Fire disaster, Hillsborough and Heysel all happened in a relatively short space of time. The fallout from all of those incidents changed football forever and most of it was for the greater good. Football is a safer day out than it used to be.

The fans of the teams I have played for have varied enormously in their outlook and there is no question that Leicester City supporters are incredibly passionate. They can be very fickle though; one day they will tell you why their club is the best in the land and the next day they will tell you why the club is crap and it's all gone wrong! But the passion is there for all to see and they are also a very knowledgeable bunch. Great set of fans. It was whilst I was at Leicester that I experienced my only open topped bus tour after we won the Second Division Championship in 1980. It was a warm day and the fans turned out in their tens of thousands and we arrived at the Town Hall. We immediately started hitting the free booze, so by the time we came out on to the balcony we were pretty merry I can tell you. I was joining in with the fans doing my song: 'He's here, he's there, he's every fucking where Alan Young, Alan Young.' So, I must have had a few. That was a wonderful day but I wish it had been captured on video by someone.

Brighton has a very laid back holiday feel to it and the fans reflect that. Football was part of the easy going feel of the town and Saturday afternoon at the match was a bit like that. Sheffield United fans were very passionate but the club was having a tough time when I was there and the crowds were down. Rochdale – if the world needs an enema then stick the tube in Rochdale! The people of Rochdale moan constantly and they're very good at it. Oldham isn't much different!

Nottingham was an odd place. Notts County fans are old! It is the only club I know where they have a club for fans that have followed the team for over fifty years. I know because I helped to get it started; they would meet once a month in the Great Hall at Meadow Lane and there might be a guest speaker and a bit of bingo and a few sandwiches. I met one fella who had been going to watch Notts County for sixty-two years. One night he met Derek Pavis and he was telling him about his early games at Meadow Lane when he would sneak in under the turnstile and Derek turned to this old guy and said, 'You owe me three fuckin' pence!'

Jimmy Sirrel was a favourite amongst this group; he would always have a dance with the ladies. We are all supposed to be living longer these days, so maybe all clubs should do this. But I have to say that all Notts County fans love their team; they are genuine people and expectations aren't high which helps. They also have the daftest song I have ever heard – The Wheelbarrow Song! There's only one line to this song and it is 'I had a wheelbarrow, the wheel fell off' and you just have to repeat this line ad nauseum. It all started when Notts County played at Shrewsbury and the barrow carrying hot dogs or something was travelling behind the goal when a wheel came off and one wag in the away end started singing this song, and so it began. They sing it when they need a goal!

On the pitch the level of gamesmanship has increased to a crazy level now. It is because the prize is so big nowadays, the demands are high as well and if you think about there aren't as many trophies up for grabs each season. So the intensity and competition have increased no end and that applies to European football as well. The European game is becoming more important than the Premiership and the chase for a place in the Champions League is more important than winning the F.A. Cup which is sad, but inevitable, because of the financial rewards available in the Champions League. The way that players move around European clubs compared to ten or fifteen years ago is astonishing and it is not unusual to see an English Premier League side with hardly any Englishmen in it. I can remember when it was a real novelty to have overseas players in any side in the English or Scottish leagues.

One of the side-effects of the new multinational look and feel of the English game is the culture of diving and cheating. They call it simulation, but it's cheating and I don't know why the media is so afraid to call it that. I think it is a direct import from outside the UK. If I ran into the box with a defender at my shoulder I would want to beat him and score, or set someone else up to score. The last thing on my mind was pretending to be hurt or pretending that I had been fouled or tripped. It is a part of the game that we hardly ever saw in this country and the whole business of falling over in the penalty area is worrying, although I must confess to playing for a penalty just once in my whole career. I was at Notts County and the opposition 'keeper miskicked the clearance. I picked the ball up on the edge of the box and pushed in. I could see the defender arriving out of the corner of my eye and I knew he would get to the ball first. I wasn't necessarily cheating, but I deliberately set myself across the ball so that he couldn't get to it. So, he had to be clever in order to get to the ball before me. Instead, what he came straight through me and I went down under the challenge and made sure that he didn't get any of the ball. Penalty!

I can categorically say that I have never tried to get a fellow professional footballer booked or sent off. I would be in a referee's ears for the full ninety minutes and I was *always* right! If it went for a throw it was our throw. If the ball went over the goal line then it was our corner and I would appeal until I was blue in the face and the referee was sick of the sight of me. And the same went for the linesman. But this was in a time when a referee would turn around and tell you to piss off. Despite that I would quite often end up getting booked for dissent and this used to make Jock Wallace go mad at me. He always thought that dissent was a daft reason for picking up a booking and I can't recall getting booked for foul play too often. I was hard and I hit people hard and tackled hard, but if I wanted to hurt someone then I would usually be able to do it without the referee realising what was going on.

The standard of refereeing in my experience has never been great, but I think it matters more now when mistakes are made at crucial times in crucial matches. The thing is, I don't believe it will ever change which is a pity because, now more than ever, we need better referees. The life of a referee has never been better from what I can see. The retainer fees and match fees mean that the top referees have a decent living now and the perks are decent as well: first class travel; decent hotels; and foreign trips to referee in lovely locations for two or three days – it's not a bad life ,but they are still basically crap!

If you are a chairman and you aren't running the club properly then the fans and the shareholders might see you off and you will be out of a job (unless you own the place in which case you can tell them all to piss off). If you are a manager and results are poor, morale is poor and the players are unhappy and the fans are giving you a hard time then the chances are that you will be relieved of your duties and quite rightly. If you are a player and you aren't playing well or you don't try and this goes on for too long then you will lose your place at the club and be sent on your way, or stuck in the reserves. But if you are a referee not doing your job properly week in, week out then nothing happens. There is no accountability and there never will be unless there are changes within the referees' governing body, which is the Football Association; and that isn't going to happen any time soon. They take care of their own and they are run by people who know nothing about football. They are in it for the wrong reasons, but they are happy to turn up in their blazers and take their trips to the big games. They will do anything to protect that privilege and that makes them too powerful. What they don't want is ex-professional footballers coming in as referees because they are not 'their own' people. But this is what it will take to increase the standard of refereeing and introduce some accountability. Only then will things begin to improve. Currently, referees are making mistakes that can cost clubs millions of pounds and that isn't good enough. Like I said before, referees have always made mistakes but now they are more costly.

FIFA are another governing body that needs an overhaul. They are ten times worse than the F.A. and they are completely autonomous. Sepp Blatter remains in power by glad-handing all of these developing nations and keeps representatives from countries like Abu-Dhabi and Swaziland on board by whatever means necessary, but if you threw a ball at one of them they would say – what the fuck is that? There has to be a more democratic way of running football. Accountability is seriously lacking at FIFA and the place looks corrup. Allegedly money has to be changing hands somewhere if Qatar can get the World Cup. This is a country where homosexuals are not allowed to go to the game; you can't buy a beer; and it's 35 degrees in the shade! How can the English bid only get two votes when we have the best stadia and pitches, the history and tradition, the transport infrastructure and the support ... it just doesn't make sense. We won't get another chance to bid again until 2026 and that means I may not see a World Cup in this country.

But the way the game is run means that change for the better is far too slow. The introduction of technology to help referees is a good example of that. Sometimes the officials aren't to blame for a wrong decision; when Spurs scored a goal at Old Trafford that wasn't given a few seasons ago and Roy Carroll pulled the ball back from behind the line, the officials were too far away from the incident because the ball was struck from the halfway line. There was no way they could know if the ball had crossed the line or not. That is when the use of technology would be right. I have a feeling that FIFA might have been resisting the introduction of technology because it would highlight too many mistakes by their match officials. Who knows? But it isn't a straightforward solution; if you install technology at the top level then what about the lower level of the game? Can they afford it?

Another solution to improve things might be the introduction of two referees – one in each half of the pitch. That way, the officials will always be up with the game because when play crosses the halfway line the other referee takes over. And is it really too much to hope that ex-professionals will one day go into refereeing? That would make such a difference. They will understand the game and the players and (hopefully) the players will have more respect for the officials. I must emphasise that not all referees are, or were, crap. I had a lot of respect for Neil Midgely when I played. He has passed on now and is up in the big referee's room in the sky and I remember coming off the pitch at Derby with my arm round his shoulder saying, 'You didn't do too bad today you little twat'. But he also showed the players respect and he would always have a smile on his face and would greet the players with a, 'Hello, how are you today lads? Do you mind if I call you Alan'. Simple touches that made a difference. When some silly bugger let a cockerel on to the pitch before our F.A. Cup semi-final with Spurs in 1982 he was saying, 'Go on then Youngy, get after it'.

I told him where to get off and said, 'You must be fucking mad. Those things are vicious!'

Pat Partridge was the same and had a human side. I remember one game I was in his face giving him a hard time about some decision or other and he turned to me and said, 'Listen. I'm doing my best, what's your fucking excuse because you're not having such a good game are you?'

I think the main difference back then was that we trusted referees.

17

GAFFERS

Jimmy Frizzel

Jim was a fellow Scot and always seemed miserable. He was never too happy with his lot, always moaning and complaining, but away from the football arena he was a nice enough bloke. Having said that, when we saw him in the football setting all he seemed to do was pick the team; Andy Lochhead took training and Jim didn't turn up until he fancied joining in the five-a-sides. I have to say that Jim was a fairly nondescript sort of guy and you might only notice him when he lost his temper. He had played for Oldham for many years as a wing-half and full-back and was part of the club in many ways.

He was not any kind of tactician and he was a very practical sort of manager. He once gave me some advice because I was doing something that annoyed him; he told me to stop dangling my leg out because when I received a ball and there was a defender coming in behind me, instead of getting my body in the way and taking the ball in my midriff I would stick my leg out and try to pull the ball back into me. He would go mental on the touchline and shout, 'Stop fishing fer it, you'll get yer leg broke!' So I stopped fishing.

I wasn't surprised when he eventually took a role as assistant to Billy McNeill at Manchester City because he was good friends with Tony Book, and it was Jim and Tony that lined up my move to Manchester City until Jock Wallace came in and scuppered it. That was what caused all the furore that followed. I can say with my hand on my heart if Jimmy Frizell had talked to me about the move to Manchester City instead of setting up the deal behind my back then it might have turned out differently.

I can remember poor Jim being on the wrong end of some rumours for a while; it was said that Chris Ogden (Oldham goalkeeper) was having an affair with Jim's wife. That was the talk all round the dressing room at the time and things came to a head one night when some of the players and their partners were invited round to Chris' house. I went with Julie and there were a few others there. Chris disappeared at one point and when he returned we were telling him that things were getting a bit heated in his absence and he shouldn't be behaving like that and so on. Eventually me and Julie left and went home to Hayside and the next thing I know there is banging on the door and the window and it's Chris Ogden carrying a knife and wanting to fight me! I told him to throw the knife away before he did anything else and I don't mind admitting I was pretty scared. So he threw the knife away and I went out and he really had a rage on and so he grabbed me but it wasn't really a fight, we were sort of rolling about and throwing punches. I can't remember exactly why he was after me; maybe I had opened my big mouth again and said something remiss.

Jim had a lot of older players at Oldham; he didn't seem to like youngsters. I was actually surprised when he picked me and so I was very disappointed when I did ok and he would leave me out for the next game. That was the pattern for a while – in and out the team. That didn't really give me the confidence that you should try and instill in a young player and he certainly never took any notice of me off the pitch. He didn't bother to find out if I was settling into Oldham ok and if my digs were alright for instance, and I know for a fact that that is the kind of thing that Jock Wallace would have checked with his young players. Jock would have his finger on every pulse and Jim was the opposite. He never took the time to sit down and chat to you; he seemed to take the attitude that you were a professional footballer so you had to be a man about it. Carl Valentine was the only other player of my age that broke into the team at that time. The rest, like Paul Edwards, Vic Halom, Ian Wood, Maurice Whittle, were decent enough players but they were all what you would call senior players. There was a lad called John Ryan who played left-back and when I went back to Boundary Park with Leicester City he was marking me at one point. Next thing I know there was a whole load of spit running down my face; he jogged past me and spat right in my face. Absolutely disgusting! Being the type of player that I am I wanted to go after him but the referee hadn't seen it and I knew that I would get myself sent off. I waited until after the game and went after him in the players' lounge instead. I had to be restrained and I was asked to leave. I told him then that I would get him back one day and funnily enough I had to wait until after I finished playing for that chance to come around. I went to see my mate Phil Stant at Mansfield when John Ryan was also playing for them. I told Phil Stant the story about John Ryan and I told him that I was going to scare him in the players' lounge, but that I needed him to pretend to hold me back. So I met him in the players' lounge after the game and John Ryan was at the other end. I started to march down to where Ryan was and Stanty was saying, 'No Al, leave it.'

I was giving it, 'Fuck off Stanty!' As I got closer to Ryan the look on his face changed to something like 'Holy fucking shit!' I went right up to his face and, said 'Hey Ryan. Spit in my face now.' Our noses were practically touching when I said, 'You fucking coward!' then I turned and walked away. I got more satisfaction out of that than if I had spat in his face. Stanty and I had a laugh about that afterwards.

Jock Wallace

I have spoken about Jock in detail elsewhere in the book but it is safe to say that he was more than the 'gaffer' to me. He looked after me like I was his son and the respect that I had in return was as if he was my father. He knew exactly how to handle me and I still remember an incident in a preseason friendly in Berlin against Hertha. They had a big black guy playing for them and at one point during the game he said, 'Your Mother sucked my cock.' I went fuckin' ballistic. I was going to kill the bastard because I had never heard anything like that before. I was used to insults and name calling between players during the game in England, but the insults to my Mother were something else; that's my Mum for God's sake, so I went after him in a red mist. I don't know who got me but the next thing I know is I'm standing on the touchline with Jock. Maybe Jock saw the incident or maybe one of the other players suggested that he take me off, but one way or another Jock got me off the pitch pretty sharpish.

We had another friendly later that season against Australia at Filbert Street and Jock put me on the bench which pissed me off no end because I want to play in every match and especially against the Australian national side; I would have had an international shirt at the end of the game. Anyway, he left me out and told me to rest. I told him I didn't want a fucking rest and so I was sulking and moody on the bench, even though he had told me that he would put me on with twenty minutes to go. With half an hour to go I was up stretching and warming up, but nothing was happening. With twenty minutes to go I was running up and down the touchline and standing near the dugout pretending to look at my watch, but he was ignoring me. Eventually I went across and said, 'Are you gonna put me on or not?'

He said, 'Nah, there's only ten minutes left now Big Man.' You bastard, I thought. I was in the sort of mood where if anyone had said the wrong thing to me then I was going to swing for them. At the final whistle I went straight down the tunnel and into the showers. I wasn't talking to anyone. I wasn't bothered about the debrief or instructions for the next day; I really didn't give a shite! I went out the players' entrance and straight to my car; for once I don't think I signed any autographs. I just got in my car and went straight home.

Now the speed limit in South Wigston is 30mph and I was doing 46, which doesn't sound that quick, but it was fast enough and I got pulled over by the police. I got out the car and the first copper got out and said, 'Stay there by your car.'

I said, 'Okay Officer'.

He then said, 'Do you know that it is a 30mph limit in South Wigston?'

I said I did and then he said, 'Do you realise that you were doing 46mph?'

I said, 'I didn't realise that, no.' But that I had noticed that I didn't have much fuel left (and I pointed to the petrol gauge in my car) and I was trying to get home before I ran out. He looked at me as if to say, what a right smart arse we've got here. So I said, 'What else can I say?'

Then he asked me if I had been drinking. Just as I was telling him that I hadn't the other copper got out the car and said, 'Alright Al?' I explained about the match and being made sub and how pissed off I was and they let me off with a warning. Thinking about it now it still rankles with me because I hated sitting on the bench, I always wanted to play. Jock would have known that I was pissed off, but he also would have known that I would be able to deal with it. I wasn't the sort to go into my shell and feel sorry for myself. He would have been smart enough to know that if he had said something to me on the night then I might have said something that I would have regretted; so he left me alone. But it was finished by the next day, over and done with.

Jock created the family feel to the club, the togetherness, and it brought everyone closer; to the extent that he found it hard to keep us away from the club at times. On Sundays any players that were injured would go in for treatment and quite often, if I needed to go in, then I would take the kids. We would fill up the big bath in the dressing room and throw the kids in and let them play in there. Players started to come in even they weren't injured. So there might be a load of us playing head-tennis in the warm-up gym and John McVey, the physio, would be babysitting all the kids!

Jock loved to be out on the training ground with the players, joining in and watching; jogging up and down with us and watching the body language and 'smelling' the atmosphere amongst the players. Sometimes we would train in silence if Jock was watching us and he was looking particularly serious because he never just blended into the background, he was a real presence. If the previous game had gone well then there might be a bit of chit-chat and he might be a bit more light-hearted. He'd ask you how your weekend was and so on, but we all knew when it was time to get serious, he didn't have to say a word, it just happened once we got out on to the training ground. The only time this changed was when he unleashed his assistant, big Ian MacFarlane. Now Ian would stride out and he would run training like a boot camp and shout out the orders like, 'Right you fuckin' lot, into pairs. NOW!!' And God help you if you didn't. For some reason he always came alongside me when we were jogging and he would whisper to me ,'See you Youngy? You are an arrogant bastard aren't you?' and he would follow this with a laugh. His language was very offensive and loud at times which didn't bother us, but it bothered some of the folks living next to the training ground and he was asked to tone it down a few times.

It is interesting to look back at Jock's preparation before the match. He would have a quiet word with everyone and he wouldn't miss anyone out: 'Make sure you get that first tackle in son. Back four, keep it tight, stay together and imagine you are held together by a length of rope, so if he goes across then you all go with him. Wally, keep them right and talk to them, sort them oot. Ted (Eddie Kelly) win your battles in midfield. Peakey, make those passes count. Stevie Lynex, you know what to do…' And so on. Then he would say, 'Ian, have you got anything to add?'

Without fail, Ian would always say, 'I would just like to reiterate everything the Gaffer just said.'

It became so predictable that the players would join in so that when Jock said,, 'Ian, would you like to add anything?'

We would all chant together, 'I WOULD JUST LIKE TO REITERATE EVERYTHING THE GAFFER JUST SAID!' Jock would be pissing himself laughing. But things like that helped to relieve the tension and I think Jock used to do it for that reason.

Big Ian MacFarlane was involved in one of the funniest things I have ever seen. It happened at Amsterdam airport when we were in transit between Berlin (where we had played the preseason friendly) and Spain. We had to collect our luggage before we could transfer to our next plane and so we are all gathered at the baggage carousel waiting for cases. We are a wee bit worse for wear because we had finished off a few sherberts the night before in a club after the game in Berlin. As the cases were coming through, Jock wanted us to stay together to check-in but Ian MacFarlance was missing and Jock started to twitch. He came across and said, 'Big Man, have you seen Ian?'

'Nope. No sign of him Gaffer,' I replied. He was cursing and pacing and we are all waiting and looking at our watches thinking about the next flight when suddenly, through the plastic curtain that separates the baggage collection room from the outside world, comes Ian sitting on the carousel and holding a can of lemon Fanta and bumping along and he shouts , 'Has emdy seen ma fuckin' cases?' He went right round the carousel and out the other side again. Well, we didn't stop laughing for days!

Jock didn't do a lot of coaching and we didn't spend much time practising corners and free-kicks. We would be trusted to do our jobs and we pretty much did that most of the time. Eddie Kelly would sometimes spot things; he was Jock's eyes and ears on the pitch, and it would be Eddie that shouted across to Jock that we needed to change something or tighten up here or put an extra man there. That was how it worked.

Jock would have loved what I did with the Community Scheme at Notts County and, in some ways, I wish I could have done it all at Leicester but that wasn't possible. Jock was already doing his own community scheme of sorts at Leicester. He would have us all attending parties and awards ceremonies whenever possible, visiting schools and so on and sometimes it was just so the kids could have their photograph taken with the players and that would make their day. I can remember how much Jock cared about stuff like that. He would have been right behind a community scheme if it had existed back then.

It's sixteen years since Jock died and I can still remember how I heard the news; Alan Bennett phoned me when I was living in Nottingham and he said, 'I've got some bad news Alan. Jock has died.' I remember just thinking –'Oh fucking hell no!' I thought he was invincible, I thought he would never die. I thought he would go on and on forever. I knew he hadn't been well and he was fighting Parkinson's disease but he was still doing alright. Anyway, it seems he had been doing a barbeque for his family in the back garden and the kids were round with their families. Towards the end of the afternoon he sat down in a deckchair and closed his eyes for a few minutes. Daphne, his wife, came over and shook him and said, 'John. I'm just off to play nine holes.'

He replied along the lines of, 'Why the hell did you wake me up to tell me that woman? Go an' play yer nine holes'. So she did and when she came back he was dead, still in the deckchair. I think his heart just gave in.

The last time I saw Jock was at Colchester after he came back from a management stint in Spain. I had gone down to London to see Gary Lineker play for Tottenham at Charlton. I said hello to Gary and Michelle afterwards and had a meal with them. Then I went over to Colchester, having told Jock I was coming. I met him in the ticket office and he came over to me, but he was a bit bent over and shuffling. I said, 'Alright Gaffer?'

He said, 'Aye. Here's your tickets, see you after the game.'

That night we went back to Jock's house after the game. He pulled out a bottle of malt whisky and poured it out saying, 'I've been keeping this for a special occasion, and now is that occasion.'

I couldn't wait any longer and said, 'What's up with you Gaffer?'

He replied, 'Alan, I'm going to tell you to shut the fuck up and don't ask me that question again tonight.'

'Fair enough.' I said. He had the first signs of Parkinson's disease. We got halfway down the bottle talking mostly about our time at Leicester City. The players, the games … I remember him laughing about young Paul Friar squaring up to Joe Jordan when we beat Manchester United 1–0 at Filbert Street. Then he said, 'Are you hungry?' It was 3 o'clock in the morning.

He took us down to the local Chinese restaurant and started banging on the windows saying, 'Get the fuck down here.'

A guy's head appears at an upstairs window and he said, 'Ahhh Mr Jock, Mr Jock.'

They let us in, got everything cooking and made us a lovely dinner and never took a penny. It was all 'Mr Jock' this and 'Mr Jock' that. It just shows you the effect he had on people.

I wish so much that Jock could have stayed around longer because I know that my life would have been better with him around to offer a few words or be a shoulder to cry on. All of the problems that I ran into I could have coped with better with his wisdom and support. He was a very knowledgeable, wise man and he could 'smell' problems. Sometimes I still talk to him.

Ian Porterfield
Ian was too nice to be a manager. He had a good chairman in Reg Brealey who supported him fully – which every manager

longs for. Ian's problem was that he was just not strong enough, he was very quietly spoken and I don't think I ever saw him lose his temper. The problem I have here is that I compare Ian to Jock because Ian was the next manager I had when I left Leicester. Now Ian was a decent man and a nice fella, but he wanted to be liked by everyone and for me that means he isn't cut out to be a manager. I watched Ian at Raith Rovers when I was a kid; he was very talented with an amazing left foot, but he had no pace.

Ian should have been smart enough to see the effect that the training regime was having on the players. Their incessant routine of running and more running from Jim the Jog created a mood amongst the squad. The players clearly didn't like it and it wasn't healthy. As a manager you have to spot that and do something about it. Ian didn't have much of a presence in the dressing room and sometimes you need a leader that will be loud and let you know what is expected in no uncertain terms. Instead we had Jim coming round to each player giving out advice and we're all thinking, fuck off, you know nothing about football. Cec Caldwell was also at Sheffield United and he seemed to do all sorts of roles at the club. He was also very quietly spoken, but he was very wise and knowledgeable and if he said something you listened. Jim never kicked a ball in anger in his life; Cec was the opposite and it showed.

Ian never got upset when we lost and that always concerned me. It wasn't as if he was too close to the players, he just didn't seem to have the passion that Jock had.

Jimmy Melia and Chris Cattlin

Jimmy was very similar to Ian Porterfield in that he was a really nice guy. He had played at Liverpool and still had a broad Scouse accent when he arrived in Brighton after the chairman,

Mike Bamber, appointed him. Jimmy's Assistant Manager was a guy called Chris Cattlin and he was nothing short of an evil conniving c*nt! Everything was fine when I started at Brighton and Jimmy wanted me to play up front and look after Terry Connor. He said that I had looked after Lineker at Leicester, Edwards at Sheffield United and now he wanted me to do the same job for him at Brighton. I often wondered who was looking after me by the way! Jimmy's wife was something else and I can still remember her reaction when she found out my star sign. She begged Jimmy to sign me because the team needed a Scorpio and Terry Connor was a Cancerian and the two of us would get along fine. Anyway, Jimmy made me an offer (£400 per week and twenty grand signing on fee) and I said I would go away and think about and sleep on it. I phoned Ian Porterfield and told him what the deal was and explained that I needed another five grand so that I could afford to move into a decent house in Brighton. Everything was twice the price compared to Sheffield. Ian (and Reg Brealey) agreed to this and so I signed the next day.

Jim loved his players and he was far too close to them – it was his downfall. Chris Cattlin knew this and used it and he never missed an opportunity to undermine Jim in front of the players. I despised Chris Cattlin even though players like Tony Grealish told me that Cattlin rated me. That didn't matter to me one bit, I had no respect for him at all. When Cattlin eventually took over he dropped Joe Corrigan and said that he wanted to give the younger lads a chance. Joe and I both knew this was bollocks because he signed Frank Worthington and said that he needed experience in the side. Make your mind up Cattlin! Anyway, Joe spoke to me one day and promised me that we would get Cattlin out before we both left. Joe hung around for ages and eventually outlasted Cattlin and was as good as his word. Now it's not in my nature to fake injuries but I had genuine injuries anyway which limited my appearances at Brighton.

There was no way I was going to stay at Brighton once Jimmy got the sack. I had signed for Jim and I had no respect for Cattlin (who seemed to be too friendly with the chairman for my liking) so it was a matter of time before I left. I would like to think that I conducted myself with dignity during this spell and I went to the local paper on one occasion to tell my story and make sure the truth was known to the fans and, surprisingly, Cattlin never came back with anything. I think he was scared that I might reveal more about the way he had had behaved and the way he had treated me so he just kept quiet. It was a relief (for him and me) when I left and went to Notts County.

Larry Lloyd, Richie Barker, Dick Bate and Jimmy Sirrel

Larry came and met me in Brighton and brought his chairman, Jack Dunnett, who did all of the negotiations. He wanted me to take a cut but only because he gave me a bit more signing-on money and so I was on £300 per week. My debut was a disaster because Tony Mowbray clattered me from behind and I was out for several weeks whilst my heel healed!

Larry (bless him) didn't have much of a clue and he used to bully players, which reflects the kind of player he was. I've socialised with Larry since then and we always get on fine, but at the time I thought he was clueless. We had a poor start to the season and he was soon on his way, which meant a return for Jimmy Sirrel. Jim was a good, wise, experienced manager and it must have been difficult for other managers coming in and following 'Mr Notts County'. Jim had a lot of eccentricities in his training and managing methods and I have covered many of them elsewhere in this book and whilst you might have a laugh with him, you would never, ever disrespect him. He once said to Mark Goodwin (a Leicester player who moved to Notts County) whilst I was still at Leicester, 'If you stop the boy Young, then you stop Leicester.' I took that as a huge compliment from a man that I respected. Jim's problem was that he didn't have the energy to do the day-to-day stuff like dealing with transfers and so on; he just liked to work with the players, so he was only meant to be a temporary appointment whilst Notts County found another permanent manager. So along came Richie Barker. I never knew the guy at all, so I waited and had a look and made my mind up then. Well, it wasn't long before I was walking out of one of his training sessions because he was talking absolute rubbish. I felt insulted being asked to play the way that Barker wanted us to; it was like pub football. It was no surprise when Barker was sacked but I have to say that I had nothing to do with it; I kept quiet and didn't speak to anyone about and I certainly didn't speak to the press. I have no idea what happened after that training session but clearly something was said to someone because Barker was on his way. There were a lot of strong characters in that side and it was never going to work.

So who should reappear as manager but Jimmy Sirrel! He kept things going for a while and then Dick Bate was appointed manager. Now Dick was a true Football Association man, complete with blazer and tie – a real member of the establishment. I have to confess that I was wary of him to start with because my natural suspicion of anything to do with the F.A. He tried to muster together a group of experienced professionals but he just wasn't up to it; he was used to taking care of players of schoolboy level. Our first training session with him started with him leading us all on a warm-up run, but he went off so fast that we were completely strung out behind him and it achieved nothing other than to show us that he could run fast. Hey! Well done Dick! It immediately alienated the players and left us all wondering what he was up to. I've since met Dick and he is a lovely guy but he needs to stick to what he does at the F.A. I saw Dick when I was doing my full coaching licence at Lilleshall and he came across really well as did another guy there called Mick Wadsworth who impressed me no end. He broke the mould of the F.A. establishment and he was able to have a laugh and, more importantly, laugh at himself. He was an excellent coach and he was prepared to listen which is so important. I would have liked to have worked with Mick but our paths never crossed after the F.A. qualification course. When I left Notts County I left behind one of the most remarkable characters in football and that was Jimmy Sirrel. Jimmy died in 2008 and it was sad news to hear. One of the quotes that was trotted out when all of the obituaries were written was so typically Jim, 'The best team always wins. The rest is only gossip.'

Vic Halom and Eddie Gray

When I went to Rochdale I found myself under the amazing leadership of Vic Halom; what a fucking twat! He hadn't a clue about football, or how to manage a team. He never seemed bothered and thought that everything was a big laugh and I don't think he had a serious bone in his body. You can't have that from a leader; he has to be seen to be doing his best at all times, he should be showing an example to the players. His nickname amongst the players was 'The Hamburglar' after a villain in a MacDonalds television advert at the time. None of the players had any respect for him whatsoever and it was a relief for everyone when he left Rochdale.

Eddie had respect for me because, a few years earlier when I signed for Sheffield United, he tried to sign me for Leeds United. I respected his knowledge and his approach (a lot of which was learnt from his time under Don Revie) and I used to enjoy chatting to Eddie. In fact, Eddie, Derek Parlane, Jimmy Lumsden (Eddie's assistant) and I used to have a lot of conversations about football and that was partly because we were all Scottish, but mostly because we were all experienced professionals that had played at the highest level. We were seen as a little bit elite at Rochdale, but that was partly because there were too many players at the club that had only ever played at a lower level. It was as if they just accepted mediocrity and didn't have the ambition or work ethic to get any further. That used to annoy me and Derek.

Training facilities were very poor and consisted of a school gym, a cow field and the hills around the town. But Eddie and Jim made the best of it and tried to make it more interesting and introduced variety and tried to break up the routine, even though it was only running at the end of the day. Eddie also had the good sense to see that older pros like Derek and I didn't need to be doing quite as much running as the younger lads, because after a certain age too much running would actually take it out of you rather than put it in. So he used to step in sometimes during the hill runs and just say quietly, 'Youngy, Derek, Brammy. That's enough, take a rest'.

Eddie inherited too many poor players at Rochdale to achieve much, but that didn't stop me admiring him immensely and he respected me as a player and as a person and that sets him apart. I occasionally see Eddie when he does media work for BBC local radio and it is always a pleasure to see him.

Alan Young

Alright so I never managed a club at full level but I know, given a chance, that I would have been a good manager. I would have been very similar to Jock Wallace, but with more tactical awareness. I have all of my coaching qualifications and I don't think that they are the be all and end all but they certainly gave me something: the knowledge and wherewithal to be able to manage a group; make progressions; understand the game more; dissect the game; observe and notice problems; and change things. Tactically, in terms of set-pieces for instance, I would have put a lot of work into them. My teams would be very fit and I know that my players would like to play for me. I would be a bit of a shouter but that has never changed; even now, during charity matches, I will be shouting and bawling at the referee and so nothing has changed there!

I've been youth team coach at Notts County and I used to shout a lot then, but I asked the kids once if it put them off when I shouted at them and young Neil Bateman said, 'We fuckin' love it when you shout Al.' And he meant it. I replied by telling him not to swear! I created a real family at Notts County and I took a similar approach to that which Jock took at Leicester. I also used a bit of psychology and man-management when it was needed. I remember we were having a lean time in terms of results and we had a match at Birmingham City. I knew that Andy Johnson was going to be having a run out in their team and playing against my kids. I asked Neil Bateman (who was my captain) for a favour and asked him to play up front instead of his usual position at centre half. He did this but insisted that he have the number nine shirt, which wasn't a problem. Now he wasn't the quickest but he was brave and strong. Anyway, he scored twice and we won 2–1, which was a remarkable result. Neil never got a contract and never became a pro, but his reaction that day was incredible, he celebrated his goals as if he had won the World Cup!

I like to think that people liked working for me, not just the players but the staff that you need around you to make things happen. I was always very fair with the other coaches and so on at Notts County and I always made sure that we socialised as often as possible. I would hold regular staff meetings with food and drink laid on, and the meeting would be followed by a good social session. This kind of approach creates trust and reliability and that is essential.

18

THE BEST XI

In goal – it would have to be Joe Corrigan. He was a huge, magnificent presence and he was very brave as well. But he could afford to be because he weighed about fifty stone! He was great off the pitch as well, very modest. Mark Wallington was a first rate 'keeper as well, but he didn't have the same presence as Joe.

Right-back – Tommy Williams. Tristran Benjamin (Notts County) and Chris Ramsay (Brighton) would run him close but Tom was unflappable. He always had a smile and very dry sense of humour. He could knock a lovely ball into the front men as well, not too fierce, so it was easy to control. I remember we played Arsenal and it was the 89th minute and Tom played a one-two with Steve Lynex and rolled it into the net and as he turned away he said, 'Fuck you Jennings!'

Left-back – It has to be Dennis Rofe with his snooker table legs. He was a great captain as well. I hadn't seen 'Sid' for about thirty years and he turned up last season at a game that featured a lot of ex-players. After the game I walked into the players' lounge and he jumped up and shouted 'Fackin' big man!!' and came across and started chatting as if we had never been apart.

Centre-halves – I would go for Dave Watson but Steve Foster is close. Dave had so much experience and even in the twilight years of his career he was still very effective. I played with him at Notts County, but I used to love playing against him as well. Alongside him would have to be Larry May. He was very quick and he would score a lot of goals as well, and was rarely beaten on the ground or in the air. I really thought he would go on to bigger and better things but it just never happened.

Wide right – Steve Lynex. Stevie was an uncomplicated player who could beat full-backs (although he didn't need to) and he put in great crosses for the likes of me to get on the end of.

Central midfield – Eddie Kelly. No doubt about this one. He was a great leader and a great communicator as well as being a great guy to have around off the pitch. Alongside him would be Jimmy Case. He was as hard as fuck and he became a great friend as well, I still hear from Jim. He got me into the sit-up routine I mentioned. He partied hard as well did Jim. Apparently all of the Liverpool lads did.

Wide left – Terry Curran, TC! He had all the skill in the world but he was a complete and utter twat – you couldn't help but love the guy. He stayed at my place for two months but it was only supposed to be for a few nights. If anyone could complicate the game then it was him, but if he was on form then nobody could touch him. Not even in training.

Forwards – Keith Edwards. The most naturally gifted finisher I ever played with. Marvellous player was Keith. I am tempted to say that the other striker would be Derek Parlane because he was a superb finisher, but he wasn't as good as Gary Lineker. For what Gary has achieved in the game I can't leave him out, but if you had asked me at the time we were teammates then I wouldn't have nominated him.

✳ ✱ ✳

There have been a number of decent players that I have played with that didn't go on to achieve what I thought they would at the time. One of these was Larry May at Leicester; I really thought he would win England caps. There was a young Irish lad at Brighton called Kieron O'Regan and he was a right-back who was hard and uncompromising, but very good. I could never understand a word he said because he had such a strong accent. I know he represented Ireland at under-21 level but never went on as I thought he might.

Funnily enough, at Leicester City under Jock we were a bit ostracised from the youth players and didn't really mix with them. One player that I did notice though was young Stuart Hamill who had a brief spell in the first team around 1981. In training he had everything including the confidence; he wasn't afraid to dish it out and take the piss, but he was yet another lad that you see with loads of talent on the training ground that can't take it on to the pitch on a Saturday afternoon.

There are a lot of players that I didn't play with that I admired. Denis Law, Kenny Dalglish, Jim Baxter and Bobby Moore. I am fortunate enough to say that I played against Bobby Moore when he was at Fulham. I was only eighteen at Oldham and he still made a fool of me. I did nutmeg George Best once though;

Leicester City played a friendly at Easter Road against Hibs and I put the ball through his legs and said, 'Mind yer legs Bestie', and he laughed.

I don't admire many players in the modern game apart from the obvious ones like Lionel Messi, who has amazing ability. If we go back a couple of decades then I think there was a lot more to admire about professional footballers. I became less concerned about other players the older I got, but I still think back to my early days at Oldham and have trouble getting my head around the idea that six weeks before my Oldham debut I was playing football at home on the Valley Primary School playing fields – England v Scotland and I was Denis Law! Then wind forward six weeks and I am making my debut in the Texaco Cup at Maine Road and who is playing for Manchester City? Denis Law. Six weeks earlier I was him and that was why I deliberately bumped into him. He always did that thing where he had his sleeves tucked into his hands, he always played like that. I remember the pitch at Maine Road seemed massive to me.

Sometimes I would put people on a pedestal when I was younger. Then when I met them it was a big disappointment. My prime example of this was Peter Osgood. I supported Chelsea as a boy and I could tell you right now the side that won the F.A. Cup in 1970. Peter was a hero of mine back then, but I played against him for Oldham when he was at Southampton and he turned out to be a right bastard, a real nasty piece of work. He threatened to break my leg and I believe he would have done if he had had the chance. I know we shouldn't speak ill of the dead but that's what I found, and I was so disappointed to find out that he was anything but a hero.

I admired Eddie Kelly as well, but in a different way. I wonder what he would have been like a few years before

I played with him, but he was a great teammate on and off the pitch. He was a good person and an inspirational captain.

I didn't admire any goalkeepers; hated them in fact and I would do anything I could to hurt them. I would batter them and jump into them and elbow them at every opportunity to try and put them off their game. Generally I would say I feel the same about centre-halves with one exception – Billy Bonds. We had some right tussles and I knew if I battered him then he would be back to get me and vice-versa. No matter what happened during the game he would always have a big smile at the end of it and we always shook hands, he was a gentleman off the pitch and a warrior on the pitch and I admired that. I didn't shake hands with many players after a game, especially if we had lost, but I made an exception for 'Bonzo'.

Kenny Dalglish was probably the best player that played in my era. You can only have admiration for him because he made fantastic use of what he had consistently, week in, week out. He would be playing to 90 per cent plus of his ability for his entire career and that is true greatness. I cannot recall a single bad game that he had. I remember being in the Scotland squad with him and we are playing five-a-side at Hampden Park. He did a simple thing and read Alan Rough's roll out. He ran one way but knew where 'Scruff' was going to roll the ball and he bent his run and intercepted it and stuck it in the back of the net. I remember thinking, 'Fuck me, that's brilliant!' And it was so simple, he got inside the 'keeper's head, knew what he was going to do, anticipated and intercepted the roll out and executed it perfectly. Not spectacular but genius nevertheless. Wee things like that stick with you and I take pride in the fact that I was on the same pitch as him when Leicester played Liverpool and beat them twice in one season!

19

REFLECTIONS

Regrets

I should never have left Leicester. That is possibly the single biggest regret I have from my professional career. The problems started when Jock went to Motherwell. It was a total shock, we knew nothing about it. My feelings for Jock go beyond anybody's. At his funeral his wife Daphne told me he thought of me as a son, which was a marvellous thing to hear, because he was like a surrogate father to me. And when he left Leicester I remember thinking, 'Jock can't go. Why has he gone? Well that's it then.'

My immediate thought was that I didn't want to stay at Leicester if Jock wasn't there. I'd had three great years under him at Leicester and couldn't face it without him. I was a wee bit hasty there I think, maybe I should have given Gordon Milne more of a chance. In my defence, I remember him coming across to me in preseason training and introducing himself.

He said, 'Hello son, how are you?'

I said, 'I'm fine Mr Milne, thank you. You've inherited a great bunch of lads, we're very, very honest and I think we'll have a great season.'

He replied, 'I'm quite sure we will Alan, and it's 'Boss' from now on.' He didn't need to say that and it stuck with me and helped sway my decision. Looking back he may have been right because it was a hard job following Jock and he had to get the players on board. He'd obviously done his homework and knew my relationship with Jock.

I went to see him in his office and I said, 'You know, I don't think this is going to work?'

We didn't fall out or anything, he said: 'Well what course of action do you want to take?'

I said, 'It would probably be best for me to go on the transfer list.'

He said, 'Okay then, son.' And that was it.

I was never happy at Sheffield United but I didn't admit it to myself at the time, that I was a fool to leave Leicester. I might have fitted into a strike force of Lineker, Young and (Alan) Smith if I had stuck around. Maybe I jumped too quickly.

Injuries

If it wasn't for injuries I might have played for Scotland; I was chosen for a match against Czechoslovakia in 1981 but there was fog and it was postponed. We stayed over hoping to play the following day. However, by then there was snow and ice. So, we hung around a bit longer and the the snow melted but the pitch was waterlogged. So snow may have cost me a cap. I'll never know for sure I guess. After that I went to QPR and did my cartilage! I have no way of knowing what might have happened; I might have gone on to win twenty caps or played in a World Cup finals. But I don't think about that often, it was out of my control – but I still blame that bloody plastic pitch.

Thinking back, I was injured more times than I care to think of. My worst spell was at Brighton after we came back from a friendly against Real Madrid, and I had injured my back.

But the back injury was related to my problematic right knee. You tend to compensate when the knee is painful so you shift your weight or maybe run differently. Despite this I still scored a good few goals.

I didn't miss many games at Leicester and this was for a variety of reasons: sometimes you had the injury talked out of you by Jock; sometimes you had a pain-killing injection to help you and sometimes you kept quiet about it and didn't make a fuss because you were so desperate to play. The majority of players at that time were the same, they wanted to get out there. Unfortunately I have paid for that mentality. I should have looked after myself more and listened to my body when I was clearly injured and not played when I shouldn't have done. All this did was aggravate the injury and it probably caused further injuries. This all comes back to haunt you as you get older once you've retired. The big problem with the right knee started at QPR and it has been degenerating ever since because it has effectively been bone-on-bone. This made training and playing very painful at times. Once my back became a problem as well then some mornings I had to get into a hot bath before I could do anything. It's still very painful today and sometimes I feel resentful because I know I have more to offer but due to my lack of mobility I can't apply for certain jobs; like the coaching position that came up at Leicester two years ago. If I was more mobile I would have been straight in for that, I would have been kicking Sven's door down for that role. I would have said that he didn't have to employ me, but just watch me work for a week.

It would be a bonus just to be able to walk properly some days, but then I think that I have been luckier than most; I have had a career. I played at Anfield and Old Trafford and I played at Filbert Street every other weekend for three years. So I try not to carry too many regrets about my knee, even though it frustrates me some days and even more so since I had a total knee replacement which didn't work as it should have done. As it stands I have the surgeon telling me that he would like to go back in and operate again. But I said no you won't, but I might change my mind. The lack of fitness and weight gain frustrates the hell out of me because I always used to pride myself on my fitness levels. Even as recently as the coaching role at Chesterfield, I was one of the fittest guys on the staff.

I am realistic enough to accept that I might end up in a wheelchair, I am in agony most days and the quality of life has diminished quite a bit.

At Sheffield United I wasn't helped by the training and fitness regime; it was very poor and all we did was run and didn't see the ball at all in some sessions. Rochdale was a joke as well; one minute we would be running up massive hills, the next we would be in a school gymnasium, then we would be in a lousy field somewhere running up and down in snow and ice. It was awful. There was no consistency and the footballs were like cannonballs. There was never a decent surface to play on and even when Eddie Gray and Jimmy Lumsden took over they found it difficult to find anything better. Wee Jimmy used to have a couple of angry pills in the morning before training, he would always turn up in the morning with a dour, miserable face befitting his strong Glasgow accent. Jimmy was a quiet, unassuming man but he was full of surprises. After I left Rochdale I lived near to Wetherby for a while and there was a pub there run by Jim McCalliog. I used to go there as well as Jimmy Lumsden and a number of retired Leeds United players such as Peter Lorimer, Eddie Gray, Arthur Graham and Gordon McQueen – all Scottish lads. Jim had done the bar out in a tartan carpet but some of the floor was still covered in linoleum. The unspoken arrangement was that the Scottish lads were allowed to sit in the plush, carpeted area and the English customers had to sit on the lino! There was fierce banter that flew between the Scots and the English at times, but it was all good fun and I had some great nights there. If a stranger walked in and walked on to the tartan carpet then they would get a tap on the shoulder (usually from Jimmy) and he would ask them, "Scuse me. Are you Scottish?'

When they answered no he would say, 'Well then fuck off this carpet! It's fuckin' Scotland over here alright'. He was only about 5ft tall but he would physically move customers off of the carpet if he thought it was necessary.

One night in the pub Jimmy had been knocking the wine back and he was a bit the worse for wear. So he decided that he was going to make an announcement. He stood up and started off, "Scuse me, I have got something to say so I would appreciate a bit of quiet ... even you fuckin' English. See this here (and he held up the bottle of wine he had been drinking) this is fifteen pounds a fuckin' bottle. Quality, quality wine. No shite. None o' that Blue Nun crap and do you know how ah can afford it? Because ah get paid £5,000 a fuckin' week!' and he promptly burst into fits of laughter and nearly pissed himself!

I roomed with Jim at Lilleshall when I did my advanced coaching licence. Jimmy has been assistant to David Moyes at Everton for several years now and I saw him last year when Leicester played at Leeds. He came across and made a point of saying hello to me and he was genuinely pleased to see me again.

Personal Discovery

I used to be the one that made sure everyone else was alright. I would put everybody else before myself and if somebody needed something doing then I was the one who did it. I was the one volunteering to help out family and friends and I look back now and think that I was fool to myself some days. I didn't put myself first often enough, but that is changing and my son, Kyle, grimaces at certain things that I say or do because I just come out with it now when I might have bitten my tongue previously. If there are things need to be said then I will say it in a forthright and honest way, and I won't let people take advantage of me anymore. I wish I had realised this a long time ago and things might have been different. Even on the pitch I was very unselfish. I would put in a lot of running for my strike partners some days, but then that was my job and it is a bit different to be unselfish on the pitch.

I guess I was always happy to be everybody's friends back then and if someone let me down occasionally, then so what? But it meant that people like Tommy Cannon got away with lying to me. He promised £5,000 to sign for Rochdale and I took him at his word and when it didn't happen I just put it to the back of my mind, didn't make a fuss and eventually I let it go. If that had been today then I would have ripped his fucking head off. Similarly I might have gone to jail for what I would have done to Chris Cattlin given the chance after he deliberately fucked up my weekend with my two boys that I had planned. I was so angry at the time but I chose to drop it and move on.

The whole business with Karen Towers' parents was appalling and they got away with far too much when we split up. They did some horrible things to me. It was the start of the worst period of my life because Karen and the kids *were* my life and it was all being taken away from me. Her Mum and Dad made it much worse but I just took it all.

I should have made more of a scene when Allardyce sacked me. I should have gone to the chairman and the P.F.A. and told them all that I wasn't settling for this,

Sam shouldn't have been allowed to take away that job that I had spent ten years of my life. He came along and destroyed all of that dedication and hard work and success. If I had been allowed to stay then eventually I would have got a shot at the manager's job. I had done a great job there and I had earned a stab at the top job. As it was Sam didn't stay long anyway, he fucked off to Bolton.

If I could give advice to players coming into the game it would be this – learn to play the piano! I remember giving that answer in a *Shoot* magazine questionnaire and the question was – What advice would you give to youngsters? In other words, don't come into the professional game and go and find something else to do. To be serious, my advice would be: be in the right place at the right time in front of the right people doing the right things. If you don't then it is damn hard work and you could be the most skilful, quickest player around, but if you aren't seen by the right people then you will struggle to make it. If the coach of the youth team doesn't like you then it won't matter how good you are, your face has to fit. You also need a bit of luck and that is mostly to do with steering clear of injuries. Don't have high expectations, get in there and try your hardest and be the biggest, the best and the fastest, every single day. Karen Hespin said something to me once that has stuck with me, it's a simple phrase: 'Do your best at all times. Have the biggest smile, have the best manners, always be first in and last to leave, just do your best always.'

I think a lot of young footballers suffer from their parents' unrealistic hopes and expectations. They get inside their children's head and set expectations that are too high, so it is important that youngsters coming into football are realistic. If things go alright at first and the kid gets some recognition then it is important to keep their feet on the ground and don't let them get carried away. It is a long journey with a lot of distractions along the way. So, it is important to remain focused and keep that hunger and desire.

I often wish I was back at school with the wisdom that I have now, but then I think most of us would settle for that, just to know then what you know now. Funnily enough I know the game better now since I stopped playing. When you play the whole time is spent on developing your game and the playing side is the most important thing (obviously) and there isn't time to be analysing the game at a different level, it's all about you and the job that you are doing for the team.

I often wish that I had had more of a business or financial mind back then, because when I moved clubs and had to sell my houses I fell short of making what I should have done. Maybe I should have kept the houses and just rented them all and sold them when the time was right, instead of selling them in a hurry because I needed to move quickly. I suppose I was focused on the football and didn't think enough about the money issues.

I should never have married Julie – we were too young, it all happened too quickly. I am not saying that I wasn't in love with Julie, but since then I have experienced a different, more intense love and that makes me thing that I shouldn't have married Julie. I remember my sister, Lyn, at the evening reception having a chat with me when we stepped out for a bit of fresh air. We were always close me and my wee sister and I hadn't seen her for about two years at the time. She said to me, 'Are you alright. I mean are you all right?'

'No. I'm not,' I said; and we both left it there. Even at that early stage I wasn't sure and that is nothing to do with Julie, it was me and my head and my thoughts. Julie was a fantastic

Mum and a genuinely nice person, but maybe we just weren't right for each other. On the other hand I have two great sons as a result of that marriage so a lot of good came from it.

My marriage wasn't great with Julie at the time when I left Leicester and I was thinking that if I moved then we would be apart and that would be better. What was difficult was being apart from my lads, Wesley and Jordan. But I had met Karen Towers by then and we had started what you would call an affair which grew into something much more. I got divorced in 1982 and that coincided with the move to Sheffield. I would travel back to Leicester every other Saturday to see my boys and take them out, without fail, and even when I moved to Brighton I still made that trip every other Saturday. I did that until I moved back up to the Midlands with Notts County and there was I thinking that seeing my boys would be easier, but they moved to bloody Rochdale!

Karen was and is a very attractive girl and was probably an early version of a WAG. She wasn't always accepted by the other wives at Sheffield United, perhaps because she wasn't a 'wife' in that sense. She found it difficult at times, and I know she would get lonely but when we had time together we were fantastic; I was completely in love with her and she with me.

I still have ambitions in life, but not in a way that I will step all over anyone who gets in the way. I'm not so driven that I don't care about who I upset on the way to getting what I want, and I have never been like that although I know what it feels like to be young and ambitious when you feel as if you have the world at your feet. These days I think I am more ambitious for others; I'd love to see Kyle achieve more because he is such a talented boy. He has represented Nottinghamshire at cricket, tennis, football, rugby and if he had picked up a golf club sooner then he would have played that to a high level as well. I went out for a few rounds of golf with him not so long ago and he has no handicap, has never had a lesson in his life, but he has natural timing and he hits the ball a mile. He went round in four over, five over and one over. Amazing! He doesn't look out of place when he plays for the Leicester City legends and my ambition for him is that he gets a bit of a break and plays sport for a living because I believe he is good enough. Putting on my coach's hat (because all Dads think their sons are good don't they) I think that he could do it. My two eldest boys are already successful in business and have done very well, but young Sophie is just starting out and I want the very best for her. She is doing the right thing at the moment and enjoying life, but she sands up for herself and I know she will achieve what she wants.

If I could put my finger on a single turning point in my life then it would be the phone call I got from Sophie when I was in Scotland, drinking, when she was in trouble back in Nottingham. That made a light come on for me and suddenly I had a purpose, a focus and every time I was tempted to pick up a can of beer I thought about that phone call. Every morning it was the first thing I thought about and that helped me to start putting my life back together. I had to do that before I could give Kyle and Sophie any kind of support and Sophie's phone call was the catalyst for that. She was sobbing her heart out and I thought, Christ almighty, that's my daughter. It took about a year but I got back down to Nottingham and I feel much closer to Kyle and Sophie now, even though Sophie eventually went to Switzerland with her Mum. I did it for Sophie, but ultimately I did it for myself. Life is full of turning points (transfers, divorce, injuries) but this one is the biggest and most significant and without Sophie's call then I might not be sitting here telling my story in a book. If it had been a shorter distance to the big pier then who knows? I went months without having a drop of alcohol after that and I needed to prove to myself that I was strong enough to beat it because I don't think I had been trying hard enough. Suddenly I had a reason to say, 'I'll show you all and prove you all wrong'. And I did.

A couple of years ago there was a documentary on television that featured Calum Best and he was talking about his father's alcoholism and how it affected him during his childhood. He told some horrific stories about George going on drinking benders when he was supposed to be spending time with Calum and how he was often abandoned whilst his Dad disappeared for a couple of days. The question that kept coming back from Calum was – why couldn't you stop drinking for a couple of days for me? Why is the drink more important than I am? It was heartbreaking for the lad and even now it still troubles him because he never got the answers he wanted. He still doesn't understand what was happening. The only thing I would say to Calum is that your Dad never put alcohol first, he just couldn't help himself. He had no choice.

The way I see it, alcoholics fall into three basic categories: the successful, presentable, well-paid businessman who drinks; the homeless, unemployed guy who drinks whatever he can lay hands on and who has no hope; and the third category (which was George Best) is the celebrity who drinks. The latter is more interesting to the public and the media when he is drunk. I think George drank to block something out. I think it is sad that Calum never got the answer he wanted, but I will say categorically that George couldn't stop. A child will ask those questions because they cannot comprehend alcoholism. When I was drinking there was nobody depending on me. The stuff that had happened to me over the years gradually wore me down and there is a gradual transition from enjoying a pint which becomes more than a pint and then before you know it, the drink is the only thing you look forward. It takes hold of you and takes over. However, it is preventable and you can recover from it and Sophie was the trigger for my recovery and I am a different person now, a better person I hope. I am never going down that road again, not in a million years.

I have discovered that when you are in the situation that I found myself in then the only person that can do anything about it is you. There is no point blaming others, that will get you nowhere and will just make you more angry and bitter and that adds fuel to the fire and so the problem goes on.

WHEN GARY
MET YOUNGY

AY – Alan Young
GL – Gary Lineker

AY: Did you miss me?

GL: I've missed you so much, I can't tell you.

AY: I didn't expect that. [laughs]

GL: It took me about ten years to understand you ... and that was just your football. Seriously, it's great to see you again; it's been a long time, about thirty years I reckon. You were one of Leicester's top centre forwards and you used to put yourself about a bit with those old bow legs ... you and Martin Henderson were established up front in the first team and I was trying to breakthrough ...

AY: Well that brings me to another point; I was asked a question the other day about when you and I first got together up front and I used to sort of resent you a wee bit because you were keeping my mate out of the side but it happened to you when he kept you out of the side as well so when you started getting in the team I was thinking,

I want my pal back alongside me, but I soon realised that you were better for me when you were in the side and I had to be ruthless about it when you established yourself in the team I thought, this is great!

GL: If you remember it was because you were pretty much an established partnership at Leicester even though Martin was never that popular because he didn't score many goals. I think Jock wanted to get me in the team because he saw something in me even though I was a bit raw. I'd always scored goals and he played me on the right wing for the first time in my life. In fact, I think my first thirty/thirty-five games for Leicester were played in the wide right berth with you two in the middle. I wasn't playing particularly well if I'm honest but I was desperate to get in the central striking position. It happened eventually.

AY: It did. How well do you remember Jock?

GL: Of course I remember Jock

AY: Can you tell me one thing about Jock that I might not know?

GL: Well the first time Jock had any real impact on me, in terms of playing, I was playing in the reserves. I remember coming at half time in this particular game and Jock came down in to the dressing room. Now he didn't usually bother much with reserve games but he came marching in at half time and he wasn't happy. Now you remember Jock when he lost his temper, it was frightening. Well he came in to the dressing room and he was raging but he was looking right at me. He was going, you English shit, you this that and the other, you lazy little so-and-so, you better do some more running and he pinned me up against the dressing room wall and I wouldn't have minded but we were two nil up and I'd scored both goals! I didn't score second half because I was a quivering wreck. He called me in the next day and had a word and really wanted to make the point that you don't stop running and working just because you've scored a couple. He taught me how to live properly in many ways and told me not to do anything silly and look after myself but he wasn't the best tactically; he was a goalkeeper for goodness sake so it was hardly surprising! That tells you everything but in terms of motivation and getting the best out of people and in terms of fitness and learning to live properly it was invaluable experience for me.

AY: I always tell people that he knew when something was wrong and he would know what was wrong with you before you did.

GL: Exactly. He did.

AY: I remember he did a similar half-time bollocking to me during a fist team game. We were playing Bristol Rovers at Filbert Street and we were two nil up at half time and I'd scored one but I had missed a bucketful and it could have been five all to be honest because we were terrible. So he stormed in to the dressing room and ripped in to me saying stuff like, who the hell do you think you are, you big-headed this that and the other and after he had finished he just walked out to the physio's room and we all sat there quietly and looked at each other until Andy Peake spoke up. He came and put his arm around me and said, it's alright big man, you're playing ok. I remember turning round and saying, Andy, you're only a bairn. Shut-up and sort your own game out. The gaffer was getting to the rest of the team by having a go at me and going through me because he knew I could handle it. He rated you very highly though Gary. I remember when I signed he told me that he had this boy Lineker who was like shit off a shovel but he was a bit raw but that he was going to be some player. That was him telling me about you and you weren't even in the first team when I signed.

GL: It's funny that because I never felt like that about my own game; everything I did in the game surprised me. I remember when I got in to the youth team I thought, well this might find me out but it didn't and I kept scoring goals. Then I made it in to the reserves and then the first team squad and I'm thinking, what the hell am I doing here? But he obviously saw something in me and the goals came spasmodically because I was playing out of position for a while in the early stages and eventually the goals flowed and I don't think we did too bad as a strike pairing did we?

AY: You know, I've got a few statistics here my friend. In three seasons our partnership brought 30 goals and by that I mean when me and you started together. That's not bad eh? In the last season I was there we played 26 games together and got 19 goals. Mind you it was always me that was knocking centre-halves over so that you could just go and tap the ball in.

GL: Well that's right and I was always very appreciative of that and I have played alongside a few players like that in my career like Alan Smith at Leicester, Graeme Sharp at Everton …

AY: He's a lucky lad that Alan Smith. He's lucky that I left!

GL: That's what he said! I remember the great wins over Liverpool in 80-81 because I didn't play in them, I was watching up in the stand. The two nil win at our place was amazing; Andy Peake smashed one in from a long way out and I think Martin (Henderson) got the other.

AY: He did. But what about the win at Anfield that season?

GL: I wasn't playing in that one either; I was sitting on the bench I think. I seem to recall that you scored a good goal that day Youngy! Talk us through It …

AY: I tell you what, here's the thing; Ian Wilson has a lot to answer for.

GL: Are you going to mention the semi-final defeat [to Spurs]?

AY: I am. And Harlow Town! But at Anfield Willy was down to mark Terry McDermott but he got injured in the centre circle and off goes to Terry Mac so I thought I had better track him so we are running back towards my own goal and Alan Kennedy hit a lovely ball to the far post where David Johnson knocked it back across goal. Terry Mac was on my inside and I'm thinking I had better get a bit of this or he's going to score but I got too big a bit of it and it went straight in the top corner. But I had a strange feeling that day that we would still win the game and we did! Little Pat Byrne got one and that guy with ginger hair got the other.

GL: Melrose was it? He was another of the many Scots players that Jock brought down wasn't he. How long had Jock been there when you arrived?

AY: One season.

GL: So you wouldn't have been there for the first time we all saw the sand hills at Wanlip. Jock was famous for getting his players fit at Rangers by taking them up and down the sand dunes but Leicester is about as far as you can get from the sea so he had these big sand hills built at Wanlip. I think it was a bit of a PR stunt to be honest but I remember Dennis Rofe being interviewed in the middle of this training session, in his high-pitched cockney accent, and they asked him what he thought of Jock Wallace and he said something like, I can't understand an effing word he says but when he says jump you don't half effing jump!

AY: It's on YouTube you know.

GL: You can see anything on YouTube these days … except a goal from me from outside the box, you've got no chance of finding that.

AY: Aye, they're like hens' teeth! So you moved on from Leicester to Everton and then to Barcelona; was that where you learnt to dive?

GL: I never dived!

AY: Come on!

GL: I would always take advantage of any naivety in any defender's tackling. If they missed the ball and hit you then I would go down. There is a difference between that and going down with no contact. I mean if you are one on one with the goalkeeper and you know that you are going to get there first then you might knock it past him and then not try to jump over him so he takes you down. There is a line somewhere between cheating and not but if a defender or goalkeeper goes diving in and you've got the ball past them, then as long as there is some sort of contact then I think it's fair enough personally. It is a totally different thing to knocking the ball and then lunging in the air like we see some players do.

AY: Simulation they call it. And it's up to the referee to interpret it. Correctly we hope. And don't they have a tough job?

GL: Especially with us on Match of the Day analysing every decision they make. I wouldn't be a referee, no chance.

AY: When I played I used to feel sorry for referees which is why I was always so sympathetic to them. (Laughs)

GL: Yeah right! That was the only reason I never got booked; because you got them all.

AY: Listen. I've got three boys and you've got four. So you've got …

GL: George …

AY: Alan …

GL: No way, Harry, Tobias and Angus.

AY: Good name that last one.

GL: It's almost an anagram of Alan Young!

AY: I've got three boys and a wee girl but none of them showed any real inclination to have a go at football as a living. How about yours? Any sign of a keepie-uppie here or there?

GL: George by his own admission is fairly hopeless and Harry can play a bit but isn't bothered, which is a shame, because he has the pace and the movement and he's eighteen now so maybe it has passed him by now. He's in to other things to be honest

AY: Does the surname Lineker cause him any problems?

GL: it makes a difference sometimes and it can be quite hard for him. My third lad, funnily enough, was at Chelsea's academy for about two years but he's had Osgood-Schlatter's (which is a chronic problem caused by irritation of the patellar ligament) for about two years which is a shame because it has affected his confidence. He is just coming out of it so he is effectively starting again, but remember he hasn't played for two years. He has grown a bit; he was tiny when he first went there so we'll see how it goes. If he's good enough then he will be ok.

AY: And of course you need that hunger and desire and self-belief to make it as well. But that brings me on to Harlow Town and Ian Wilson again. In the first match at Filbert Street we were one nil up and we had a free kick in their half. I gave it to Willy and moved to one side and said, give it back Willy, but he didn't ...

GL: He knew better ...

AY: We'll ignore that one ... and he lost the ball and Harlow took it up the other end and scored. Eddie Kelly went ballistic at me, it was twenty minutes to go, we were winning and I played a short free-kick etc. etc. he wasn't happy. But it was Willy not me, he lost the ball ...

GL: Passing the buck again! But we should still have beaten Harlow Town and I played in the replay I'm afraid. Jock hadn't picked me for the first one so I didn't expect to be involved in the replay but he brought me in on the wing. On the morning of the game I had tonsillitis and I felt so rough but I didn't tell anyone because I didn't expect to be picked. Anyway, when he picked me I didn't dare say anything because I was scared stiff of him. I played for ninety minutes and could hardly put one foot in front of the other so I should have said something but if Jock told you that you were in then you didn't tell him you don't want to play! I still get reminded about that game every season when they discuss giant-killings.

AY: It was a bizarre result; we absolutely battered them but we just couldn't score. Anyway, we mentioned him earlier and I want to talk about a guy we both played with called Jim Melrose. You mentioned that I didn't get on with him.

GL: That was always the rumour and it was probably true as I recall, I was there at the time! So what was it with you two? I know could be a bit …

AY: Arrogant.

GL: Well he was confident alright …

AY: I didn't like some of the stuff he did off the pitch. I remember one occasion at the training ground when we were having a keep-ball session and he was in the middle and getting hammered. The ball landed at your feet and he went in on you and ripped your sock open.

GL: I remember that …

AY: He tried to hurt you and you just don't do that to a teammate, no two ways about it…

GL: I try and give people the benefit of the doubt …

AY: But he ripped your sock open …

GL: I treasured those socks, I've still got them! It was my shins I was more worried about.

AY: But he got a good hiding from the lads after that. Jock let us for a while and then said, right that's enough!

GL: I think he wasn't getting a game at the time and it can get to you like that.

AY: The other problem with him was that he was great friends with a certain journalist in Leicester.

GL: That would be Bill Anderson of the Leicester Mercury of course who was there for a hundred years, good guy Bill, but Jim was too pally with him and that makes it difficult because Bill is writing things that will influence the thinking of the Leicester public so it did cause a bit of friction when certain stories appeared.

AY: Gary, would you ever have considered going to Motherwell?

GL: On holiday? To play?

AY: To play

GL: Well that would have been a tough decision … Barcelona … Motherwell … Barcelona … Motherwell …??

AY: The reason I ask is that when I left to go to Sheffield United I called Jock when I had the offer to go to Sheffield. Before I get on to that I have to say that I was as shocked as anyone when Jock left to go to Motherwell. So I called him and told him about the offer from Sheffield United and he stopped me and said, if I can get you and Lineker up to Motherwell then I really will have a great side, the only problem is I can't afford your wages. Lineker is fine, no problem!

GL: How times change!

AY: Jock went to Seville for a while and then back to coach at Colchester. I remember going to see him over there after Karen and I had been to see you play at Charlton for Spurs. We went to reception at Layer Road and he came through to the ticket office and sorted out our tickets but I remember how badly he was stooped and shuffling and it was more noticeable because he was such a big man.

GL: I know what you mean. I saw him around that time at a charity golf day and he was a shadow of the giant that I knew and it was awful to see.

AY: So did you never fancy management?

GL: No, definitely not. I didn't think it's me. I was always more interested in journalism to be honest and I thought there was a bit of niche back then because there weren't many ex-professionals in the media. When I was playing for England in the 1990 World Cup I was nicknamed 'Junior Des' because that's how I was. I think management is a really difficult job; it's 24 hours a day, you are dealing with players, agents, media, fans and you know at some stage, almost without exception, you will get the 'tin tack'.

AY: What age were you when you retired? You were young weren't you?

GL: I was thirty-two when I went from Spurs to Japan and I played there for a couple of years but not much because I got injured. My thirty-fourth birthday was my last game! I relied a lot on my pace as you know and I had a bad injury on my toe in Japan and had all sorts of problems after that and eventually got back playing in the second half of my second season in Japan and in one game the ball was knocked through and I knew I was in. I looked to my side and suddenly the central defender was staying with me … and he stayed with me … and he stayed with me … and when a Japanese centre half is keeping up then it's all over and that helped me to make my mind up.

AY: Well, here's a complete contrast for you. I was up at Rochdale and Eddie Gray pulled me aside one day and said, big man I think it's time you had a rest. I was 31 then. When you were moving to Everton and Barcelona and Spurs I was doing a shift at Sheffield United, Brighton, Notts County and Rochdale. But I don't envy anything from anybody because I have got my health back apart from dodgy knees and a dodgy back. It's strange how life has a path for you but you going in to journalism and Match of the Day and filling some big shoes with people like Des Lynam.

GL: Oh Des was great and very supportive. I think it takes people a while to get used to you then they decide whether they like you or not. You talk about paths in life but if you had told me when we played together that I would play in a World Cup for my country then I wouldn't have believed them because I wasn't that good when I was young

AY: But you had pace and scored goals ...

GL: Yes but I wasn't like Rooney or Michael Owen when they first came on to the scene, I could finish and I could run but that was it. And I spent half that first season on my backside because I was nine stone wet through! In the end I could think quicker than I could run and I worked out how to score goals. Simple as that!

AY: But you also worked out how to play alongside other players like Graeme Sharp, to play off someone. My strength was the ability to keep a ball that I was given and give it to one of my own in a way that they didn't have any problems when they received it. I had a good touch. And I think that helped you when you were started.

GL: No, you're right. Unquestionably and what I've achieved I would never have imagined in my wildest dreams. Things have happened at the right time for me during and after my playing career.

AY: When you look back at the time we played together at Leicester they were great times and you were good for my career, no question, but I was saying to someone the other day that one of the things I remember most about playing with you was when you scored; you had the biggest grin on your face …

GL: I loved scoring …

AY: We all did Gary, you would wheel away with the arm in the air but I could never catch you!

GL: You still can't and especially with your dodgy knees. You were a bit slow getting in to this room mate; you couldn't keep up with me! So what happened when you retired anyway?

AY: It was 1987 and I had just got my preliminary coaching badge and I wrote to all 92 football clubs. I got replies from about forty odd but no offers of work so I moved back to Leicester in a rented house but couldn't get back in to football. After I worked at a local indoor cricket school for a while I got in at Notts County and built up the community football programme for 12 years, something I am immensely proud of. We produced some good players like Jermaine Pennant and Will Hoskins and then Allardyce sacked me. I went to Chesterfield for a while and when that finished I worked in a factory cutting metal pipes.

GL: I bet that made you appreciate how lucky you were to have played football. You had some dark times as well didn't you.

AY: I did. Very dark times. Some days I didn't even get out of bed.

GL: You see I can't imagine that happening to you because you were such a big, positive personality around the football club; you were Youngy!

AY: I played in some very big games but none more important than this one, and I've won this one!

GL: What was the turning point?

AY: Sophie, my daughter. Her Mother was going to Switzerland and she didn't want to go with her. She had been crying her eyes out and sleeping on friends' couches and stuff and a light just came on for me. I thought that I had to do something for her. I never say that I will do anything for anyone unless I know I can do it and that night on the phone I made her a promise that I would come back down to England. And I did, but it took a year! My Dad was fantastic in all this; he never judged me at all. He wouldn't ever tell me to pull myself together or anything like that. He was just there for me. But I'm fine now and I like what I'm doing covering the football on local radio as well.

GL: Are Leicester going up? I want them back on Match of the Day! The money they've spent they ought to get out of that league. Come on The Foxes!!